RICHARD DANBURY read philosophy at Cambridge University and trained as a barrister before practising in criminal law. In a bid for freedom in 1998 he escaped to South America to reinvent himself as a travel writer.

Married to Trailblazer author, Melissa Graham, with whom he wrote *The Rough Guide to Chile*, he now lives in London and works for the BBC.

The Inca Trail, Cuzco & Machu Picchu
First edition: 1999, reprinted with amendments January 2001

Publisher
Trailblazer Publications
The Old Manse, Tower Rd, Hindhead, Surrey, GU26 6SU, UK
Fax (+44) 01428-607571
Email: info@trailblazer-guides.com
www.trailblazer-guides.com

British Library Cataloguing in Publication Data
A catalogue record for this book is available from the British Library

ISBN 1-873756-29-1

Editor: Patricia Major
Layout: Bryn Thomas
Typesetting: Anna Jacomb-Hood
Cartography and index: Jane Thomas

Every effort has been made by the author and publisher to ensure that the
information contained herein is as accurate and up to date as possible. However,
they are unable to accept responsibility for any inconvenience, loss or injury sus-
tained by anyone as a result of the advice and information given in this guide.

Printed on chlorine-free paper from farmed forests by
Star Standard (☎ +65-861 3866), Singapore

THE
INCA TRAIL
CUZCO & MACHU PICCHU

RICHARD DANBURY

TRAILBLAZER PUBLICATIONS

To the memory of my parents

Acknowledgments

At the risk of sounding like an Oscar winner, there are many people, both in the UK and in Peru, to whom I owe thanks. For providing help and information in London: Giovanna Salini at the Peruvian Embassy, the DTI and FCO, and Marcia Walker at the Peru Support Group. In Peru I must thank the INC, the SAEC and Infotur. The staff at Humanities 1 in the British Library provided great help with general research, and in more specific fields Samya Beidas Emanuel gave a hand with economics, and doctors Chris Danbury and Gus Gazzard helped with medical stuff. I was also lucky enough that another type of doctor, Dr Ann Kendall, found time to help with information about the Cusichaca. Thanks also to the Arequpia tourist office, and the La Reyna hospedaje in the same town: sorry that we had to cut you out. Thanks to Richard Derham for checking the maps and not getting lost, and to his sister Katie for secretarial work (keep that forehead stiff). An enormous thank you to Bryn for letting down the lifeline, and all at Trailblazer, particularly Patricia Major for sensitive editing, Jane Thomas for the index and all the hard work and inspiration involved in turning my sketches into maps, and Anna JH for typesetting.

For walking with me, Paul Vick, and to Simon (from Wall Street) and Nell (from Sesame Street) for putting up with our bickering. Thanks also to Ladia and Jitka for company, photographs and the invitation to Prague. Gustavo Rivera Basurz, Lima for friendship and a lift (*Defiende a la Republica: Esribe a tus amigos de todo el mundo!*). And thanks to Melissa, for so much and I'd better stop now or I'll get sloppy.

A request

The author and publisher have tried to ensure that this guide is as accurate and up to date as possible. However things change quickly in this part of the world. Prices rise, new hotels are built and trails are rerouted. If you notice any changes or omissions that should be included in the next edition of this book, please write to Richard Danbury at Trailblazer Publications (address on p2). A free copy of the next edition will be sent to persons making a significant contribution.

Updated information will shortly be available on the Internet at
www.trailblazer-guides.com

Front cover: Machu Picchu (photo: © Richard Danbury)

CONTENTS

GOLD BREASTPLATE FROM CUZCO

INTRODUCTION

Declared both a natural and a cultural World Heritage Site by UNESCO, the **Machu Picchu Historical Sanctuary** is truly a rare and wonderful place. Where else in the world can you walk for days through cloud forests and over razor-sharp passes, in country that's been inhabited for thousands of years by civilisations only discovered by Europeans less than five hundred years ago? Where else could you have such a breathtaking goal to your trek: the magical, lost city of Machu Picchu which rises from a high spur of mountain, like a stage set in a green amphitheatre of forest-clad hills?

THE INCA HERITAGE

For thousands of years the people of South America developed separately from the rest of the world. Their culture culminated in the Incas, a people whose empire was centred on Peru and which stretched further than that of the Romans, yet who governed without having discovered iron, the wheel or writing. Like the Romans, the Incas left behind them monumental stone constructions, built for the most part without mortar yet strong enough to withstand centuries of earthquakes that have toppled more modern edifices. Also like the Romans, they left behind them one of the most extensive road networks in the ancient world, for the most part paved and drained, which linked every part of their realm.

Many of these roads have been rediscovered, and some of them have been cleared. The **Inca Trail** is one such road, part of a network that once penetrated the thick rainforest which grows either side of the river Urubamba. Walkers who follow it today pass over high-altitude wind-blown grassland and down to steamy encroaching jungle. At the end of the road is **Machu Picchu**. On these grasslands and in this jungle are a multitude of plant, bird and animal life, and beside this ancient Inca road are recently rediscovered castles and remote fieldstone inns.

The Incas also left their capital, **Cuzco**, which for the most part has been spared the complete destruction suffered by Mexico, capital of that other great ancient American people, the Aztecs. It's still possible to wander along Cuzco's Inca alleyways which run between walls of perfectly hewn stone and visit the remains of the magnificent Sun Temple, once the religious heart of an empire. And the 'new' buildings such as the Cathedral and the Compañía, built in the sixteenth century by the Spanish colonisers, are beautiful in their own right.

VISITING CUZCO AND MACHU PICCHU

In the days of the Incas, Machu Picchu was a long hard walk from Cuzco. *Chasquis*, Inca messengers, ran the roads of the Inca Trail and herders drove llama trains laden with maize and potatoes over the high passes. Today Machu Picchu is only a couple of hours from Cuzco by train, along a railway that's been pushed through the jungle along the banks of the Urubamba river.

However, you can still walk. The high tableland around Cuzco leads down to the fringes of the Amazon rainforest, and the area is criss-crossed with roads and tracks ancient and modern, passing through unrivalled natural and ancient beauty. As you walk you'll pass dazzling high glaciers and remote corries, along trails lined by ancient Inca canals and dotted with remote unvisited ruins where a multitude of orchids grow in the clear Andean air.

ABOUT THIS BOOK

The book is designed to take you from your armchair to these cities of the Incas, Cuzco and Machu Picchu, and to guide you along the Incas' trails, stretches of some of the best hiking in the world. The book includes information on getting to Peru, a guide to Peru's capital Lima, background material on modern Peru, there's a chapter devoted to the Incas and their predecessors, and chapters on Cuzco and Machu Picchu. Detailed trekking maps are included, as are site plans and descriptions of what's known about the abandoned ruins you'll pass on your way.

RESPONSIBLE TRAVEL

Sadly, as with many tourist sites, the paradox of tourism means that the trails, ruins and cities of the Sanctuary are at risk, threatened by their own beauty. It's this beauty that draws the tourists who bring much needed money but at certain times of the year the main trails have become overcrowded and the fragile environment and ancient stones damaged by thoughtless visitors who fail to behave with sensitivity. Such damage is not inevitable and this book contains a section suggesting how on your visit you can help preserve this beautiful environment.

Peru is full of wonders. Its beauty is breathtaking, and its culture fascinating. If you are sensitive to the place, it can have a greater impact on you than you have on it. So, in the words of Rudyard Kipling:

> 'Something hidden. Go and Find it. Go and look behind the Ranges –
> Something lost behind the Ranges. Lost and waiting for you. Go!'

(From *The Explorer*, which inspired the man who rediscovered Machu Picchu, Hiram Bingham).

PART 1: PLANNING YOUR TRIP

With a group or on your own?

So you've decided to take one of the greatest walks on the planet. The first question to ask yourself is how are you going to do it: are you off on your own or will you go with friends, and are you going to arrange it yourself, or take a tour?

THE PROS AND CONS OF INDEPENDENT TREKKING

Independent trekking

It won't be difficult to buy a ticket to Peru, pack your rucksack and just go. When you get to Peru, it's easy to get to Cuzco and the trailheads using public transport, and if you're carrying proper hiking gear you can just head off into the hills.

The wonderful thing about independent trekking is that you can go where you want at your own pace. You can wander up an interesting-looking hill just to see what's on the other side. You can spend a morning high up at the head of some valley, watching the shadows retreat as the sun rises, or press on quickly through a village full of people pestering you to buy things. These are freedoms you don't have when you're trekking in a tour.

Taking a tour

On the other hand, by arranging things like transport and porters for you, tours take a lot of the hassle out of travelling. In the mountains, they can also take the responsibility and stress out of walking – it's much easier if you're not the navigator who has to decide whether this is the valley to take, or whether it leads into impenetrable jungle.

There's also the question of whether you've the experience to walk these mountains alone. The routes aren't going to present particular difficulties to a fit, experienced trekker (except for the fact that they are very high – see p159), but it wouldn't be safe or sensible to simply head on out there if you've little or no experience of this kind of thing. It's a matter of common sense.

On your own or with friends

Many people are confirmed solitary wanderers, and you can understand why when you read this extract from one of Bingham's books: 'The teapot was found to be frozen solid, although it had been hung up in the tent. It took an hour to thaw and the tea was just warm enough for practical purposes when I made an awkward move in the crowded tent and kicked over the teapot. Never did men keep their tempers better under more aggravating circumstances.' (*Inca Land* Hiram Bingham, 1922).

However, there are risks in taking to the mountains alone, and I wouldn't recommend it. The risks are reduced if you hike with others: larger groups of people deter thieves, and you help each other if one of you gets injured. This doesn't mean you shouldn't leave home unless you can drum up a group to go with, as it's easy to meet someone to walk with in Cuzco.

The middle way
The answer might be to do a little independent trekking as well as taking a tour, or, perhaps, to arrange flights, transport, food and kit yourself, but hire an *arriero* (muleteer) in a local village to carry your bags and act as a guide. What's going to be best for you is something only you can answer. This book will give you all the information you need.

Just the ruins
You can, if you don't want to do the walk, just visit the ruins. Most of the companies mentioned below do straightforward tours to Machu Picchu, and you need never see a pair of hiking boots and a rucksack.

It's as easy to get to the ruins by public transport as it is to get to the trailheads. A passenger train runs regularly between Cuzco and the valley floor below Machu Picchu (see p227), and there's also a helicopter. From the valley floor there's a bus up to the ruins, and they're even planning to build a cable car.

TOURS AND TREKKING AGENCIES

There are agencies in both Lima and Cuzco; see p104 and p129.

Agencies at home can sort everything out for you. Prices are in the region of US$2500-3300/£1500-2000 and tours range from two to three weeks. The Peruvian consulate in your home country (see p236-7) can supply you with the names and telephone numbers of other operators.

Agencies in Britain and Ireland
● **Exodus Walking Holidays** (☎ 0181-673 0859, 🖹 0181-673 0779, email: sales@exodustravels.co.uk, website: www.exodustravels.co.uk), 9 Weir Rd, London SW12 OLT. Also in **Ireland** at Silk Road Travel (☎ 01-677 1029, 🖹 01-677 1390), 64 South William St, Dublin 2. Walking specialists, they offer a four-day hike.
● **Explore Worldwide** (☎ 01252-760000, 🖹 01252-760001, email: info@explore.co.uk, website: www.explore.co.uk) 1 Frederick St,

Aldershot, Hants GU11 1LQ. Also in **Ireland** at Maxwells Travel (☎ 01-677 9479), D'Olier Chambers, 1 Hawkins St, Dublin 2. This is a large company, doing five-day hikes and ruins-only trips.

● **Guerba Expeditions** (☎ 01373-826611, 🗎 01373-858351), Wessex House, 40 Station Rd, Westbury, Wiltshire BA13 4JN. Agents for GAP (see USA, p14).

● **Journey Latin America** (☎ 0181-747 8315, 🗎 0181-742 1312, email: sales@journeylatinamerica.co.uk), 12-13 Heathfield Terrace, Chiswick, London W4 4JE. One of the market leaders in Britain for tours to South America, Journey Latin America offer a range of hikes from three to five days.

● **Hayes and Jarvis** (☎ 0181-222 7844, 🗎 0181-741 0299, email: Res@Hayes-Jarvis.com), Hayes House, 152 King St, London W6 0QU. A large, well-established firm offering ruins-only tours.

● **Ramblers Holidays** (☎ 01707-331133, 🗎 01707-333276, email: ramhols@dial.pipex.com), Box 43, Welwyn Garden, Herts AL8 6PQ. Established over 50 years ago this company is one of the few operators who offer the Mollepata trek.

● **South American Experience** (☎ 0171-976 5511, 🗎 0171-976 6908, email: sax@mcmail.com), 47 Causton St, Pimlico, London SW1P 4AT. Mainly do flights, but operate some tours too. See p17.

● **World Expeditions** (☎ 0181-870 2600, 🗎 0181-870 2615, email: worldex@dircon.co.uk), 4 Northfields Prospect, Putney Bridge Rd, London SW18 1PE. See p15 for a description of this company.

Agencies in Continental Europe

● **Belgium Divantoura**, Gent (☎ 09-223 00 69), Antwerp (☎ 03-233 19 16), St Jacobsmarkt 5, 2000 Antwerpen. Agents for Explore Worldwide – see Britain and Ireland, above.

● **Denmark Inter-Travel** (☎ 33-15 00 77), Frederiksholms Kanal 2, DK-1220 Kobenhavn K. Inter-travel are agents for Explore Worldwide – see Britain and Ireland, above.

● **Germany Aequator Tours** (☎ 089-314 2025, 🗎 089-314 9945, email: aequator-tours-gmbh@msn.com), GmbH, Schleissheimerstrasse 439, 80935 München. Agents for the North American company, GAP – see USA, p14.

● **Netherlands TCT travelconsultants** (☎ 043-350 0308, 🗎 043-350 0287, email: trotamundos@wxs.nl), Post-box 1695 - 6203 BR. Agents for GAP. **Adventure World** (☎ 023-5382 954), Haarlem. Agents for the British company Explore Worldwide.

● **Spain North, East, West & South** (☎ 91-531 4028, 🗎 91-531 5565, email: NEWS@infotravel.es), SL, C/Mayor 6, 6 Ofic.1, 28013 Madrid. Agents for GAP – see USA, p14.

Agencies in USA
● **Adventure Center** (☎ 510-654-1879, toll free ☎ 800-227-8747, ▤ 510-654 4200), 1311 63rd St, Suite 200, Emeryville, CA 94608. Agents for Explore Worldwide (see Britain and Ireland, above).
● **GAP (USA)** (☎ 914-666-4417, ▤ 914-666-4839, toll free ☎ 1-800-692-5495) 706 North Bedford Rd, Suite #246, Bedford Hills, New York 10507. This is a very large, well-run organisation that offers many tours on the Inca Trail – they do the Km77 walk.
● **Holbrook Travel** (☎ 352-377-7111, ▤ 352-371-3710, email: Travel@holbrooktravel.com, website: www.holbrooktravel.com), 3540 NW 13th Street, Gainesville, FL 32609-2196. Ruins-only tours, but they do stay in the Machu Picchu Pueblo Hotel (see p152) which is the region's best.
● **Sunny Land Expeditions** (☎ 1-800-783-7839, email: Tours@Sunny-Land-Tours.com, website: www.Sunny-Land-Tours.com). They offer the trek from Chilca (Km77).
● **Tawantinsuyu Explorations** (☎ 800-862-9294, ▤ 303-543-2256, email: incatour@indra.com, website: www.incatour.com). A small organisation with knowledgeable guides; offers the four-day route.
● **Wilderness Travel** (☎ 800-368-2794, ▤ 510-558-2489, email: info@wildernesstravel.com, website: www.wildernesstravel.com), 1102 9th St, Berkeley, California 94710-1211, USA. A very good operator, illustrated by the fact that they include the Mollepata trek.

Agencies in Canada
● **GAP (Canada)** (☎ 416-922-8899, ▤ 416-922-9822, toll free ☎ 1-800 - 465-5600, email: adventure@gap.ca, website: www.gap.ca 266), Dupont St, Toronto, Ontario M5R 1V7. See GAP (USA) for description.
● **Westcan Treks** (toll free ☎ 1-800-661-7265, website: www.trek.ca), offices in **Calgary** (☎ 403-283-6115, 336 14th St NW, Calgary, Alberta T2N 1Z7, **Edmonton** (☎ 780-439-0024, 8412 109th St, Edmonton, Alberta T6G 1E2), **Toronto** (Adventure Centre: ☎ 416-922-7584, 25 Bellair St, Toronto, Ontario M4Y 2P2) and **Vancouver** (☎ 604-734 1066, 1965 West 4th Ave, Vancouver BC, V6J 1M8. Agents for Explore Worldwide – see p12.

Agencies in Peru
See p104 for Lima and p129 for Cuzco.

Agencies in Australia and New Zealand
● **Adventure Associates** (☎ 02-9389 7466, ▤ 02-9369 1853, email: advassoc@ozemail.com.au), 197 Oxford Mall, (PO Box 612), Bondi Junction, Sydney NSW 2022. Mainly do long tours, but one of their South American options is the Km88 trek.
● **Adventure World** (☎ 02-9956 7766, ▤ 02-9956 7707), 73 Walker Street, North Sydney, NSW 2060, and in **Adelaide** (☎ 08-231 6844, 7th

Floor, 45 King William St, Adelaide, SA 5000), **Brisbane** (☎ 07-3229 0599, 3rd Floor, 333 Adelaide St, Brisbane, Qld 4000), **Melbourne** (☎ 03-9670 0125, 3rd Floor, 243 Little Collins St, Melbourne, Victoria 3000), **Perth** (☎ 08-9221 2300, 2nd Floor, 8 Victoria Ave, Perth, WA 6000). This company offers **Tucan** tours: Tucan are one of the largest operators in the area, and offer a three-day hike.
● **GAP** (☎ 03-9663 8611, 🖹 03-9663 8618), Peregrine Head Office, 258 Lonsdale St, Melbourne, Victoria 3000. See North America for a description of this company.
● **Suntravel Ltd** (☎ 09-525 3074, 🖹 09-525 3065, email: suntravl@suntravl.co.nz407), Great South Rd, PO Box 12-424, Penrose, Auckland, New Zealand. A company offering GAP tours – see USA, p14.
● **World Expeditions** (☎ 02-9264 3366, 🖹 02-9261 1974, email: enquiries@worldexpeditions.com.au), Level 3, 441 Kent St, Sydney NSW 2000, also in **Melbourne** (☎ 03-9670,8400, 🖹 03-9670 7474) 1st Floor, 393 Little Bourke St, Melbourne, Victoria 3000 and **Brisbane** (☎ 07-3216 0823, 🖹 07-3216 0827), Shop 2, 36 Agnes St, Fortitude Valley, Queensland 4006. This is a very good company, and they offer the Mollepata trek.

PORTERS, ARRIEROS (MULETEERS) AND GUIDES

Although you can tackle any of the walks in this book independently without **porters** or **arrieros** and their mules, it can make your trek more pleasurable having the load taken off your back. It also doesn't cost much: about US$5-7/£3.50-4.50 per day if you arrange things yourself.

If you want someone just to show you the way, you'll be able either to find help locally or through an agency in Cuzco. However, because it's so difficult to get lost on these trails there aren't that many **guides** around – you might be better off hiring an arriero.

Where to hire porters and arrieros

I prefer finding help in the villages on the trail rather than using a tour agency for a number of reasons: you know you're not exploiting the locals and are paying a fair price for a fair service. Also, you're putting your tourist dollars directly into the local economy and not lining the pockets of already flourishing Cusqueños or Limeños. And anyway, it's more personal.

The villages where you can pick up help are: **Mollepata** and **Soray** on the Mollepata trek, **Chilca** on the Chilca circuit and **Huayllabamba** on all the treks (though you're most likely to meet rogues at this last one).

The going rate (at the time of writing) for a porter and for an arriero is s/15-20 per day, which is about US$5-7/£3.50-4.50. A tip is expected. Five to ten per cent is customary but porters are usually very ill paid so be generous.

□ **Hiring arrieros**
It sounds simple enough, but it took no end of argument and persuasion...to convince these worthy arrieros that they were not going to be everlastingly ruined by this bargain. Hiram Bingham 1922 *Inca Land*

Some things never change. Even today arrieros drive a hard bargain and will convince you that, however much you pay, you're stealing the bread from their children's plates.

Arrieros – one mule or two?

If you're hiring an arriero, don't be surprised if he insists on taking two mules. Since the dawn of time, muleteers all over the world have refused to take only one animal. It's not a rip-off, it's an insurance policy should one of the mules go lame or should you become exhausted and need a ride.

Porters

No mules are allowed on the trail from Huayllabamba to Machu Picchu, so if you don't want to carry your bags you'll have to hire a porter.

These guys are amazing – even if you don't hire one yourself, you'll see them on the trail. They carry two, sometimes even three backpacks, loosely bound to them with rope, and they travel at a phenomenal speed.

Getting to Peru

BY AIR

The following main airlines fly to Lima: Aeroflot, Aerolíneas Argentinas, Air France, American Airlines, Avianca, Continental, Copa, Delta, Ecuatoriana, Iberia, KLM, Lan Chile, Lloyd Aéreo Boliviano, Lufthansa, Servivensa, Saeta, United Airlines and Varig. Many of the tour operators mentioned above (pp12-15) can get you tickets. Note that AeroPeru, which used to operate international flights, went out of business in March 1999. A new operator, LanPeru, should begin services soon.

Airpasses covering Peru are available, and as the exact details of the offers change regularly, you should check with your travel agent. At the time of writing, a five-coupon airpass cost US$359/£230, and a two-coupon pass US$162/£100.

For a detailed website guide to all flights to and from Lima, visit www.trafico.peru.com.

From Europe

The main gateway is Madrid, but there are flights from Paris, London, Amsterdam, Frankfurt and Shannon. The main market for discount flights is the UK, and the cheapest cost from £450 to £650.

● **USIT Campus Travel** (☎ 0171-730 8111), 52 Grosvenor Gardens, London SW1, and with branches all over the country.
● **Journey Latin America** See p13. These people often have good deals on flights, as well as running tours.
● **STA travel** (UK telesales: ☎ 0171- 361 6262). This is one of the largest budget-flight companies in the world, and they have branches all over the place.
● **South American Experience** (☎ 0171-976 5511, ▤ 0171-976 6908, email: sax@mcmail.com), 47 Causton St, Pimlico, London SW1P 4AT. A specialist in South America, this company mainly offers flights.
● **Trailfinders** (☎ 0171-938 3366, 42-50 Earls Court Rd, London W8 6EJ; ☎ 0161-839 6969, 58 Deansgate, Manchester M3 2FF; ☎ 0141-353 2224, 2 McLellan Galleries, Sauchiehall St, Glasgow, ☎ 0117-929 9000, 48 Corn St, Bristol BS1 1HQ). Also in **Ireland** (☎ 01-677 7888), 4-5 Dawson St, Dublin 2.

From USA and Canada
The main gateways are Miami and New York, though there are flights from Dallas, Los Angeles and Houston. Expect to pay US$1300-1500 from the States, CDN$1000-1500 from Canada.
● **Air Brokers International** (☎ 1-800-883-3273), 323 Geary St, Suite 411, San Francisco, California 94102.
● **Sky Link** (☎ 212-599-0430), 5th Floor, 265 Madison Ave, New York, NY 10016.
● **STA Travel** (☎ 1-800-777-0112), 10 Downing St, New York, NY 10014, and in Boston and on the West Coast.

From Australia and New Zealand
There are currently no direct flights to Peru from Australia or New Zealand. From Australia, the cheapest fares about A$2000, and an extended stay will cost about A$3200. From New Zealand, expect to pay NZ$2500-2700.
● **Flight Centres** (☎ 03-9650 2899), 19 Bourke St, Melbourne and all over the country. Also in **New Zealand** (☎ 09-209 6171) 205-225 Queen St, Auckland.
● **Thomas Cook** (☎ 02-9248 6100), 321 Kent St, Sydney and branches in Melbourne, and around Australia and New Zealand.
● **Trailfinders** (☎ 07-3229 0887), 91 Elizabeth St, Brisbane 4000, Queensland. Also in **Sydney** (☎ 02-9247 7666), 8 Spring St, New South Wales, Sydney 2000.

OVERLAND

It's very difficult to get to Peru overland from Central America, because of the swampy region in Columbia known as the **Darien Gap.** The Pan-

American highway, which links most of the rest of the two continents, stops either side of this fearsome natural obstacle.

It's much easier to get to Peru and Cuzco overland from neighbouring countries. There are buses from La Paz in **Bolivia** that cross lake Titicaca on a ferry and reach Cuzco via Puno (which rather disproves the Martin Stevenson and the Dainties' song, *You can't take a boat to Bolivia*).

From **Brazil**, there's a ten-day ferry ride up the Amazon from Manaus to the Peru's Amazonian port of Iquitos, from which you can fly to Cuzco. In times past you could also take a boat up the river to Cuzco but it's currently not safe because of bandits.

From **Ecuador** in the north and **Chile** in the south there are major bus routes into Peru along the Pan-American highway.

Budgeting

You can survive on around US$10-15/£6-10 a day, and on US$30/£19 a day you will have a very comfortable time. To get some perspective on the costs below, a housemaid gets paid on average US$115 a month, and a doctor about US$1500.

ACCOMMODATION

The cheapest hotels cost US$2.80/£1.75 per person per night. At the other end of the scale, the most expensive hotel I found was charging US$190/£120.

FOOD

A local will pay around US$0.70/£0.45 for a filling lunch and a backpacker will pay about US$3.50/£2.20 for a light one. You can easily eat more expensively though not necessarily much better: breakfast at the Machu Picchu Ruinas Hotel costs US$17/£10.75, and dinner at one of Lima's more flashy restaurants can cost US$35/£22 per person (without wine).

TRANSPORT

A 14-hour luxurious bus ride from Lima to Cuzco will set you back about US$20/£12.65, and a flight to Cuzco will cost you up to US$80/£50.

THINGS TO BUY

You're inevitably going to be tempted to buy souvenirs. The cost of these will depend on how good you are at bargaining and the quality of the thing you're buying: cheap Andean pan-pipes cost about US$2/£1.25 but prime quality handwoven textiles can cost hundreds of dollars.

When to go and for how long?

WHEN TO GO

The best time to go is in April or May. The trekking season is April/May to October. In June/July the trails become very, very busy, and it's sometimes difficult to find a spot to pitch your tent. At other times of the year the trails will be less crowded but be prepared for some serious rain and impassable roads.

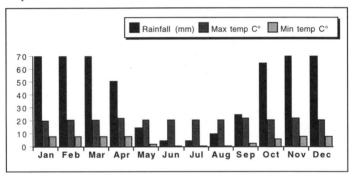

Cuzco climate chart

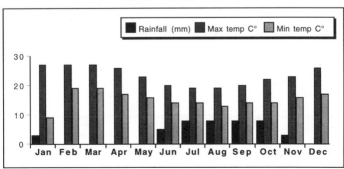

Lima climate chart

FOR HOW LONG?

The longest walk in this book takes two weeks and the shortest only two days. The basic Inca Trail from Km88 takes four days – see below for more details.

To work out how long your Peruvian trip's going to be, you've got to add five days to the length of the trail you're thinking of walking. This allows a day to fly to Cuzco from Lima (more if you're travelling overland), a day to fly back, a day just in case there's a problem with the flights, and a couple of days acclimatising to the altitude in Cuzco.

Acclimatising is very important. If you don't spend a little time allowing your body to get used to Cuzco's thin air you can expect is a thoroughly miserable and exhausting time, and you might also be risking your life. See p159 for more information.

Route options

All but one of the trails in this book end up following the ancient Inca road from the village of Huayllabamba to Machu Picchu, the route trekkers call 'The Inca Trail'. In 1911 the Hiram Bingham expedition began to uncover this route and Dr Paul Fejos discovered more of it in 1944. The trail that doesn't follow this route is the new two-day route to Machu Picchu from Km104; see 'The shorter trail' below.

THE CLASSIC INCA TRAIL (3-4 DAYS)

The classic Inca Trail starts at kilometre 88 (Km88) on the railway line that runs from Cuzco to the jungle town of Quillabamba – the foot of Machu Picchu mountain is at Km113. The first part of the walk, from Km88 to the village of Huayllabamba, is a relatively gentle stroll taking you through eucalyptus groves and past the extensive ruins of Patallacta. The hike from Huayllabamba is more gruelling but it's a superb walk through varied scenery and vegetation, travelling from barren grassland to encroaching jungle, through stone-hewn tunnels and over 4200m (13,750ft) high passes. At the end of your journey lies the legendary Machu Picchu, Lost City of the Incas.

> ❑ 'OLD MARTIN: *You call them the Andes. Picture a curtain of stone hung by some giant across your path. Mountains set on mountains: cliffs on cliffs. Hands of rock a hundred yards high, with flashing nails where the snow never moved. Scratching the gashed face of the sun'.*
> **Peter Shaffer,** *Royal Hunt of the Sun* (Act 1 Scene 7)

The walk's tough: it's only 43km (26.6 miles) long but you walk up 2150m (7000ft) and down 2100m (6880ft).The quickest time, if you're interested, for doing the whole route from Km88 to Machu Picchu is six hours. See p167.

VARIATIONS ON THE CLASSIC TRAIL

Chilca (Km77) along the Urubamba (4-5 days)
Instead of starting at Km88, you can start further up the Urubamba at a village called Chilca (at kilometre 77 on the railway, so it's also known as Km77). It's a small place – blink and you'll miss it.

The hike from here along the Urubamba to Huayllabamba takes a full day, but it's not really worth it – you'll see nothing along this route that you wouldn't see if you started at Km82. The only reason to do this trek is if you've got time to burn, or if your tour starts from here. Agencies like starting here because the road is good as far as Chilca, and so they can drive out instead of relying on the railway. See p183.

Km82 along the Urubamba (3½-4½ days)
The compromise between starting at Km88 and Chilca is to start at Km82. This walk takes further along the banks of the Urubamba than the Km88 hike, rewarding you with wonderful views down the valley, and isn't so wearing as starting at Chilca. You'll also pass the Inca hill fort, Inca Raccay, which provide a breathtaking view over Patallacta. See p186.

THE SHORTER TRAIL: KM104 (1½ DAYS)

The recently-built short path from the Inca site of Chachabamba (at Km104) to the last part of the Inca Trail is an exposed walk across an exposed hillside, not worth doing if you can afford the time to walk one of the other routes.

Although the path from Km104 is a recent construction, there's an original Inca road a couple of kilometres up the rail track at Choquesuysuy, but you can't follow this old route because the hydro-electric plant is in the way. See p187.

CHILCA (KM77) UP THE SILQUE VALLEY (6-7 DAYS)

This is the first of two alternative hikes that take you away from the crowds. This is a very beautiful valley walk on which you're unlikely to meet many gringos. The area around here was once the land of the Bethlemites, the richest religious group in the province, and the walk up the verdant Silque valley takes you through their rich and fertile old farm-land. There's a 4800m (15,740ft) high pass to climb, and if you tell peo-ple that you're walking that way they'll think you're mad – it's much quicker to get to Huayllabamba along the Urubamba. See p190.

The Inca Trails

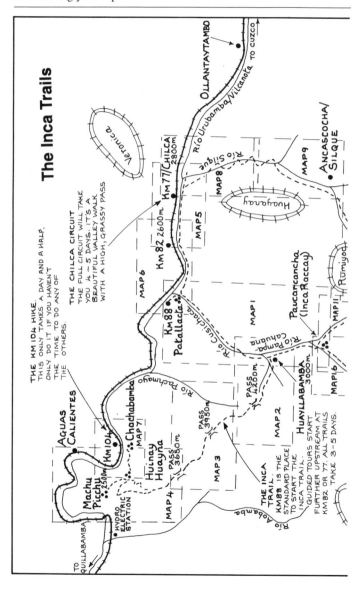

THE KM104 HIKE.
THIS ONLY TAKES A DAY AND A HALF.
ONLY DO IT IF YOU HAVEN'T
THE TIME TO DO ANY OF
THE OTHERS.

THE CHILCA CIRCUIT
THE FULL CIRCUIT WILL TAKE
YOU 4-5 DAYS. IT'S A
BEAUTIFUL VALLEY WALK
WITH A HIGH, GRASSY PASS

THE INCA TRAIL.
KM88 IS THE
STANDARD PLACE
TO START THE
INCA TRAIL.
GUIDED TOURS START
FURTHER UPSTREAM AT
KM82 OR 77. ALL TRAILS
TAKE 3-5 DAYS.

OLLANTAYTAMBO

TO CUZCO

Río Urubamba/Vilcanota

Verónica

Río Silque

Km 77 (Chilca) 2800m

MAP 9

ANCASCOCHA/
SILQUE

MAP 8

Huayanay

Km 82 2600m

MAP 5

MAP 6

MAP 1

Rumiyoc

Km88
Patallacta

Río Cusichaca

Paucarcancha
(Inca Raccay)

MAP 11

Río Pampa-
cahuana

PASS
4200m

MAP 16

HUAYLLABAMBA
3000m

Aguas
Calientes

Chachabamba

Río Pachamayo

KM104

Huiñay
Huayna
MAP 7

PASS
3650m

PASS
3950m

MAP 2

MAP 3

Río Aobamba

Machu
Picchu

2500m

MAP 4

HYDRO
ELECTRIC
STATION

TO QUILLABAMBA

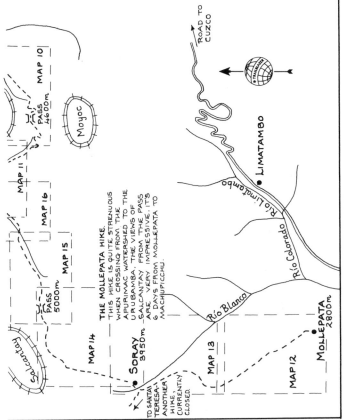

ROAD TO CUZCO

N TRAILBLAZER

LIMATAMBO

Río Limatambo

Río Colorado

Río Blanco

MAP 10

PASS 4600m

Moyoc

MAP 11

MAP 16

MAP 15

PASS 5000m

MAP 14

Salcantay

SORAY 3950m.

THE MOLLEPATA HIKE.
THIS HIKE IS QUITE STRENUOUS
WHEN CROSSING FROM THE
APURIMAC WATERSHED TO THE
URUBAMBA. THE VIEWS OF
SALCANTAY FROM THE PASS
ARE VERY IMPRESSIVE. IT'S
6 DAYS FROM MOLLEPATA TO
MACHUPICCHU.

MAP 13

MAP 12

MOLLEPATA 2800m.

TO SANTA
TERESA-I
ANOTHER
HIKE,
CURRENTLY
CLOSED.

THE MOLLEPATA TREK (6 OR 7 DAYS)

This is the most difficult and most dramatic of the hikes in this book. You start in the village of Mollepata, and walk from the valley of the Apurímac to the valley of the Urubamba, over the shoulder of Mount Salcantay. There's a 5000m (16,400ft) high pass, and you pass within touching distance of the glacier that gives birth to the river Cusichaca.

If you're a glutton for punishment, you can start in the desert heat down by the river Apurímac and add another day to this hike.

COMBINING OR ALTERING ROUTES

There's scope for linking together these routes, or doing different bits of them, or doing them in a different order. See the map on p22-3. There are so many other hikes you could take in these hills, so many other places to explore. However, you should know that the park authorities don't allow you to start at Machu Picchu and walk in the direction of Huayllabamba.

Two obvious alternative hikes are a **Chilca circuit**, and a hike from **Mollepata to Machu Picchu via Chilca** (see p208).

What to take

The golden rule is to travel light. If you're in doubt, leave it out and take more money with you. The more that's in your bag, the more weight you'll have to carry and the more you'll curse yourself. Wherever you go in Peru, don't wear military clothes or carry military-style equipment as people might mistake you for a soldier or a terrorist.

For hiking, it's still a good idea to travel light, but if you want to be fully equipped, you're going to have to carry much more. What follows is a list of what you'll need for safe and comfortable hiking.

> ❏ **The bare necessities?**
> *From here to the top, we were to carry only such things as were absolutely necessary. They included the Mummery tent with pegs and poles, the mountain-mercurial barometer, the two Watkins aneriods, the hypsometer, a pair of Zeiss glasses, two 3A Kodaks, six films, a sling psychrometer, a prismatic compass and clinometer, a Stanley pocket level, an eighty-foot red-strand mountain rope, three ice axes, a seven-foot flagpole, and American flag and a Yale flag. In order to avoid disaster in case of storm, we also carried four of Silver's self-heating cans of Irish Stew and mock-turtle soup, a cake of chocolate, and eight hard-tack, besides raisins and cubes of sugar in our pockets.* **Hiram Bingham, 1922,** *Inca Land*

BOOTS

Good boots, well broken in, are essential. Don't skimp on them – the more you pay, the better quality you'll get. There are two main types on the market. **Fabric boots** are generally lined with gore-tex (if they're not, don't even look at them) and are waterproof and immediately comfortable. They're not as tough as leather boots and don't last as long. **Leather boots** are tough and last ages, but to keep them water-resistant you have to keep rubbing in dubbin or some other waterproofing agent.

Plastic boots for mountaineers are not necessary or suitable for the hikes in this book.

CLOTHES

Back in 1922, to avoid frostbite Bingham had to order each man in his party to put on four pairs of thick woollen socks and three pairs of longjohns. Modern fabrics, however, are light and keep you warm and dry without being too bulky.

Most hikers wear several layers of clothing, rather than just a thick jumper or an enormous jacket. The advantage of doing this is that you can peel off layers as you walk and still keep comfortable, or you can combine the layers to prepare yourself for all kinds of weather from damp heat to dry cold.

● **Jacket** If you can afford it, buy a waterproof jacket made from gore-tex, a material that is breathable (ie it lets your sweat out) and highly waterproof. It's effective but not quite the all-purpose fabric the advertisements would have you believe. There are other similar fabrics on the market that are similar and almost as good, such as sympatex.

● **Down jacket/fleece top** Under your waterproof you should wear a warmth layer. Some people wear fleeces (tightly woven nylon) because they're light and warm, but I find them bulky. The alternative is a down (feather-stuffed) jacket, very light, very warm, very compact but also very expensive.

● **Jersey** I'm not convinced that there's anything better than a woollen jumper and a cotton shirt, although there are some good micro-fleeces around.

● **Shirts/blouses** Light cotton shirts with long sleeves and collars are best. Many people take T-shirts and end up with burnt necks in the fierce sun. Two or three shirts or blouses should be enough.

● **Trousers/pants and skirts** Poly-cotton travellers' clothing of the sort sold by Rohan is good since it dries quickly but it's expensive. Don't take jeans. They absorb water and sweat like a sponge, and take ages to dry. They're heavy and bulky and for the same weight you can pack both a pair of warm and a pair of light trousers. Women should not wear shorts or short skirts.

● **Inner layer/underwear** The important thing about a skin layer is that it draws away sweat from your body and dries quickly. Cotton isn't very good: T-shirts get sopping wet and then cling to you, and the moment you stop walking you freeze. I recommend thermal underwear – silk thermals are warmest but most expensive.

For normal underwear, three changes of whatever you usually wear is fine.

● **Socks** Three pairs of thick socks is enough.

● **Hat** A sun hat with a wide brim is important protection against the heat during the day. A woolly hat (the locally-knitted hat is known as a *chullo*) is essential at altitude and on cold evenings.

● **Gloves or mittens** Cheap woollen gloves are available in the tourist shops in Cuzco and are essential.

● **Swimsuit** Useful when you're washing in the open.

EQUIPMENT

Backpack

If you're not hiring porters or arrieros this is another thing that you shouldn't skimp on. You'll be wearing it for days on end so make sure it fits your back well, is tough and has the right capacity for you.

There are two types of rucksack, **internal frame** (the bag incorporates a rigid back-piece) and **external frame** (with the bag hung from a frame). You hardly ever see external frame rucksacks in Europe anymore, but they're still common in the US. Leading makes are Karrimor, Berghaus and Lowe.

It's vital to line your backpack with at least one strong plastic bag to keep everything dry, and a good idea to pack everything inside it in plastic bags, too.

Sleeping bag and mat

Down **sleeping bags** are lighter and pack up tighter than foam-filled ones but they're more expensive and difficult to dry if they get wet. You'll need at least a three-season bag, possibly a four-season if you feel the cold. Some people bring a **sleeping bag liner**, made from a folded sheet sewn up on two sides. This can be easily washed and so helps keep the sleeping bag clean; it also makes it warmer.

Sleeping-mats do two things: obviously they cushion you, but more importantly they insulate you from the chilly ground. A **foam sleeping-**

mat is ok, but the self-inflating air-mats made by **Therma-rest** are much more comfortable. They do tend to puncture, however, so take a repair kit, too. You can hire mats and bags in Cuzco.

Tent

Don't bother with anything but a free-standing tent – the ones with metal poles that you can pitch anywhere. These are so much better than old A-frame tents which are a waste of money these days. Make sure you buy one that packs up tightly and is light, and don't forget to seal the seams before your first night out in the rain.

Tents are expensive, and if you're not planning many other trekking holidays it's not really worth buying one. You can hire them in Cuzco.

Stoves, pans and crockery

Although **butane gas stoves** like the camping-gaz ones that run on the little blue cylinders don't normally work at altitude, you can buy cylinders for them containing a butane-propane mix which is completely satisfactory. They sell these cylinders in Cuzco.

Unless they're able to run on a wide range of fuels, **liquid fuel stoves** are next to useless in Peru, because the proprietary fuel on which they run is unobtainable and they get clogged up on Peru's filthy petrol. If you bring a liquid fuel stove it must be able to run on as many fuels as possible, and be easy to clean.

Bring a couple of **aluminium pans** that can be stored nestling inside each other. Some people don't bother with plates, as you can eat out of the pans. Do bring **cups** and **cutlery**, and a wire scrubber for cleaning off your burnt-on porridge. You can hire or buy these things in Cuzco.

General equipment

Other essential items include **matches** and a couple of **lighters, sunglasses** (mountain or skiing sunglasses are good because they enclose your eyes and reduce glare), a **torch** (a head torch is recommended because it leaves your hands free), **spare batteries** (easy to forget, impossible to do without), a **whistle** (to summon help), a **small sewing kit, plastic bags,** a **penknife** (with scissors and a tin opener), **water bottles** (carry two litres capacity per person), **water purifying tablets** (chlorine doesn't kill all the bugs, iodine's much better – see p163) a **sun hat, toothpaste, toothbrush, loo paper, sanitary towels** (for what they're designed for, and to deal with any serious bleeding injury), **sun block, lip balm, soap** and a **medical kit** (see p29). All toiletries are readily available in Cuzco.

If you're planning to walk the Mollepata trek or from Chilca up the Silque valley a **compass** is essential.

Useful items include **spare bootlaces, spare buckles** for your rucksack, **candles** (for when your spare batteries run out), **string** (for a clothes line), **compact binoculars**, **paper and pen** (many hikers bring a **diary**), **insect repellent**, a **small trowel** for burying your turds, and a small, thin **towel**. You could bring **biodegradeable washing liquid** although you can clean just about anything from your pans with a wire scouring pad. Some people find a **collapsible plastic bucket** useful for washing so as not to pollute the water source.

You don't need mountaineering equipment (ice-axes, ropes, crampons) on these treks.

Cameras and photography

Some people don't carry cameras, feeling that carrying a camera turns them from a participant into a mere observer, but whenever I've left my camera at home I've regretted it. A slim **compact camera** will be fine for snapshots, but if you're more ambitious you should take an **SLR** with a polarising filter and a wide-angle lens. It'd be good to take a portrait lens too, but you shouldn't weigh yourself down too much.

As for **film**, because the light's so strong you needn't bother with anything faster than 200ASA. It's best to bring all the film you need from home. You should also bring a replacement set of batteries for your camera. Although print and slide film can be bought in Cuzco and Lima, you can't be sure that it hasn't been left lying around in the sun (which degrades the chemicals in the film). When flying never put film in baggage that goes in the hold as this may be X-rayed (or even lost). Remove film from your hand luggage before it is X-rayed. The official may simply point to a label on the machine that says 'Film Safe' but you should not believe this and request a hand search.

Because of the strong light, the best time to take photos is in the early morning or late afternoon. If you want to take someone's picture always ask them first. Like you they value their privacy (see p156).

If you're buying videos in Peru note that the system used is NTSC not PAL. This is used in USA, and not compatible with the UK's system.

FOOD

Bring some dehydrated or vacuum-packed trekker's food from home and use it as emergency rations or a treat, but don't load yourself up as you'll be able to buy all the main food you need in Cuzco.

When you're off up the mountains, take food that doesn't weigh much, but which provides large amounts of carbohydrate, sugary food and little treats to raise your spirits. Examples of good food to take, all of which you can buy out there, are dehydrated potato, polenta, *quinoa* (an Andean grain), porridge, milk powder, dried noodles and packet soup. Also take some dried fruit and nuts, chocolate, sugar, stock cubes, salt, pepper (keep them in used film canisters), dried sausage or tinned meat. Ground cinnamon and cloves go well in the porridge. All of this is light and nutritious. It helps greatly if you divide the food into a separate plastic bag for each day, and then you won't have to empty your whole rucksack looking for the last packet of soup.

MEDICAL KIT

Mine contains: assorted **plasters**, different sizes of **sterile gauze**, a **triangular bandage**, a **crepe bandage**, an **elastic support**, some **moleskin** or **compeed** (for blisters), **antiseptic** cream and wipes, **antihistamine** cream, **ibuprofen**, soluble **aspirin** tablets (for sore throats), a **spare lighter**, **spare needle and thread**. You might also want to take **acetozelomide** (Diamox) for altitude sickness (see p161) and for diarrhoea **loperamide** (Imodium) and **re-hydrating powders**.

Some people carry a course of antibiotics which they get from their doctor at home. Note that over-use of antibiotics can create super bugs that are resistant to treatment so you should only use them if it's really necessary.

MAPS

The IGN (Instituto Geográfico Nacional) in Lima sell good maps of the region, which you can also buy from the South American Explorers' Club (see p106). The maps you want, which are on a scale of 1:100,000, are: 2444 (27-r) and 2344 (27-q). The bottom of 27-q is incomplete, which is a problem as this contains Mollepata, the starting point for one of the treks.

There's also a 1:200,000 map of the region to the north of Cuzco that's of no use for hiking because the scale's too great and it's inaccurate. However, it does give a general overview of the region.

RECOMMENDED READING
Guidebooks
My favourite guidebook is *The Rough Guide to Peru* but *Peru Handbook* (Footprint) and the Lonely Planet's *Peru* are both excellent.

Hilary Bradt's *Backpacking and Trekking in Peru and Bolivia* (Bradt Publications in the UK, Globe Pequot Press in USA) is the classic guide to trekking in these two countries. Charles Brod's *Apus & Incas* (Inca Expeditions, 1989) is a very good guide to hiking in the area around Cuzco but difficult to obtain. There's also Peter Frost's *Exploring Cuzco*. The only widely available phrase book in Quechua is published by Lonely Planet.

General books on Peru
The Peru Reader (Duke University Press 1995), edited by Orin Starn and others, is an interesting introduction to all of Peru, past and present. For analyses of modern Peru, read *Fujimori's Peru* edited by John Crabtree

and Jim Thomas (Institute of Latin American Studies 1998), and *Shining Path,* Simon Strong (HarperCollins 1992). *A Fish in the Water* by Mario Vargas Llosa (English translation Faber & Faber 1994) is a description of his 1990 election campaign.

The Incas and their ancestors
Richard Burger's lavishly illustrated *Chavín and the Origins of Andean Civilisation* (Thames and Hudson 1992) is the seminal book on how it all started. *The Incas and their Ancestors* by Michael Moseley (Thames and Hudson 1992) is a good survey of where it went from there.

In the nineteenth century, Prescott and Markham wrote famous histories of the Incas but the best book on the subject is John Hemming's *The Conquest of the Incas*, (Penguin 1983, Papermac 1993). This book is excellent reading and a thorough piece of scholarship.

There are hundreds of other books on the Incas, ranging from children's pop-up books to academic tomes. The best place to start looking for a reading list is in the bibliography of Rebecca Stone-Miller's art-history book *Art in the Andes*, (Thames and Hudson 1993). *The Cities of the Ancient Andes* by Adriana von Hagen and Craig Thomas (Thames and Hudson 1998) also has a good reading list.

Machu Picchu
Machupicchu, Devenir Histórico y Cultural Efrain Chevarria Huarcaya, (UNSAAC 1992) is a guide to Machu Picchu and its position in Peru's history and culture (only available in Spanish). *Machu Picchu* by John Hemming (Readers' Digest *Wonders of Man Series* 1981) is the best book in English on the subject. Worth a read are *The Sacred Centre* Johan Reinhard (Nuevas Imágenes 1991), which gives an alternative view of

---

❑ INTERNET SITES

Peru
www.rcp.net.pe (a general guide to Peru), **www.peruonline.com** (another general guide to Peru) and **www.travel-library.com** (an excellent travel site with listings and links for Peru).

Cuzco
www.chaski.unsaac.edu.pe/cusco (home page of a cybercafé in Cuzco, and a good information source for the area, including Machu Picchu), **www.city.net** (a good general site providing listings for Cuzco).

General information
www.traficoperu.com (detailed information on as diverse things as flights and restaurants, lodging and car hire), **http://paginasamarillas.telefonica.com.pe** (Peru's yellow pages online). **www.samexplo.org** is the website of the South American Explorers' Club (see p106).

what Machu Picchu's about, and Jim Bartle and Peter Frost's attractive coffee-table book, *The Machu Picchu Historical Sanctuary* (Nuevas Imágenes 1995).

Travelogues and expedition reports

Early descriptions of Peru include *Peregrinations of a Pariah* by Flora Tristan and the beautifully illustrated 1877 book *Peru. Travel and Exploration in the Land of the Incas* by E George Squier (Macmillan & Co).

Hiram Bingham's most accessible account of his travels is *Inca Land* (Constable & Co, 1922) and of the discovery of Machu Picchu is *The Lost City of the Incas* (Duell, Sloan and Pearce 1948). This last book is now available in a reprint all over Cuzco. Gene Savoy, the man who finally established the location of the ancient capital of the rebel Incas (see p99) wrote up his explorations in *Antisuyu* (Simon and Schuster 1970). Dr. Paul Fejos explored what's now called the Inca Trail and published the results in *Publications in Anthropology #3: Archaeological Explorations in the Cordillera Vilcabamba* (The Werner Gren Foundation, The Viking Fund 1944).

Cut Stones and Crossroads (Penguin 1984) is a good modern travelogue written by Ronald Wright (sadly now out of print); and Matthew Paris has published a characteristically well-written book called *Inca Cola* (George Weidenfeld & Nicholson, 1990).

Other books

The *Royal Hunt of the Sun*, Peter Shaffer, is a play about the fall of the last Inca Atahualpa (see p95). *The Heights of Machu Picchu* Pablo Neruda, (Jonathan Cape 1966) is an extended piece inspired by the ruins by the Nobel Prize-winning Chilean poet.

Two good books on keeping yourself healthy are *Bugs, bites and bowels* Dr Jane Wilson Howarth (Cadogan Books 1995) and *Medical Handbook for Mountaineers* Peter Steele (Constable 1988).

For more information on the effects of high altitude, there's an accessible guide aimed at non-medics: *Altitude Illness, Prevention & Treatment* by Stephen Bezruchka MD (Cordee 1994).

Pre-departure health preparations

FITNESS

Obviously it doesn't need saying but one of the most important health preparations is to get reasonably fit. You don't have to be a marathon runner, but you'll enjoy yourself much more if you're in good shape.

INOCULATIONS

Before you travel you should make sure that you've been immunised against the following diseases: **tetanus**, **polio** and **diphtheria**, **tuberculosis**, **yellow fever**, **hepatitis A** and **typhoid.** Check that the shot you had is still effective and that you do not need a booster. There was a serious outbreak of cholera in Peru in 1991 but there's not much point being inoculated against it as the cholera germ has become resistant to the vaccine. If you're going to the jungle (below 2000m) then you should take a course of anti-**malaria** tablets.

If you're walking the longer trails, consider having a **rabies** inoculation too. It's expensive and you need to leave a month between injections, but as you will be a couple of day's walk from the nearest transport to the nearest hospital and the locals' dogs aren't usually friendly, it's wise to have one. The inoculation won't, however, prevent the disease, it'll only buy you more time to get to hospital.

> **❏ Dealing with dogs**
> It's worth noting that if a dog does run up to you barking you should do as the locals do: pick up a stone and throw it in the dog's direction. If there's no stone nearby simply making as if to pick up a stone will usually scare off the dog.

To check on the latest requirements, look at the **US Center for Disease Control** website: www.cdc.gov, or ask a doctor. Travel clinics are usually better informed than your local doctor, however. Up-to-the-minute health information and an on-the-spot vaccination service is available in London at **Nomad Travellers Store & Medical Centre** (☎ 0181-833 4114, STA Travel, 40 Bernard St, WC1N 1LJ). There are also clinics run by **Trailfinders** (see p17) and **British Airways** (☎ 0171-606 2977 to find one near you). Note that while some inoculations are available on the NHS in the UK, you'll have to pay for all inoculations at travel clinics.

HIGH ALTITUDE TRAVEL

The effects of high altitude

You should be aware of the possible ill effects of high altitude before you go, and people with heart and lung problems or high blood pressure should get advice from their doctor before travelling. Children are more susceptible to altitude sickness than adults so should not be taken above 3000m or 10,000ft. Young adults (in their teens or early twenties) are also more susceptible and extra days should be allowed for acclimatisation. Cuzco is at 3360m (11,000 ft) above sea level, and the highest pass

---

(Opposite): A Quechua woman at Chinchero market. The Quechua are the direct descendants of the Incas. (Photo © Ladislav Blazek).

described in this book is 5000m (16,400ft). The altitude can do funny things to you. The first thing you'll notice is that you're always short of breath, but you may also lose your appetite, have difficulty sleeping and sometimes wake up feeling as if you've been slightly smothered. You might also notice your companions' breathing becoming increasingly shallow as they sleep, before an enormous grunting breath reassures you they're still alive. Don't worry, all this is normal. It's caused by your body having to deal with less oxygen at a lower pressure than it's used to at lower elevations. Almost everyone who comes to Cuzco notices some of these things, and it's so common that the better restaurants and hotels have oxygen available.

You might notice other things happening, too, in your first days up there with the gods. Your hands, face and ankles may swell up, and you may fart and burp more than usual. You'll probably get a headache. Rarely, some people suffer from fainting fits, but these aren't serious on their own.

Having given you all the bad news, I should reassure you that the most obvious effect of altitude you'll notice, once you're acclimatised, is a feeling of clearness and health.

Acclimatisation

Altitude sickness can be fatal but is entirely preventable. The key to avoiding problems is to acclimatise (see p159). The biggest mistake to make is to belt up from Lima (which is at sea level) and then expect your body to do everything that it normally does when you're breathing richer air. Take a couple of days lazing around Cuzco while your system catches up with you. After two weeks, you'll hardly notice the altitude.

For more information on health and safety while trekking see p158.

INSURANCE

You should take out travel insurance before you leave, or check you're covered by your domestic policies. In the US and Canada, your domestic health insurance or home owners, or rental insurance may cover you on this trip; check with your insurer.

Many travel insurance policies will cover you for trekking the routes described in this book but some won't. Check the small print before you sign up. For added safety, take out insurance specially tailored for trekkers or mountaineers. The British Mountaineering Council (☎ 0161-445 4747, ▤ 0161-445 4500), 177-179 Burton Rd, Manchester M20 2BB, do this sort of insurance for members.

(Opposite): At the colourful market in Pisac (see p148), which takes place on Sunday, Tuesday and Thursday mornings, you can buy anything from a bunch of carrots to an alpaca sweater. (Photo © Melissa Graham).

PART 2: PERU

Facts about the country

Peru is an amazing country. Within its borders there's part of the largest jungle on earth, the planet's driest desert and a large section of the world's second highest mountain range. The seas around Peru are no less impressive – there's a thousand times more food in Peru's coastal waters than there is the average ocean. Because it's a land of such extremes, Peru has an immense range of life forms: you can find 20 out of the planet's 34 life zones in Peru, more than any other country in the world.

Peru's attractions are not only geographical: it possesses a rich cultural tradition, both ancient (Peru is the source of ethereal Andean music) and modern (exemplified by the novelist, Mario Vargas Llosa, and the poet César Vallejo).

But Peru's not just a place of fascinating geography, natural history and cultural interest: it's also a country that's emblematic of modern South America. Climbing out of the pit of hyperinflation and attempting to establish economic stability, Peru is trying to live with the atrocities of a past conflict while struggling to entrench democracy.

GEOGRAPHICAL BACKGROUND

Peru covers 1,280,000 square kilometres and is divided into three basic zones: *costa* (coast), *sierra* (highlands) and *selva* (jungle).

Geographical regions

The Pacific Ocean is circled with a ring of fire of soaring mountains and active volcanoes, caused by the massive plates that form the skin on the earth's core of molten rock ramming into each other. These plates can rise into the air and form mountains or can sink deep into the planet's crust and melt. When this melted rock rises to the surface again it causes volcanoes to form. This is how the Andes, the mountain range that separates Peru's Amazon rainforest from the Pacific coast, were formed.

Costa The geography of Peru's coast is dominated by the **Humboldt (or Peru) current**. This is a cold stream of water, so cold that it creates above itself a wide mass of chill coastal air. This air forms a barrier that the warm moist winds of the Pacific can't penetrate, and so scarcely any rain falls on the coast. Because the coast's so parched, the **Atacama desert**

has formed – a long thin strip of scorched land that extends far down into Chile. The Humboldt current is also rich in nutrients and supports a vast amount of sea life.

Sierra There are two branches of the Andes in Peru, the *Cordillera Blanca* (White Range) fronting the Amazon and the *Cordillera Negra* (Black Range) which parallels the coast. Between the two ranges is the *altiplano* (high plateau), an enclosed plain 800km long, which is characterised by high grasslands called *puna* whose fertile topsoil has been scraped off by glaciers. It's too cold up here for this soil to be replaced naturally, and so it's pretty barren land.

Selva The eastern slopes of the Andes are covered by the edge of the Amazonian rainforest, which the locals call the *cejas de la selva* or eyebrows of the jungle. The selva itself is largely unexplored.

Climate

Peru carries the curse of El Niño. Usually the country's climate is predictable; it's always dry on the coast and there's regular rainfall in the mountains but a couple of times a decade El Niño hits.

El Niño is a change in the weather brought on by a change in the currents of the Pacific Ocean. What happens is that the coast becomes bathed in warmer waters that have made their way across the Pacific. The Humboldt current disappears, and the fish that bless Peru's coast swim south to colder waters. Damp winds roll from the sea over the desert, causing heavy rains that drench the land and cause serious flooding. Many people die or are made homeless. The effects aren't limited to South America. On the other side of the world, El Niño inverts usual weather patterns and causes devastation. Whilst the mechanics of this scourge are understood, the cause isn't. It seems to come in seven-year

---

❏ **El Niño and the fall of the Moche and Tiahuanaco**
The periodic climactic upheaval of El Niño causes great damage. The last major one, in 1998, killed at least 900 people, destroyed hundreds of thousands of domestic animals and caused an estimated US$90 billion worth of damage across the world. In the past, however, El Niño's done worse. It's probable that it finished off two ancient Peruvian civilisations and prompted the expansion of a third.

Samples of ice taken from a Peruvian glacier suggest that there was an El Niño about the time of the decline of the Moche civilisation (see p72), which supports theories that the Moche were wiped out by massive climactic change. It's also likely that the same phenomenon caused the fall of the greatest of pre-Inca civilisations, the Tiahuanaco, and a similar environmental catastrophe destroyed the fertile lands of Chimú and spurred them on to conquer their neighbours (see p79).

cycles but until we know why El Niño happens, there's no way of predicting exactly when it will come back.

The phenomenon was first noticed to occur around Christmas, and so called *El Niño* (the boy) after Jesus. El Niño has an opposite called *La Niña* (the girl), when the seas are unusually cold.

El Niño shows that Peru's climate isn't static, but there's more to it than just these short term disturbances. About 12,000 years ago most of Peru was covered by massive ice sheets, and even within the past 4000 years there have been cycles of heating and cooling; just 300 years ago Peruvians were growing plants at 4200m that you can only grow today at 3700m. The only thing that's static about Peru's climate is the fact that it changes.

● **Costa** Summer is from December to April. The temperature ranges from 25°C to 35°C, and rainfall is extremely rare. Winter comes from May to November, when the temperature drops by about 10°C and there's lots of fog and cloud and a little rain too.

● **Sierra** There isn't really a summer and winter in the sierra, more like a rainy and a dry season. April or May to October is the dry season, when temperatures range from 25°C by day to -20°C by night. November to March is the wet season; the temperature's pretty much the same by day, but it's much warmer at night.

● **Selva** The wet and dry seasons are the same as the Sierra, but it's hot just about all the time.

HISTORICAL OUTLINE

For Peru before the Spanish see Part 3, pp67-100.

Peru under the Spanish

In 1542, after the Spanish authorities consolidated their power by mopping-up a brief revolt by some rebellious *conquistadors* (the name given to the Spanish conquerors of the Americas), they created the Viceroyalty of Peru. It was a massive, immensely rich place, governing all of South America except Venezuela and Brazil. Peru was the jewel in the crown of Spanish South America, the centre of law, administration and commerce for a whole continent. Lima became one of the most important cities in the hemisphere; the highest court in the continent was in Lima, and if you were a trader anywhere between Quito and Chile your goods could only leave the continent through Lima's port, Callao. Things only got better for the Spanish Peruvians with the discovery in 1545 of a mountain of silver called Potosí, in what's now Bolivia.

Spanish rule in theory The Spanish Crown tried to rule humanely, protecting the Indians from the excesses of the settlers. The principles of rule were fiercely Roman Catholic and profoundly nationalistic, not surprising considering that Spain had just emerged from under the heel of the Moors. The theory was that the Crown was supreme, and no government should be left to the locals, be they conquistadors or *cabildos* (town councils). Everything was owned by the Crown, and was supposed to revert to the Crown. Spaniards were only permitted to hold *encomiendas* (land, and with it the benefit of the labour of any Indians who lived on it) if they spread Christianity, and they were not permitted to live on their property, nor could they leave it to their children. Indians were not slaves; they were equals who simply hadn't learnt of the Gospels, and they should be treated as such. Crown agents called *corregidors* were appointed to keep a watch over things.

Spanish rule in practice It didn't, of course, work like that on the ground. Spain was making too much money to really want to emancipate the Indians, and even if its intentions had been uncompromised by greed, it was too far away to supervise the implementation of its laws. In any case, the *encomenderos* (owners of encomiendas) were out for all they

---

❑ La Leyenda Negra

The stories of the great atrocities inflicted by the Spanish on the Incas are called by some *La Leyenda Negra* (The Black Legend). Anglo-Saxons, looking south with envious eyes, have always been prepared to believe the worst about the Spanish Empire, and stories of great evils perpetrated on the noble Peruvians have been frequently told by historians such as Markham and Prescott. In the nineteenth century, the Inca civilisation became for many in the Romantic movement a golden age of harmony, violated by the conquistadors.

Spaniards maltreating Incas
FELIPE HUAMÁN POMA DE AYALA

The truth is more complicated, of course. The Incas didn't run a perfect society: they were ferocious and merciless in war, and Atahualpa (see p95) admitted that if he'd captured the Spaniards he would have enslaved them and had them castrated. But the bottom line has to take account of the horrors of Spanish rule, especially the horrors associated with the silver mines of Potosí, Bolivia. It was there that hundreds of thousands of Indians met their deaths, suffocated in the depths of the mountain or maddened by the chemicals used to extract the silver itself. Convoys of pressed labour made their way here from all over the old Inca Empire, men separated from their families, and tied together by the neck. If these poor sufferers were too weary to continue, or if they fell, the Spaniards didn't waste time loosening their bonds, they simply cut their bodies from the yoke with swords. These were days of great suffering.

❏ Bishop la Casa, a contemporary supporter of the Indians, wrote: '...long before they [the Indians] had heard the word Spaniard they had properly organised states, wisely ordered by excellent laws, religion and custom... [they were ruled by] laws that at very many points surpass ours, and could have won the admiration of the sages of Athens... Now what belief will be placed in the Spaniards – greedy, violent, and cruel men who put unarmed and harmless Indians to the sword and rob them with extraordinary avarice?'

could get, wouldn't have obeyed laws that deprived them of their labour force. Consequently many Indians were worked to the bone (the silver mines at Potosí – see boxed text, p37 – were particularly horrific places), and much of the glory of Imperial Spain was built from the sweat and blood of the children of the Incas.

However, it wasn't simply a case of the European power raping Peru and Peruvians (though there's no doubt they did both), and from Don Cristóbal Paullu Inca onwards some Indians did very well out of the conquest.

The empire in decline The flower of Peru and Lima's glory held the seeds of the decline of the Viceroyalty, and Peru's pre-eminence was one of the causes of the decline of the Spanish Empire. For example, it was incredibly inefficient to have the continent's only port in Callao, and this caused smuggling to become commonplace and Spain's laws to be flouted. Disregard for the mother country extended further: the colonists did not like the benevolent attitude of the Crown to Indians or the fact that locally born Spaniards (Creoles) were denied any power – such positions were reserved for newcomers from Spain. It didn't help matters that less money was coming in from mining and that pirates were scourging the coast.

The empire rallies and Peru declines A historian has described the eighteenth century, when the Bourbons replaced the Hapsburgs on the Spanish throne, as a second conquest. The colonies were once again ruled with vigour, and South America was transformed. Power was consolidated by the tightening of the regulations prohibiting Creoles from holding public office, and the Jesuits were expelled. Peru ceased to be the only Viceroyalty in the continent, and became just one of many: the Viceroy of new Granada deprived Peru of its northern territory in 1718, the Viceroyalty of Río de la Plata (Argentina, Paraguay and Uruguay) cut off its eastern provinces in 1776 and Chile became a virtually autonomous captaincy general. The trade system was reformed removing Lima's monopoly as a port, and old taxes were put up and new ones imposed.

Days of rebellion This caused problems. In 1780 a prosperous Indian called José Gabriel Condorcanqui took the name of the last Inca Tupac

Amaru (see p139), and revolted against the authorities. He said – to start with at least – that he was loyal to the Spanish Crown and church, and was rebelling against increased taxation and oppressive labour. Then his movement began to mean something more: it began to be an attempt to recreate the rule of the Incas. He was captured and executed in 1781 (his execution took seven hours), but his revolt carried on till 1783.

These events were seen amongst Europeans (for example Baron von Humboldt, the German naturalist after whom the sea current was named) as a war waged by the forces of civilisation against those of barbarism. It's now seen rather differently as the stalking horse of Peruvian Independence.

Liberation

The turn of the eighteenth century was a time of revolution in America and France – something that wouldn't have escaped the notice of the Spanish colonies in South America. Then, in 1808, Napoleon invaded Spain who, desperate to resist the French, asked for help from its empire, and the price of Spanish American support was more recognition of the rights of Creoles. And so, partly because of the revolutionary atmosphere of the time, and partly because of the abasement of Spain, Spanish America began to taste independence.

Peru was very loyal to the Crown, because it had done very well out of the empire. It's no surprise then, that it was liberated by outsiders rather than being the seat of sedition. What is surprising is that in the wars of liberation there were more Peruvians in the monarchist army of Spain than in the liberating army of South America.

Peru was freed by the two great South American liberators: **San Martín** and **Simon Bolívar**. Two more different men it's difficult to imagine. San Martín was a refined, cautious, cold Argentinian; Bolívar was a heated, hairy, impulsive Venezuelan but both were equally brilliant generals. San Martín started the ball rolling by kicking the Spanish out of Argentina and Chile, but he needed to secure his victory by denying Spain the wealth of Potosí and access to the port of Callao. In other words, he needed to liberate Peru. He landed in Pisco from Chile in 1818 and fought his way up to Lima, entering the city and declaring Independence in 1820 just as the Viceroy was escaping with the remains of the royalist army.

San Martín travelled north to meet Bolívar, from whom he asked for help in defeating the Viceroy. Bolívar refused, wanting all the glory for himself, and so San Martín abandoned the country to his northern colleague. Bolívar finished off the royalists at the battles of Junín (6 August 1824) and Ayacucho (9 December 1824).

First steps in independence

Bolívar was made political supreme chief in 1824 but the Peruvians feared absorption into his 'greater Colombia' and abandoned him soon thereafter. Sadly there was a reluctance by civilians to take power because there was no tradition of self-government in the country and so, in a coup that was to mark a pattern in the rest of Peru's history, the *caudillos* (military leaders) seized control. A soldier called **Gamarra** became president, and the die of Peru's history was cast.

In 1835-6, Peru was promptly invaded by the dictator of Bolivia, Santa Cruz, who planned to create a confederation with Bolivia. Chile and Argentina put a stop to these plans at the battle of Yungay in 1839, and recreated Peru's independence. Gamarra became president again, and retaliated by invading Bolivia; his army was defeated and he was killed at Yngavi in 1841.

One revolt later an honest and tolerant man, **Ramón Castilla**, became president. His presidency coincided with the exploitation of *guano* (bird excrement fertiliser) in the Chincha islands and the nitrate of Tarapacá, so he had wealth to play with. He built railways and invested in the education of the Indians, abolished the system of tribute, and emancipated black slaves. Prosperity and stability weren't to last, and the next president, **Balta** (1868-72), encouraged by Castilla's example, spent vast sums on the Andean railways, money the country could ill afford. He hung the albatross of Peru's national debt around its neck.

War with Spain
Then in 1864 came war with Spain, which had never formally let go of its colonies. A Spanish squadron seized the valuable Chincha islands. The Peruvian president, Pezet, would have been happy to pay a ransom to get them back, but he was quickly replaced as leader by a man called Prado, who went to war against the Spanish in alliance with Chile, Ecuador and Bolivia. The Spanish bombarded Callao and the Chilean port of Valparaíso in 1866 then slunk off home, but it wasn't until 1871 that an armistice was signed. Spain finally acknowledged Peruvian independence only in 1879.

War of the Pacific
Having beaten off the Spanish, Peru didn't have much time to enjoy itself. The price of guano, a main Peruvian export, fell after the invention of chemical fertilisers and so Peru's finances got worse. Prado decided to make the sale of nitrates a government monopoly and he arranged compensation for the mine owners. The Chileans who owned the mines didn't think he paid them enough.

Their government was spoiling for a fight anyway, and Prado's action antagonised them. Bolivia and Peru, aware of this, had entered into a half-secret alliance against the Chileans in 1873.

War broke out between Chile and Bolivia in 1879, and surprisingly, when Peru offered to mediate between the two the Chileans declared war on Peru. To start with, all went well for the Peruvians. They won the battle of Iquique sinking the Chilean ship, the *Indepencia*, but then it all went wrong and they lost Arica. By 1881 the Chileans had occupied Lima, and a humiliating peace treaty was signed at Ancón in 1883, which ultimately resulted in Peru losing its southern provinces.

Picking up the pieces

If Peru was in a bad way before the War of the Pacific it was desperate after, and by 1890 it couldn't pay its foreign debt. The British bondholders who held this debt formed the **Peruvian Corporation**, an organisation which undertook to pay it off in return for annual payments, a 66-year lease of the railways and guano concessions. The Peruvians hated this arrangement but despite the humiliation, relative peace followed, and the country was buoyed up by rising copper production. Reforms were introduced such as direct suffrage, public education programmes and municipal elections. One of the main presidents of this time was **Leguía**, who ruled from 1908-12 and then from 1919-30. He began well, but when he was conciliatory to Chilean claims for Peruvian land in the south and Ecuadorian claims in the north he lost the sympathy of his people.

The dance of APRA and the army

The Depression finished off Leguía, and he was ousted in a coup in 1931, but a more interesting fish was being fried far from the centre stage of Peruvian politics. This was the **APRA party** (*Alianza Popular Revolucionaria Americana*) formed by Victor Raul Haya de la Torre. APRA was to dominate Peru right through to the 1980s, either through being in power or being suppressed by the army.

APRA started off Marxist and was bent on integrating the oppressed minorities of Peru, resisting what they called the economic imperialism of the US, and founding a union of Latin American states. Haya de la Torre first stood for president in 1931 and lost. APRA cried foul, and in 1932 staged an **uprising in Trujillo**, during which they killed 50 army hostages. Up to 5000 people were then taken out into the desert by the army and shot. APRA retaliated by assassinating the president in 1933.

Banned by the authorities, APRA continued to operate covertly and endorsed a presidential candidate in the 1936 elections. However, just as their candidate was about to win, Congress annulled the elections and gave General Benavides dictatorial powers. He was followed by Dr Manuel Prado Ugarteche who, except in his relations with Ecuador, was a pan-Americanist – Peru followed the USA and declared war on Germany and Japan, if a little late, in February 1945.

In 1941 Ecuador and Peru had a **border war** which Peru won, causing Ecuador to cede parts of its southern territory. The war still festers, and it last erupted in 1995, but a recent peace deal looks as if it may hold.

In the 1945 election, APRA was legalised and got a majority of the seats in the lower house and half of the seats in the upper house.

However, shortly after the election, President Bustamente (elected on an APRA ticket) went independent and so APRA staged an uprising in Callao. They were banned again, and suppressed so fiercely that Haya de la Torre had to seek sanctuary in the Colombian embassy for the next five years.

Land reform – 1963
In the fifties, the power of APRA declined. In a bizarre marriage of convenience, they sided with their old enemies the army in support of Manuel Prado in the 1956 election. About this time the pressures from landless *campesinos* (peasants) increased, and there was a bloody revolt in the Cuzco area led by Hugo Blanco.

After the 1962 election was inconclusive, a military junta rather predictably seized power but they permitted another election in 1963 that was won by **Belaúnde Terry**. By this stage everyone was worried by the campesinos' volatility, and so agrarian reform was implemented, with 500,000 acres of land being distributed. This was an important step, and the campesinos of Peru, who had from time immemorial worked the land for a distant landlord – the Incas, the encomenderos, the hacienda owners – finally worked the land for themselves. Whether you think they have thrived or withered since depends on your politics.

The military take control
The military didn't hold back for long, and in 1968 they forced the resignation of Belaúnde, imprisoned politicians and suspended rights. It was a time of friendship with Soviet Russia and of censorship. Nationalisation of industry followed, and with the Agrarian, Mining, and Industrial Laws the government seized control of Peru's industries. More land was given to the campesinos and in 1973 the government reformed the education system, recognised the equality of women, built rural schools (permitting children to be taught in Quechua and Aymara) and gave autonomy to the University. The national debt grew, increased by the cost of agrarian reform and a decline in the price of fishmeal and copper.

Things fall apart
The army allowed elections again in 1978 and after a new constitution was drafted, Haya de la Torre was finally elected President. However, he didn't last long, beaten in the 1980 elections by Belaúnde Terry who reorganised the economy along free-market lines.

It was about now that things started to go seriously wrong. In 1982-3, an El Niño hit the fishing industry, and the terrorist movements **Sendero Luminoso** (The Shining Path) and the **MTRA** (*Movimiento Revolucionario Tupac Amaru,* Tupac Amaru Revolutionary Movement) built up a head of steam. Peru's currency, the sol, collapsed, and inflation ran riot. In 1983 APRA were elected and **President García** tried to remedy the situation by not paying more than 10% of Peru's foreign debt, a move that caused the international banks to refuse to make any further loans to Peru. The situation got steadily worse. García's administration became increasingly characterised by graft and human rights abuses, which peaked when the *Rodrigo Franco Commando* (a right-wing death squad) started fighting the terrorists with extreme violence. The people who suffered were those caught in the middle, the campesinos.

The economy got steadily worse, and in 1987 García moved to nationalise the banks, a move that caused strikes and inflation. The country descended into a spiral of misery.

1990s – Peru under Fujimori

The 1990 election was, therefore, one of the most important for a century. With the economy and society in tatters, the novelist **Mario Vargas Llosa** (see p48) stood for President as a moderate right-wing candidate against APRA. Hardly anyone noticed another contender, a provincial agricultural engineer of Japanese ancestry, called **Alberto Fujimori**. Against the odds, Llosa lost, and Fujimori won.

In 1992 Fujimori shut down the Congress and dismissed the Supreme Court, and in 1993 the constitution of Peru was rewritten. Fujimori then

---

❑ Terrorism in Peru

The two main terrorist groups in Peru are the Communist party of Peru, (Sendero Luminoso or Partido Comunista de Perú) and the Tupac Amaru Revolutionary Movement (MTRA).

The **Sendero Luminoso**, founded in the 1970s by philosophy professor Abimael Guzmán Reynoso (aka 'Comrade' or 'Presidente Gonzalo'), are Maoists intolerant of global capitalism and the Peruvian government. They draw their support from dissatisfied campesinos (of which there are many), particularly those who live in the highlands around Ayacucho. The Sendero ruthlessly persecute those who don't support their ideology. If you're not with them, you're against them, and any other group is a target: in 1991, for example, they killed four mothers and their children because they were distributing free milk to children. Guzmán has been in prison since 1992; Nicholas Shakespeare's book, *The Dancer Upstairs*, is based on his arrest.

The other Peruvian terrorist organisation, the **MTRA**, was little-known abroad until they took over the residence of the Japanese ambassador in December 1996, having got in disguised as waiters. (It was only by chance that the Peruvian president, Alberto Fujimori, himself of Japanese ancestry, wasn't there.) The MTRA are a more moderate left-wing terrorist group, but they've never been as strong as the Sendero. The Japanese ambassador's siege gained them notoriety, and then won Fujimori support when in April 1998 he sent in the military. The building was stormed and all but one of the hostages were released unharmed. All the terrorists were killed, as were two soldiers.

embarked on economic and legal reform which he claimed would enable the country's economy to grow and assist in the crushing of the Sendero Luminoso. It also, surprise, surprise, allowed him to stand for another term in office.

This has been called the **President's coup**, and it was either a master stroke of development or a bloodless coup d'état, depending on your point of view. However, in 1992 Abimael Guzmán, the leader of the Sendero, was arrested by the police, and the economy has now been brought under control. The Peruvian people obviously thought that Fujimori was justified, and endorsed his actions when nearly two in three of them voted for him in the 1995 elections, in which he beat the ex-head of the United Nations, Javier Perez de Cuellar.

Since then, Fujimori's government has negociated peace with Ecuador and managed the economy to the satisfaction of the IMF and USA.

THE PEOPLE

Most (70%) of Peru's 23.9 million people live in modern cities, but the society is deeply rooted in its past; about half the population is **Quechua,** the descendants of the Incas. The blood of the Incas was mixed with that of the Spanish from the first days of the conquest, and a third of the people are the products of these unions: **mestizo**; only a fifth are **white**.

The others that make up Peru include the significant minority of **Aymara** around Lake Titicaca, and about 250,000 indigenous **jungle tribespeople**. There's also a small **black** population, based south of Lima, who are the descendants of those unfortunates brought to Peru as slaves (in the first century alone after the conquest as many as 10,000 were brought to Peru).

The Quechua who farm the highlands prefer to be called *campesinos* (peasants) and not *indios* (Indians), which they consider an insult.

Education and literacy

About one in ten adult Peruvians is illiterate. Over a third of Peru's population is under 14 and education's now free and compulsory up to the age of 16. It's difficult to enforce this in rural areas, but the government estimates that most of Peru's children have primary education, two thirds of children go to secondary school and a quarter are in tertiary education. The government spends 9.3% of its budget on education, but publicly-funded schooling doesn't have a good reputation and those who can afford it send their children to private schools.

Language

(For useful words and phrases see p229). Spanish is the main language today, but **Quechua** (or *Runasimi*, 'the people's mouth') is spoken by about 10 million people concentrated around Cuzco and southern Peru, two million of whom don't speak anything but Quechua. In the main tourist areas in Lima and Cuzco English is understood by some people. Around Lake Titicaca, the ancient language *Aymara* survives; it dates from before the Incas.

Quechua, the language of the Incas, was not written down till the sixteenth century so there are many different ways of transcribing it. It's difficult to be consistent, as different words have become familiar in different spellings: Inca can be written Inka, Sacsayhuaman as Saq'saywaman, and Cuzco as Cusco or Q'osqo. I've tried to be consistent in my spelling of Quechua words, except where a particular spelling of a word has become so familiar that spelling it another way looks bizarre.

Religion

Ninety-five percent of the population are **Roman Catholic**, and the Peruvian church is the cradle of 'liberation theology', a socialist interpretation of Christianity. However, in more rural areas the people have been better described by the anthropologist, Robert Randall, as '**Pagan Catholics**' whose Catholicism is mixed with indigenous beliefs, placing a veneer of Christianity on ancient ceremonies and substituting saints for local spirits.

There are various **Protestant** churches active in Peru, and they're considered predatory by some Catholics: you'll often see stickers in people's front windows telling Protestant canvassers to go away. Some of these churches are the charmless North American imports that have spread all over the world, but some are indigenous, such as the IEP (Evangelical Church of Peru) which has been in the country for a hundred years. Protestant churches have formed a solid base of support for President Fujimori.

POLITICS AND ECONOMICS

Politics

The president hires and fires ministers and is elected every five years with the 120 members of congress. The country is divided into 25 departments, governed by prefects who are also appointed by the presi-

> ❏ **Pilgrimage to Qoyllor Riti**
> This pilgrimage is a good example of what has been called Pagan Catholicism. Qoyllor Riti is a village in the *Nevado* (snow-capped peak) Ausangate near Cuzco, and once a year in early June many people climb the hills on a pilgrimage there. The Christian basis for the festival is that Christ appeared here to a young shepherd called Marianito in the eighteenth century but the festival dates back to the days before Christianity arrived in Peru, back to the days when pilgrimages were made to the *Apus* or spirits of the mountains who needed to be placated with human sacrifice. Some say that to this day there's always a death on the pilgrimage: a baby freezes to death on the glacier, or a campesino falls from a precipice and the Apu is satisfied.

dent. Departments are divided into provinces, which are sub-divided into districts, each governed by a mayor elected every five years.

Current politics Fujimori's party holds 67 out of the 120 seats in the Congress, and he looks unassailable in his control of Peru. The constitution states that he can't have three terms in office, but he wants his third term and he doesn't want to step aside. When the Constitutional Tribunal told him this was illegal he dismissed them.

Fujimori's party is called *Cambio 90* and the main opposition is *Somos Peru*. Other political parties are: *Accion Popular* (AP) – centre right; *Alianza Popular Revolucionaria Americana* (APRA) – originally a revolutionary left-wing party, now in tatters after Alan García's (see p42) disastrous presidency; *Izquierda Unida* (IU) – a left-wing umbrella group, now split by internal division and the *Partido Popular Cristiano* (PPC) – a right-wing, pro-business party centred around Lima. There is widespread disillusionment with traditional political parties in Peru.

The northern border war Ecuador claims that a large portion of Peru's north is by rights Ecuadorian territory; Ecuador wants access to the Amazon and its Atlantic ports. Peru fiercely rejects Ecuador's claim, and the they went to war over the area in 1942 and again as recently as 1995. After long negotiations, however, they finally worked out a peace deal in late 1998.

Human rights

The situation has improved since the dark days of Sendero Luminoso activity and government death squads, when whole villages were punished by the army for giving support to the Sendero and by the terrorists for helping the army. In 1996 a commission was set up to investigate miscarriages of justice incurred in the fight against terrorism, and 450 prisoners have been released: their records, however, remain marked with their convictions, and the life of the commission is limited.

Indeed, the culture of abuse hasn't died out, and Amnesty International endorses claims that the regime in Peru is an authoritarian civilian-military government, stating that torture and ill-treatment of those detained is widespread and systematic, and that those responsible are not punished. They also say that people working against Fujimori's campaign for a third term have received death threats.

There have been other non-political issues, too. In the early part of 1998 newspapers were reporting that the government was giving doctors mandatory monthly quotas of sterilisations to perform, and bribing illiterate campesino women to have the operation.

The economy

Peru is blessed with abundant mineral resources, seas teeming with fish and a wide range of climates that means just about anything can be grown there, but in the past hyperinflation and political instability practically ruined the country. The situation's better now and the economy is thriving, but there are still enormous differences in wealth and opportunity between the richest and poorest Peruvians.

The Fujimori administration has privatised large chunks of state-owned industry, reforming the tax system and eliminating many price controls and import tariffs. The economy is now largely free market and, following the reforms, the growth rate for real GDP was as high as 13%; it was a more realistic 7.4% in 1997. However, with the catastrophes of 1998 – El Niño and the Asian economic crisis – this halved.

Peru's chief exports are minerals and metals; it's traditionally been a mining economy but fishmeal and agricultural products are also impor-

---

❑ **Coca and cocaine**

It's been said that coca leaf has as much to do with cocaine as elephants have to do with ivory – it's the raw material from which the refined product comes, nothing more. Coca leaf has been chewed in the Andes for thousands of years, and it's as central to Andean culture as coffee is to the Arabs and tea is to people from the Indian subcontinent. Once, coca leaf was reserved for the Incas themselves, but in the days of the Spanish Empire it was chewed almost incessantly by overworked labourers.

The quid of leaves is chewed with a mixture of lime or quinoa and potash called *llipta*, releasing a natural anaesthetic which relieves hunger, and, in some way that's not understood, relieves the effect of altitude. Coca leaf has a long history in Andean culture, and you can see the characteristic quid in the cheeks of some portrait pots from the days of the Nazca (see p74), and implements associated with its use have been found from the Moche culture (see p72).

But the coca leaf is most famous around the world today because of its derivative, cocaine. This alkaloid was first isolated by a scientist called Gaedake in the nineteenth century, and when it was discovered it seemed an unalloyed benefit to humanity – a pain-relieving drug of great potency. However, over the years its abuse and restriction have created the demon that cocaine is today. In Peru, the main problem is the enormous profits that cocaine production can bring, and the growing of coca leaf to produce cocaine is organised by largely Colombian gangs of narco-terrorists, whose anarchic rule subjugates swathes of Peru's remote jungle.

The United Nations, and the USA's Drug Enforcement Agency (DEA), seem set to try and solve the world's cocaine problem by eradicating all coca leaf growing in the Andes. Sadly, this ignores both the traditional nature of the leaf in Andean society and the poverty that drives campesinos to try and make money from growing it. When the DEA torch remote fields that campesinos have spent months cultivating, they create hatred. The campesinos see cocaine as a problem of the urban West rather than rural Peru, and believe that the US's 'War On Drugs' is cynically fought in the highlands of Peru rather than where it could have more effect – in the USA itself – because there are no votes to lose in Peru.

tant. The largest proportion of Peru's trade is done with the United States and Japan (37%), but Germany, Italy and the UK are all heavily involved.

Domestically, manufacturing makes up the biggest individual slice (22%) of GDP, followed by trade and agriculture. Other significant activities are mining and construction. Annual inflation is around 7%.

Continuing economic problems   Until recently a staggering 94% of Peruvians didn't have a proper job, and Peru's wealth and income are still highly concentrated in the hands of a few old families, a source of festering discontent. According to the Peru Support Group (a NGO), just under half the population earn less than a dollar a day. For those that are in work the position is a little better. The average monthly wage for a housemaid is just US$115/£73, but a factory worker can expect to earn US$350/£220, and a doctor US$1575/£990.

On the international side of things, Peru's national debt is still large at five times the annual income from exports – a fifth of all the money Peru makes from its exports is spent on paying the interest on this debt.

The environment
Peru has its share of environmental problems as the country tries to balance the need for economic growth with ecological sensitivity.

The current hot potatoes are proposed oil developments in the jungle. The largest one of these is the Camisea Project. In 1998 Shell considered the exploitation of oil reserves in the selva to the north of Quillabamba, and this caused concern amongst environmental NGOs. There's 11 trillion cubic feet of oil and gas under the forest, and exploiting it would create US$500 million to US$1 billion. However, the area is rich in biodiversity and is populated by indigenous people who have little or no contact with the outside world. Shell, stung by international reaction to their Nigerian activities, abandoned the project but the government is still keen to develop the region.

CULTURE
Writing
Peru has a vibrant and powerful literary tradition, from the days of the conquest on. Many of the conquistadors left records of their battles, and on the Inca side there's the work of **El Inca Garcilasco de la Vega**, and **Felipe Huamán Poma de Ayala**.

Today **Mario Vargas Llosa** is Peru's most famous writer, a man whose books can stand up against the South American Titan, Gabriel García Márquez. Vargas Llosa was born into a middle-class family and is related to an ex-president of Peru. He writes narratives woven with the complexity of Andean fabric: try *Conversación en la Catedral* (Conversation in the Cathedral), or *La casa verde* (The Green House).

César Vallejo (1892-1938) is one of the Spanish language's greatest modern poets. Vallejo broke linguistic rules to write poetry that appears rough but has magnificent imaginative power.

Visual arts

The most significant form of **painting** to come out of Peru is the **Cuzco school**, which flourished in the seventeenth and eighteenth centuries. The Cuzco school consists of paintings of formal European subjects, such as religious themes, which have been re-interpreted by indigenous artists. There is a lot of decorative flower and bird patterns, and the use of applied gold on the canvas pre-empts Klimt, but the things that most tourists notice are the bizarre details such as angels armed with muskets. These paintings are still made and sold in the San Blas district of Cuzco (see p141). Christopher Isherwood came across these pictures and commented in *The Condor and the Cows* (1948): 'In the lounge, there are some beautiful and absurd Colonial religious paintings. My favourite represents an angel, a fairylike little girl with a sword and golden butterfly skirts, who has her foot coquettishly planted on a sprawling demon. The demon, who is old enough to be her father, is obviously loving it. He is leering and caressing her foot with the enthusiasm of a boot-fetishist'.

Peruvian **cinema** has never reached the heights of other Latin American countries such as Mexico or Brazil, but in Cuzco in 1955 Manuel Chambi set up a pioneering film club. The name Chambi is also famous in **photography** – Martín Chambi was a pioneering Cuzqueño photographer, who took, in 1920, the first iconic shot of Machu Picchu.

Music and dance

Music and dance are a breathing part of everyday campesino culture. The music's going to be familiar to you, either from Andean buskers who play in shopping malls all over the world, or from songs like Simon and Garfunkel's hit *El Condor Pasa*. Many people think that they composed the tune, but it's in fact a traditional Andean melody that was written in the eighteenth century to mark the execution of the rebel Tupac Amaru II, (see p38-9).

The basic instruments played are the *quena,* a simple flute with a notched end, and the *charango,* a mandolin originally made from the shell of an armadillo. You'll also see panpipes, drums, guitars and – occasionally – harps. Pipes of old didn't have the full scale, so tunes jumped from one player to another, but today they're made with a full complement of notes. The most widely available modern version of traditional Andean music is the Chilean group Inti Illimani.

More traditional musical styles come in different forms, such as the almost waltz-like *huayno* from the highlands or the *crillo* from the coast; a song called *La flor de la canela* sung by Chabuca Granda used to be the soul of Lima. Today they play *chicha* in the *pueblos jóvenes* (shanty towns), a music that's a fusion of Colombian dance with Andean music. Also watch out for brass bands pumping out oompa-oompa music at any major festival; it's usually an unforgettable cacophony of a dozen or so different bands blasting away at different tunes in different tempos all at the same time.

Media

The main **newspapers** are *El Commercio*, *del Expreso* and *La Republica*, and there are numerous tabloids that decorate their front pages with bare-bottomed women and fill their insides with gruesome stories of car crashes (with pictures) and horrific murders. The airwaves are packed with **radio** stations, and in the mountains they're the only way people can get the news. In Lima and Cuzco there is a wide range of cable **TV** stations including the predictable CNN and BBC World.

Sport

This is South America, so **football** (soccer) is all that matters. The main teams are Alianza, Universitario and Sporting Cristal. Don't mention the world cup: Peru missed out in 1994 and again in 1998. The 1998 campaign was particularly gutting for Peruvians, as Chile squeezed into the finals ahead of Peru by the smallest of margins. Learn the names of a couple of Peruvian footballers and you'll never be at a loss for conversation.

Practical information for the visitor

DOCUMENTS AND VISAS

To stay in Peru for up to 90 days no tourist visa is needed by citizens of EU countries, the US, Canada, Australia, and New Zealand. Nevertheless, check with a Peruvian embassy (see p236).

You should have proof that you've got enough money to finance your stay in Peru and a return ticket to show you're going to leave again, though you're not likely to be asked for these. You'll be given an Embarkation and Disembarkation card (TED) when you arrive, valid for 60 to 90 days. Always keep it, or a copy of it, on you and don't lose it or you'll be fined s/10 (US$3.50/£2.20). You can extend your stay by applying at the Immigration and Naturalisation Department (DIGEMIN, see p107 and p130), or by leaving and re-entering the country. They'll give you another 30 or 60 days, and charge US$20 (£12.50).

For those that need a tourist visa, it will cost around US$15 (prices vary according to your nationality), and two passport photos, a return ticket, and 'proof of economic solvency' are required.

AIRPORT TAX

When you leave Peru, you'll have to pay US$25 (about £16). On some internal flights (like Lima-Cuzco) there's an airport tax of s/10.

MONEY

Currency

The currency is the *nuevo sol*, often just called the sol, whose symbol is s/. A nuevo sol is divided into 100 *céntimos* (or cents), and is pretty stable: as a guide, it was s/3.32 = US$1 in May 1999, s/2.85 = US$1 in May 1998 and s/2.52 = US$1 in December 1996.

Notes in circulation are s/200, s/100, s/50, s/20, s/10. Coins in circulation are s/5, s/2, s/1, s/0.50, s/0.20 and s/0.10.

Hoard your s/10 and s/20 notes and avoid any with a value of over s/50 as you'll have difficulty getting change, but don't accept 'no change' as an excuse to rip you off. Don't get landed with damaged notes, as no one else will take them off your hands.

❑ Rates of exchange		
USA	$1	s/3.32
Europe	Euro 1	s/3.57
UK	£1	s/5.41
Canada	$1	s/2.28
Australia	$1	s/2.23
New Zealand	$1	s/1.87
Chile	$1000	s/6.99
Ecuador	S10,000	s/3.82
Bolivia	B10	s/5.77

For up-to-the-minute rates of exchange visit **www.xe.net/currency**

You can often use US dollars instead of soles, but watch out for forgeries; there are many in circulation.

There was horrendous inflation in the early 1990s (7600% in 1990), and the currency was twice devalued. Be careful that you don't get handed these worthless old notes when you exchange money. They are called *intis* and, rather confusingly, *soles*; there's no need to worry because they look completely different from nuevos soles. All mentions of 'soles' in this book mean nuevos soles.

Other forms of money

There are many **ATM**s (cash machines) in Lima and Cuzco where you can get money on your Visa or MasterCard, and many shops where you can use them as **credit cards**. Visa is the more useful. Using your bank card through an ATM linked to the Cirrus, Maestro or Plus systems it should soon be possible to get cash advances direct from your bank account. Check the logos on your card and the logos on the ATM.

It's much safer to carry **travellers' cheques** than cash but avoid the less well-known brands and take only US dollars – the number of soles you can buy for one pound sterling is sometimes half the amount you can buy for one US dollar because of high commission charged on most foreign currencies other than US$. American Express dollar travellers' cheques are by far the most commonly accepted.

Banks and cambios

Exchanging money and travellers' cheques is easy; there are many **banks** (opening times vary, but are generally weekdays 9am-12pm, 4pm-6pm) and **cambios.** Take your passport with you when you change money as you will need to prove your identity. There are often *cambistas* (money changers) on street corners, some of them wearing waistcoats that say they're regulated by the municipality. They seldom provide a better rate of exchange than the banks and cambios, and they're more likely to short-change you.

GETTING AROUND

Travelling between cities

The main way of travelling overland is by **bus**, and they're very cheap. Buses range from Chilean-style comfort wagons, the most luxurious road transport I've ever used, to broken old rattletraps. Always check where the departure terminal is, as it's often in a different place from the ticket office. There are hundreds of different bus lines competing with each other, but the main ones are **Cruz del Sur**, **Ormeño**, and **Civa**, although this last one is picking up a bad reputation for safety.

Where no buses run you can often **hitch** on a truck, but payment is often expected. It's wiser not to hitch alone.

There are some passenger **trains** still operating, notably the run from Arequipa and Puno to Cuzco (called the Southern Railway) and the run from Cuzco to Machu Picchu. There are also the remains of a railway from Lima to the highlands (the Central Railway) which recently restarted passenger services (see p119). There are many classes in Peruvian trains (see p120 and p142), you get the quality of ride you pay for.

Planes run regularly between Cuzco, Lima and other towns (see p119 and p142), and there's a **helicopter** that connects Cuzco with Machu Picchu (see p227). The main domestic airline is AeroContinente. AeroPeru went out of business in March 1999 and Faucett wasn't flying at the time of writing. A new airline called Lan Peru is scheduled to start operations in mid-1999.

You can sometimes cadge a lift with Groupo Ocho – the Air Force – but they don't have reliable schedules.

Local transport

In Peru **taxis** don't use meters, and will normally charge what they can get away with, so fix the price before you step into the cab. If you're not sure what the price should be, either ask a passer-by or offer to pay one half to three quarters of the price the *taxista* is asking. Tipping isn't usual nor expected.

Buses in cities tend to be beaten-up old crocks, but they're cheap; they charge flat fares. Disorganised though the system may appear, they'll cover just about every part of a city, and travelling by bus is a great way of meeting people, but beware of pickpockets and bag-slashers.

You can also travel by **colectivo** – enormous, chuntering old Dodges or spanking new Japanese minibuses that speed along set routes filled to the gunwales with paying passengers. They'll have their routes written on the windscreen.

Hiring a car

Don't drive in Lima unless you've got a strong stomach and a forceful personality, and if you drive outside Lima expect bad roads and aggressive drivers. For car hire companies and rates, see p104 (Lima) and p125 (Cuzco). You need an international driving licence valid for 30 days; you can get one from your country's automobile association.

ACCOMMODATION

Price

The hotels listed in this book are divided into three classes: **budget**, **mid-range** and **expensive**. All prices change, and hotel prices change particularly quickly, so the chances are they'll be higher when you visit than they were when this book was researched. To compensate, the prices listed are always the cheapest double room available, so you'll be able to make comparisons between the relative expense of different hotels. The hotel price is always followed by information in brackets: '**att**' means there is an attached bathroom and '**com**' means there is a shared or communal bathroom. If breakfast is included in the cost of the room, that's mentioned too, although in Peru it's normal for breakfast to be extra.

In the **budget** class are hotels that charge up to s/30 for a room. **Mid-Range** hotels are those that charge from s/30 (US$11) to US$60. The class is wide, so hotels of a similar price are listed together within the class. **Expensive** hotels charge more than US$60, and sometimes add another 10% for service and 18% for tax on top of the price of the room (prices in this book include this extra charge). The cost of a room is usually negotiable, and you should get a bargain if the hotel is empty. Try saying '*tiene usted algo un poco más económico*' (have you got one a little cheaper)?

Standards

A Peruvian hotel can call itself a *residencial*, a *hostal*, a *hotel*, a *pensión* or a *hospedaje* – it makes no difference to the standard of what's on offer. The cheapest hotels offer a plank bed in a dirty room in a dangerous part of town run by a threatening manager, or they may provide a sunny room in an old colonial mansion, so ask to see a room before you part with your money. You won't get plank beds in any hotels listed in this book and expensive hotels will be up to the international standard you'd expect.

Availability

You'll have no problem finding somewhere to stay unless you turn up on a major holiday or festival (see facing page), and even then you'll probably find somewhere, it'll just be more expensive.

ELECTRICITY

220 volts AC, 60 cycles. Expect power cuts and power surges, and don't touch the bare wiring you'll see in your shower!

TIME

Peru is five hours behind GMT (UK winter time).

POST AND TELECOMMUNICATIONS

Telephone and fax

You can dial international calls directly from public phones in the street, but you'll need a phonecard to pay, which you can buy from women who hang around phones selling them or in shops that display a sign saying *tarjeta telefónica* (telephone card). You can also make a call from telephone company offices but this will be more expensive. The number to dial for the operator is 100, for information it's 103 and for the international operator it's 108.

To phone Peru from abroad dial your international access code, then 51. Add 1 for Lima, or 84 for Cuzco. To dial home from Peru, first dial the international access code 00, then add your country code (UK 44, USA and Canada 1, Australia 61, New Zealand 64), then your STD and number required.

You can send and receive faxes from many hotels and the telephone company offices.

Email

Email is rapidly replacing other forms of communication for travellers. Cybercafés spring up like mushrooms and die like mayflies, so check **www.cybercaptive.com** for the latest picture. If you don't already have a free address with one of the companies such as hotmail, rocketmail or yahoo you can easily set up an account at a cybercafé.

Post

Post is slow but generally reliable, and a letter outside the Americas will cost about s/2.50. Stamps are sold where you buy your postcards. Main *correos* (post offices) have **poste restante**, and American Express offices also hold letters addressed to their clients. It helps if the people who are sending you letters underline your surname, and when looking for your letters check under *all* the names on the envelope; they're often misfiled.

HOLIDAYS AND FESTIVALS

1 January	New Year (all Peru).
6 January	*Fiesta de Ollantaytambo* (Cuzco).
14 January	*Feria de Pampamarca* (Cuzco): a large agricultural fair.
April	Maundy Thursday, Good Friday and Easter (all Peru).
1 May	Labour Day (all Peru).
7-9 June	*Qoyllur Riti* (Cuzco): an Apollonian pilgrimage to the glaciers of the high Andes.
June	Corpus Christi (all Peru, but especially Cuzco): statues of saints are paraded around Cuzco's packed streets. It takes place on the Thursday after Trinity Sunday (ninth Thursday after Easter).
24 June	*Inti Raymi* (Cuzco): the old Inca festival of the winter solstice, which was suppressed by the Spanish and recreated in 1944. Elsewhere the celebration is called Peasant's Day.
29 June	St Peter and St Paul (all Peru).
15-17 July	*Fiesta de Paucartambo* (Cuzco): a Dionysiac festival to honour the Virgin of Carmen of Paucartambo (a village near Cuzco) with masked dancers.
28/29 July	Independence Day (all Peru).
30 August	*Santa Rosa de Lima* (all Peru).
7 October	Battle of Angamos (all Peru).
18 October	*El Señor de los Milagros* (Lima): a day of religious processions.
1 November	All Saints' Day: (all Peru): the day when Peruvians remember their dead.
8 December	Immaculate Conception (all Peru).
24 December	*Santorantikuy* (Cuzco): originally a market which sold objects for Nativity Scenes, this is now a large market for practically anything. Elsewhere, the day is a pre-Christmas holiday.
25 December	Christmas (all Peru).

FOOD AND DRINK

Peruvian food can be excellent. There's a tradition of good eating and drinking that goes back to the days of the Incas. Pedro Pizarro reported that when the Inca Atahualpa ate: 'Ladies brought in his meal and placed it before him on tender thin green rushes. ... They placed before him all his vessels of gold, silver and pottery on these rushes. He pointed to whatever he fancied and it was brought. One of his ladies took it and held it in her hand while he ate.'

Meats

You will get bored with *lomo* (beef loin steak) cooked *cordon bleu* (stuffed with cheese and ham), *milanesa* (beaten into a thin steak, rolled in breadcrumbs and fried), and *a la pobre* (fried with an egg on top). Chicken is often cooked in these ways too, or just plain roasted. *Parilladas* (a mixed grill and a restaurant that sells grilled meat) are generally very good and filling, if lacking in imagination.

> ☐ **Pet food**
> In the Cuzco area, you'll see *cuy* (guinea pig) on offer – it tastes a bit like duck and has a tough skin. Cuy is laid flat on your plate, as if it had been run over by a bus then peeled off the wheel. They say it's cooked in one piece to prevent someone trying to dish you up cat.

More interesting dishes are *lomo saltado* (strips of beef cooked in onions, peppers, tomatoes and soy sauce, served with rice), *anticucho* (beef-heart kebabs), *causa rellena* (a very slightly spiced potato cake mixed with tuna or chicken) and *aji de gallina* (shredded chicken stewed in a gently spiced cream sauce).

Fish

The coast of Peru has truly excellent fish: *congrio* (a pacific conger eel), *lenguado* (sole), *corvina* (sea bass) and shellfish. Try *jalea* (fried whitebait), *chupe de camarones* (special prawn chowder), and especially the traditional Peruvian dish *ceviche* (raw white fish marinated in lemon and onion and served with two types of maize). Ceviche originated when coastal slaves weren't allowed to cook food on fires and had to prepare their fish in another way – they invented cold cooking with lemon juice.

Other dishes

The potato was first cultivated in Peru (indeed Sir Walter Raleigh introduced it in Elizabethan England from that country) so not surprisingly there are hundreds of different varieties and many ways of cooking them. Some of the waxy, firm beauties you eat out here will put to shame the humble spuds you get at home. You could also try *chuño*, which is potato that's been freeze-dried. Freeze-drying is a traditional way of preserving potatoes for leaner times by leaving them out in the bitterly cold Andean nights.

Peruvians are good at replicating other country's cuisines: pasta is often freshly made and first-class (Cuzco is famous for its pizzerias) and Chinese food (*Chifa*) is also good.

Dessert

For dessert, there are *picarones* (light fried doughnuts on a plate of honey) and *mazamorra morada* (a sweet tasting dish derived from purple maize) which looks like jelly.

Drink

Non-alcoholic Tea is usually served without milk but with sugar and lemon. **Herb teas** are often available. In Cuzco you should try *maté de coca*, which is made from coca leaves and said to help alleviate the symptoms of altitude sickness. It's available in most restaurants.

> ❏ **Maté de coca**
> Coca leaf, even in tea bags, is a prohibited drug in most countries, and if you try and take some home you risk jail (in the UK coca leaf is a Class A drug, the importation of which carries a long prison sentence).

Coffee is usually served as coffee essence that you add to hot water; instant coffee is better. In some places you can now get a cappuccino or espresso.

Don't drink the **water** from taps or streams without first purifying it (see p163). Alternatively you can buy bottled mineral water.

Coke, Pepsi, Fanta and Sprite are widely available. You're going to have to try the ubiquitous home-grown soft drink, **Inca Cola**, at least once – the name's too intriguing to miss. It tastes like bubblegum.

Alcoholic Avoid Peruvian **wine**, it's not very good, and drink Chilean or Argentinian wine instead. However, the Peruvian spirit **Pisco** (distilled from grapes) is a gift from the gods. Be prepared: it's strong though usually drunk diluted in the refreshing cocktail Pisco Sour. The Chileans claim that they were the ones who invented Pisco, but it's probably Peruvian.

> ❏ **Pisco Sour**
> 2 fl oz Pisco
> ¹/₂ lemon
> 1 egg white (whisked)
> 2 dessertspoons of sugar
> The spirit, egg and lemon juice are shaken together then served over crushed ice with a dash of Angostura bitters.

The **beer** is watery lager and it all seems to taste the same; brands include Cristal, Cusqueña, and Arequipeña.

Chicha (see p58) is a **maize wine/beer** that dates back to the time of the Incas – you can identify houses that have chicha for sale because they fly red flags or bin-bags from sticks. The historian Prescott described it as sparkling champagne, but then he'd never tasted it. Another historian, John Hemming, more realistically describes it as murky pale cider.

Health (see p163)

Drink only purified or bottled water and avoid ice in drinks. If you can't peel it, wash it in purified water, cook it or shell it, then don't eat it, otherwise you run the risk of getting diarrhoea. Avoid things like salads, raw vegetables, unpeeled fruit, ice cream, unpasteurised dairy products and anything that's not been freshly cooked. You can make a solution for washing vegetables by putting 12 drops of iodine in a litre of water.

❑ **Chicha**
The 'champagne of the Incas' is still widely drunk today. Different areas of Peru make chicha in different ways, and the chicha from the Cuzco region is made as follows. Maize grains are soaked overnight, and then put in the sun to germinate. When they are part-germinated, they are boiled up, and then strained through a sieve. The liquid produced is called *upi*, and it's put to one side. The maize grains left in the sieve are boiled once more, and then sieved again, which produces a liquid called *seque*. The seque and the upi are then mixed to produce chicha, and the residue is fed to animals. Chicha is often flavoured with cinnamon and cloves, and sweetened with molasses.

Tax and tipping
Expensive restaurants sometimes add another 10% for service and 18% for tax to the bill. The service element in this should make its way to the waiter, so theoretically there's no need to tip, although the reality is that the money will go straight into the manager's pocket.

SHOPPING
Fabrics
Fabrics are profoundly important to Andean peoples, and they always have been. The Inca wore clothes made from the most delicate and beautiful fabrics possible. Pedro Pizarro described Atahualpa's clothes: 'He was ... wearing a dark brown tunic and cloak. I approached him and felt the cloak, which was softer than silk. I asked him "Inca, of what is a robe as soft as this made?" He explained that it was from the skins of [vampire] bats that fly at night.'

You can't get bat skin anymore, but woollens made from *alpaca* (a relative of the llama, domesticated for its beautiful wool) are widely available. The quality varies greatly: if you burn a couple of fibres and it smells of plastic, it's not made from alpaca but acrylic, and if it stinks when slightly wet, it's not alpaca, it's **llama**. You might also find fabrics made from *vicuña* wool, a beautiful, fine silken fibre that used to be reserved for the Inca himself. This stuff is incredibly expensive (the poor beasts are rare and were almost hunted to extinction), but very beautiful.

Arts and crafts
You can buy other traditional Peruvian crafts such as Andean pipes and cheap copies of Moche erotic pots (see p73). Never be tempted to buy the framed insects and stuffed animals you'll be offered in Cuzco, as the trade in them depletes the resources of the forest. Many of them are protected species anyway, and either Peruvian Customs or your own will confiscate them. Any 'Inca' artefacts you're offered are probably fake, and if they're not it's illegal to try to export them.

Rip offs

Peru's not, as a character said in Peter Shaffer's play *The Royal Hunt of the Sun*: 'a silent country, frozen in avarice', but if you feel you've been taken for a ride contact the **Tourist Protection Service** (☎ 0800 4 2579, and it's a free call, not available from pay phones). This organisation is run by the government to deal with tourists' complaints.

SAFETY

'The Prefect had been very solicitous about our welfare, and, although we assured him that we preferred to travel without a military escort, he insisted that a sergeant and at least one soldier should accompany us as long as we were in his Department…. There was no danger, and highway robbery is unheard of in Peru.' *The Lost City of the Incas*, by Hiram Bingham, 1948. Whatever it was like in Bingham's day, Peru now has a crime problem, so you need to be careful. But being careful doesn't mean being paranoid, and most of the guide books to Peru are so liberally spiced with warnings that it seems you're entering a war zone. You're not, and you will have no trouble provided you take sensible precautions:

● **Don't flaunt your valuables**. It's wisest not to travel with anything you might be upset to lose. Leave expensive jewellery at home and bring a wrist watch that looks obviously cheap. Leave your passport and wads of money in your hotel safe.

● **Be aware** Don't go to dodgy areas, take care when travelling at night. Be aware of people around you and beware of any who are paying you undue attention. It helps to walk around in groups, at least until you've got your bearings and feel secure. Take taxis when you arrive in a new place.

● **Take precautions** Wear a money belt and carry your money in a couple of different places on your body. Some people stick a US$100 bill under the insole in their shoe for emergencies, or put one in an elastic bandage on their leg. Make sure your luggage is secure – you could put chicken wire inside your bag to prevent slashing razors, or buy a flour sack and sew your rucksack into it to secure easily opened pockets. (Don't use a fishmeal sack for this, as predictably they stink.)

● **Don't fall for tricks** Common scams involve catching your attention and then picking your pocket; someone might spit on you or stick chewing gum on your shirt, or an old lady might collapse under your feet. There'll be an accomplice who's standing behind you, and when you're not on your guard they will whip out your wallet and that'll be the last you see of it. Also be on your guard against fake policemen; always ask to see an ID. Whilst on the subject of the police, be careful of corrupt policemen as they might try to plant drugs on you, and never get into a police car if you can avoid it, but insist on walking to the police station.

In Cuzco they've taken the art of distracting you to the limit. Be on your guard. As in all countries there is the occasional mugging.

● **If the worst happens** Remember, they're probably after your money, so stay calm and hand it over – it's worth much less than your health. If you are unlucky enough to be a victim of crime, go to the **Tourist Police** (see p107 and p129) who speak English and are helpful. Get a police report for insurance.

Having said all that, you should remember that hundreds and thousands of people visit Peru each year without any problems at all. Nothing's likely to happen to you if you take care.

As for the risk from **terrorism**, as the SAEC (p106) say, you're more likely to be run down by Lima's mad traffic than come to grief from the Sendero Luminoso or the MRTA.

DRUGS

For many people, there's nothing that needs to be said about this. But for others, you should know that buying or using drugs can land you in prison for the next 15 years, and the person you're thinking of buying them from may be a police informant. Think long and hard about it – is it really worth the risk?

Flora and fauna

FAUNA

Mammals

The star of the Sanctuary, but an animal you'll be extremely lucky to see, is the **Andean (or Spectacled) bear** (*Tremarctus ornatus*). These bears pose no threat to hikers as they are both shy and herbivorous; and on the contrary they are the ones who are threatened by the inroads we make into their habitat.

Whilst on the subject of large, frightening animals, don't expect to see any **puma** (*Felis concolor*), the fanged cat of Peru, because they are very, very rare. You're more likely to see the **Colpeo fox**, a scavenger that lives in these hills and preys on the ill and the dying, or an Andean **skunk**, a **weasel**, or if you're lucky a **White-tailed deer**. The Sanctuary also boasts **pudú** (pigmy deer), timid little nocturnal beasts which are rarely seen during the day.

❏ **The Peruvian Paso**

Horses were native to South America, but they died out many thousands of years ago. They were re-introduced by the Spanish, who used them to great effect in battles against the natives.

Some of the descendants of the mounts of the conquistadors have been developed into a breed of horse called the Peruvian Paso, or Peruvian Stepping Horse. It's famous for its characteristic way of walking, with high stepping forelegs and powerful hind legs, which makes it comfortable to ride. It has great stamina, being able to maintain a regular speed of about 11mph (18kmph) over rough country.

Keep a look out for **mountain viscachas** – there are hundreds of these rabbit-like rodents living in the Machu Picchu ruins, and you'll see their pellet-like droppings everywhere, even if you can't see the viscachas themselves.

The animals (apart from horses) which you'll see most frequently are **llamas** and **alpacas**, cousins of the camel that have been domesticated for thousands of years for their meat, wool and ability to carry cargo. They have two wild relatives, **guanacos** (big with a white belly) and **vicuña** (gentle-looking with inquisitive eyes and a furry chest), both of which are rarely seen in the Machu Picchu Sanctuary but are more common in the south.

Reptiles

Also keep a look out for snakes: **coral snakes** and **bushmasters** are both reasonably common in the selva and are poisonous.

❏ **Paddington Bear**

If you were to say 'Lima' to a British reader between the ages of 25 and 40 they'd probably immediately think of Paddington Bear. For those not familiar with this character, he was the star of a string of books written by Michael Bond.

Paddington, a small, fat bear with a duffle coat, a love of marmalade sandwiches and an extraordinarily hard stare, was found by the Brown family on London's Paddington station (hence his name), with a note around his neck written by his Aunt Lucy, saying 'Please look after this bear, thank you'. Aunt Lucy (also a bear), you see, had grown old and could no longer look after young Paddington herself, so she'd had to pack him off to England, after which she'd retired to the Home for Retired Bears, Lima, in deepest Peru.

Aunt Lucy is no more but you can, however, still see some Retired Bears (Andean spectacled bears) at the Parque de Leyendas (see p117) in San Miguel, Lima.

Birds

The Incas considered birds to be the messengers of the apus, the spirits of the cordillera (mountain range), and the mighty condor represented the great snow peaks while the lesser birds represented lesser mountains.

● **Andean condor** The Andean Condor (*Vultur gryphus*) is enormous, averaging over a metre from bill to the tip of the tail and much more across the wings. In the air a condor is identifiable (apart from by its sheer size) by the characteristic forward-pointed finger-feathers at the end of its wings, its white ruff and bald head.

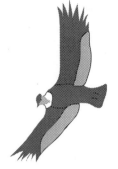

ANDEAN CONDOR

Despite its reputation as a mountain bird it's not common here and is more usually found on the coast where it can find more carrion. It's had a bad press over the years, and stories have been told of its attacking travellers, carrying away goats and killing small children. The great writer and traveller Bruce Chatwin relates in his book, *In Patagonia,* an unlikely story about being harried by a condor, and George Squier (*Peru – Travel and Exploration in the Land of the Incas*, 1877) includes a picture of himself almost being attacked by one of these massive birds, just managing to see it off with a shot from his pistol. Just one glance at the feet of a condor (usually only possible when you come across a stuffed one) tells you this is impossible, as instead of sharp, evil talons condors have what look like oversized chicken feet. They couldn't grasp anything, let alone carry away a struggling small child up into the air.

GEORGE SQUIER FENDS OFF A CONDOR

● **Other birds of prey** The large birds that you'll see are, more often than not, birds of prey. You're likely to catch a glimpse of an **American Kestrel** (*Falco sparverius*), an **Aplomado Falcon** (*Falco femoralis*) or a **Mountain Caracara** (*Phalcoboenus megalopterus*). The kestrel is quite a small bird, averaging just under 30cm from beak to tail, with grey wings, a grey head, white cheeks and a brownish breast and tail. The falcon is about 10cm longer, and has

light brown wings and tail and a paler breast. The caracara is larger still, 50cm from beak to tail, and has characteristic black, white and grey wings and a black and white tail.

You might also see the **Black-chested Buzzard Eagle** (*Geranoaetus melanoleucus*) and various different types of **hawk**. The buzzard eagle is big, 70cm from beak to tail, and is

MOUNTAIN CARACARA

predominantly a grey colour, with black edges to its wings and a black neck and head. The feathers on the tips of its wings do not spread forward as much as those of the condor. Hawks generally range from 40 to 50cm long, and range in colour from grey and white to brown and beige.

BLACK-CHESTED BUZZARD EAGLE

● **Waterfowl** If you're interested in birds, you shouldn't only be looking upwards, as the Sanctuary also boasts many different types of birds in the trees and on the water and ground. In streams, lakes and ponds you can find the famous **Torrent Duck** (*Merganetta armata*) of Matthew Paris' book *Inca Cola*. Male torrent ducks are a stripy black and white with red beaks, and females have reddish-brown chests and grey backs. You can also see **Andean (or Ruddy) Ducks**, red with a spiky black tail, dark head and wide bill, and the **Crested Duck**, a sleek grey with a touch of red on the wings. **Andean Geese** can sometimes be seen, with a rather menacing grey stripe around the eye, while black and white **Giant Coots** are common.

● **Humming birds** Of the smaller birds, the ones that cause the greatest excitement are the various types of beautifully named humming birds: **Sunangel**s (*Heliangelus amethysticollis*), **Great Sapphirewings** and the world's largest, the **Giant Hummingbird** (*Patagonia gigas*), a surprisingly dull brown bird but a massive (for a hummingbird) 24cm from the tip of its bill to the end of its tail.

● **Other birds** One of the most famous birds in the Sanctuary is the **Cock of the Rock**, with its stunning head-dress of red feathers that reminds some of the red fringe that the Inca used to wear as a badge of his rank. This is Peru's national bird. On the ground you can see **partridge**s, which at one stage were so common that they gave their name to a town (Pisac, the name of a town in the Sacred Valley, means partridge). In the skies, keep a watch for **swifts** and **swallows** with their characteristic swept-back wings and pointed tails. In woodland look out for **woodpeckers**. You're more likely to hear than to see a woodpecker called the **Andean Flicker**, a largish bird (33cm from beak to tail) with a beige head, grey and dark brown body and a yellow breast.

FLORA

Many of the plants you'll see in the Sanctuary have relatives that are commonly grown in Europe and North America.

There are **begonias**, **lupins**, **fuchsias**, **daisies**, **elders**, **buttercups**, **lilies**, and **cacti**. You'll also see **calceolaria** (ladies' slipper), which is very common and has bright yellow flowers. **Salvia** is quite common in some areas, and you may see **kantu**: Peru's national flower (see photo opposite, bottom right).

Bromeliads, relatives of the pineapple, can be seen in the Sanctuary. One of the most impressive Peruvian plants (sadly not native to the Sanctuary) is the puya Raimondi, that lives for a hundred years, grows ten metres high and flowers just once before it dies.

Orchids

One type of plant that you will come across in the Sanctuary is the orchid. The place is blessed with about 200 different varieties, and there are said to be up to 3000 orchid species just in Peru. New species are discovered each year.

You may see the **Huinay Huayna** (the name means 'forever young') orchid or *Epidendrum secundum* a small pink star-burst of a flower, which gave its name to the Inca ruins just near the Trekkers' Hotel (see p181). Also in this area, keep your eyes peeled for *Masdevallia veitchiana*, locally called **Huakanki** (the name means 'you'll cry') which has extremely beautiful purple-and-orange coloured flowers with three delicately pointed petals (see centre photo opposite).

Orchids are, however, in danger in the Sanctuary. They are at risk from plant hunters and also from the destruction of thier habitat. The recent fires have destroyed large areas of virgin forest.

Medicinal plants

Some plants have medicinal uses. For example, a tea from the leaves of a plant from the *Labiateae* family (a shrubby family that includes sage) called **muña** (*Minthostachyys glabrescens*) relieves the effect of altitude. However, be careful about playing around with plants which you may not recognise – the tea made from the seeds of a lupin known as **Q'era tarwis** (*lupinus mutabilis*) is used as fish poison.

Compositae
Yellow daisy

Leguminosae
Lupin

Calceolaria engleriana
Ladies' slipper

Bromeliaceae
Flowering bromeliad

Masdevallia veitchiana
Huakanki orchid

Labiateae
Salvia

Datura arborea
Moonflower

Begoniaceae
Begonia

Cantua buxifolia
Kantu

Centre photo © Bryn Thomas
All other photos © South American Pictures/Tony Morrison

Forests

An important part of the ecology of the Sanctuary are the forests, especially the **cloud forests**. Cloud forests, as you might be able to guess from their name, get most of their moisture from fog and clouds rather than the rain: look for stumpy trees (such as the *polylepis* species) and shrubs loaded down with moisture-absorbing moss and lichen. There's one of these forests on the section of the trail between Huayllabamba and the first pass.

FIELD GUIDES

It's difficult to find a good but compact field guide for Peru. For birds there's John Dunning's *South American Birds*, or the comprehensive *Birds of the High Andes* (Jon Fjeldsa and Niels Krabbe).

There's a good section on orchids and birds in Peter Frost and Jim Bartle's *Machu Picchu Historical Sanctuary*, (part-written by the expert birder, Barry Walker, who runs the Cross Keys bar in Cuzco).

(Opposite): A young Quechua llama-herder.

PART 3: THE INCAS

Pre-Inca civilisations

Peru is a place of great antiquity. The Incas were only the third empire to dominate the Andes. Before they built their roads and terraces, before they counted on their *quipus* (string used for record-keeping – see p85) and before they worshipped the sun, other cultures had flourished in the barren deserts and soaring mountains of this part of South America. The first pan-Andean civilisation, the **Chavín**, thrived about 2500 years ago, the second, the **Huari-Tiahuanaco**, about 1000 years ago, and between these times of cultural unity many smaller peoples rose and fell. The glories of the Incan state, the architecture, the textiles, the roads, the agriculture, the social organisation were developed out of the foundations of these more ancient civilisations of Peru.

IN THE BEGINNING

Paleo-Indians, the first settlers of the Americas, walked over the tundra some 20,000 years ago, chasing their migrating food across the land bridge that joined the continents of Asia and North America. This was possible because in those days the world was much colder than it is today, and massive ice sheets froze the oceans into glaciers, making the sea level much lower. The waters have now risen again, and the land bridge is lost beneath the Bering Straits.

Early days in South America

How long it took for humans to work their way down to South America is something about which archaeologists don't agree, but the generally accepted view is that we've been on the continent for between 9000 and 11,000 years. It has been suggested that the first settlers arrived in South America about the same time as they arrived in North America, making a pretty swift migration down the two continents. This view is disputed.

There's more agreement about what the first people were like: they hunted to survive, eating ancient American horses, which are now extinct, mastodons and the wild relations of the llama. After about 2000 years, differences developed between people on the coast and those living in the highlands.

The highland people

Digging in the floor of a deserted old cave in the Callejón de Huaylas called the Guitarrero Cave, archaeologists have discovered that agriculture began here in the highlands in about 8500BC. By 4000BC animals were being domesticated, and by 3000BC highlanders were planting and eating a wide variety of foods such as maize, gourds, squash, some tubers and grains. As well as telling us about the foundations of agriculture, the Guitarrero Cave has also unveiled what may be the first example of Andean art: a small rock wrapped in textile in about 5500BC. It's from these humble beginnings that arose the glory of South American cloth.

The coastal people

The coastal settlers had the benefit of the lush pastures of the Pacific Ocean (one archaeologist has suggested that as many as 6,500,000 people could have been fed by the anchovy schools swimming in the chill Pacific), and so they didn't need to develop agriculture or domesticate animals until much later than the people living in the highlands. At first the coastal dwellers caught their food by angling and scavenging for shellfish but in time they fished with a spear headed by a delicate stone point. This spearhead, which was carved like a slender willow leaf, is called a Paiján point.

Chinchorros About this time an interesting people, the Chinchorros, lived on the desert coast around Tacna and Arica. They were quite sophisticated, inventing bone fishhooks and living in stable communities. In 6000BC, long before the ancient Egyptians, they started to mummify their dead. The mummies have been preserved, partly because they were buried in the dry sands of the Atacama desert, but partly because of the preservation techniques used by the Chinchorros. The bodies of the dead were wrapped in fabric, bound with reeds and a face mask of clay was placed over their skulls. Some of these mummies, the oldest in the world, are on display in the museum near Arica in northern Chile. The Chinchorros mummies started a Peruvian tradition, continued by the Incas some 7500 years later.

❏ **Earliest mummies**
The custom of mummifying the dead to prepare them for the after life goes back at least 8000 years in South America. Bodies were usually placed in a foetal position, seated in a basket and wrapped in many layers of embroidered textiles.

PRE-CERAMIC PEOPLES (3000 TO 1800BC)

Unlike the rest of the world, civilisation evolved in Peru before the invention of pottery. This wasn't realised at first. There are many large temples on the coast in which archaeologists couldn't find any ceramic remains, and these temples were dated by other pottery that was found nearby, pottery that was scattered around by much later inhabitants. Carbon dating, however, showed that the old temples were far more ancient than these ceramics, and the civilisations that built them must have existed without pottery.

The oldest temples were built about the time of the Old Kingdom of ancient Egypt (about 3000BC), many years before the rise of the other most ancient American civilisation, the Olmecs of Mexico. Some of these structures are almost as huge as the Egyptian Pyramids; it's estimated that 2,000,000 work-days were needed to use 100,000 tons of stone in constructing the nine vast complexes at El Paraíso by the river Chancay to the north of Lima.

Kotosh

Most of the decoration of these temples hasn't survived but at one site, Kotosh, by the headwaters of the river Marañon, you can still see the type of thing that adorned these places. Kotosh dates from 1000 to 2000BC and consists of two mounds, in one of which there's the **Temple of the Crossed Hands**. This is an adobe room with trapezoidal niches, a design that was to become so characteristic of the Incas. Under one of the niches there's a sculpture of a pair of crossed arms. The decoration has survived because, for some reason that's not understood, at some stage in the past the sculptures were carefully protected with sandbags before the whole complex was buried.

What were these people like?

There's evidence that these people were traders and travellers, shown by the finding of Ecuadorian shells in a grave at a site called Aspero, between the rivers Chancay and Huarmey. They had reasonably advanced techniques for dealing with their environments: in the highlands a 4000 year-old irrigation canal has been found, and on the coast archaeologists have dug up the remains of fine cotton fish-nets and floats made from gourds. Delicate textiles have been reconstructed from debris found at Huaca Prieta, north of the river Moche, with painstaking work recreating complicated patterns showing birds of prey with snakes on their breasts and crabs that dissolve into smiling snakes.

All this is informative but it's the imposing temples that tell us most about these people. To build the temples, these cultures must have been sophisticated enough to have developed a system of division of labour that provided enough surplus food to supply the workers; but archaeologists disagree as to whether the enormous temples indicate centralised, authoritarian regimes or a loose confederation of peoples performing communal labour. Perhaps there was a mixture of both systems as with the Incas themselves.

THE INITIAL PERIOD (1800 TO 1000BC)

The years from 1800BC to 1000BC are called the 'Initial Period' because it used to be thought that this was when Peru's cultures started becoming more sophisticated; the rise of sophisticated cultures always being linked with the development of pottery and these were the days in Peru's history when pottery was being invented. The ball of civilisation actually started rolling long before but the name's stuck.

The invention of pottery

The coastal people cracked the problem of pottery at a different time from those who lived inland, but both were quite late considering that people had been firing clay dolls for hundreds of years (one was found above the niche of the crossed hands in Kotosh) and the Ecuadorians had been making pottery for a thousand years or so.

Pottery styles of the coast On the coast the first pots were fired at places like La Florida in Rimac but they're pretty basic as ceramics go, thin-walled and with a mottled finish, their shape based on the gourds that they replaced. In time they became more sophisticated, and the northern Cupisnique culture developed the stirrup-spout pot (two arms leading to a single spout, which prevents the pot making a glugging noise). The Cupisnique are also famous for their hallucinogenic-inspired portrait pots, psychotropic drugs derived from the San Pedro cactus being very important in ancient Peru.

The making of pottery coincided with the development of coastal agriculture, metalwork and smelting (small bits of beaten copper dating from before 1000BC have been found at Mina Perdida, just south of Gargay), and the construction of even larger public buildings than had hither to been built. The largest such as the La Florida complex would have taken one man about seven million days to build, and the structure at Moxeke is thirty metres high and has a base that covers the same area as three and a half football pitches. There are two basic designs of building – those south of the Chancay river were built with 'U' shaped courtyards, and north of the river they have sunken circular courtyards. They're all grey-brown mounds now, but originally all these buildings were painted with bright dazzling colours: reds, pinks, yellows, white and greyish-blue, which illuminated the clay sculptures that were moulded onto the walls. These buildings were either tombs of important people, centres of religion, or sites of oracles.

Inland pottery styles Highland pottery was influenced by the styles and techniques of the jungle where the standard was apparently quite advanced; as an early example of ceramics the highland style at Kotosh is relatively sophisticated. Shards of these early pots (indicating a trade connection) have been found in the jungle in a place called the Cave of the Owls, which makes archaeologists suspect that there's a lost jungle civilisation from which the highland people learnt the art of pottery. This suspicion is strengthened by the fact that these pots are often decorated with jungle animals like jaguars, spider monkeys and snakes.

Goldwork was being discovered inland at the same time as pottery. At Waywaka, in the south-central highlands, the body of a man who lived sometime between 1900BC to 1450BC has been found holding in his hands foils of beaten gold. In the same way as the coastal people, the inlanders left significant footprints, both literal, two footprints were carved into a boulder at a place called Pacopama during this period, and metaphorical, such as a 9km-long irrigation canal cut into the bedrock.

The people

These were pretty violent times. In the Río Casma valley, north and east of Huanuco, there's a site called **Cerro Sechín** that consists of over 300 carvings of mauled soldiers: heads lie on the ground, bleeding from their eye-sockets, and severed torsos try to stop their guts from spilling on the ground. In the **Huaca de los Reyes** mound at a place called Caballero Muerto (Dead Horseman) in the lower Moche valley, there are the remains of a two-metre (six-foot) high clay head of a snarling catman.

However, it was not all blood and gore. On the south coast, the **Paracas** left behind some of the most beautiful fabrics ever to be discovered in Peru. These people wrapped their dead in layers of cloth, and the dry sands of the Atacama desert preserved both the dead and the textile. The fabric is stunning, made from alpaca wool and rich in colour and intricate pattern.

CHAVÍN (1000 TO 200BC)

The Chavín were the first pan-Peruvian civilisation, unparalleled in their unification of the multitude of peoples of Peru. They lived in a society that venerated gold, used llamas for cargo carriers, had highly developed textiles and built enormous public buildings in dressed stone. Their influence lasted about 800 years, and it was from this source that the Incas grew.

The cult of Chavín

The Chavín extended their influence over an area twice the size of modern Portugal, but they probably weren't a trading empire or a military power. They were a cult group. Characteristic Chavín iconography, such as the Chavín fanged cat, spread out from the centre of the culture, an oracle called Chavín de Huantar. What sort of cult were they?

Some have suggested they were evangelists and say that the icons of Chavín made their way into many different places in the same way as the cross of Christianity makes its way today into places as different as the Vatican and small altiplano villages in Bolivia. However Richard Burger (the author of a beautiful book on the Chavín, see p30) thinks that the cult was rather like the Pachacamac cult in Inca times: it was an organisation superior to but also complementary to domestic religions just as the Oracle of Delphi in ancient Greece did not supplant other pagan faiths.

The essence of the Chavín style of carving is found on objects at **Chavín de Huántar** such as *El Lanzon*, the Tello Obelisk and the Raimondi Stela, all of which can be seen today in museums in Lima (see p117). The Chavín style may be adapted by local cultures, but it's all essentially the same and can be found in various guises on pottery, goldwork and textiles across Peru.

Skilled engineers

The spread of the Chavín influence indicates that trade was becoming more common and people were moving around. Rare Ecuadorian shells are often found in tombs of the Chavín era, as is precious lapis lazuli from the Atacama desert in Chile. There were other developments too. The construction of the Castillo (castle), the central building at Chavín de Huantar, shows not only that the people of this time could organise labour forces, but also that they had engineers. The Castillo is a high structure that is honeycombed with water courses, which would make the whole building resonate and rumble with sound when water flowed in them. Designing a building that could 'speak' like this would have needed well-developed engineering skills.

The **Raimondi Stela** depicts the duality of the Chavín god of agriculture and fertility. Here he stands with his feet firmly placed on the ground. Turn the picture upside down to view the god as a many-faced animal figure descending from heaven to earth.

❏ **The role of hallucinogenic drugs in Chavín religious life**
Hallucinogenic drugs, from the San Pedro cactus or the Vilca seed, have been used in Andean religion since the earliest times. In the capital of the Chavín civilisation, there's a fascinating representation of their use.

The walls of the sunken courtyard of **Chavín de Huantar** were decorated with carved heads, set deep into stone, resembling gargoyles that are found on European cathedrals. These carvings, fixed onto a wall in tiers, are three dimensional carvings of men and beasts, showing the transformation of a man into a snarling feline. Some of the carved heads have mucus pouring from the nose, something that happens when hallucinogenic snuff is snorted. This has led Chavín scholar, Richard Burger, to suggest that these heads represent a drug-taking shaman transmuting from man to possessed prophet.

MASTERCRAFTSMEN (200BC TO 700AD)

From about 200BC the time of the Chavín peace was over. A village was built on the site of the Castillo at Chavín de Huántar, whose stones were reused as hut walls, fortifications were built where previously none had been needed, and trade diminished. These were days of violence, made manifest in the discovery of headless and armless bodies buried during this period. Chaos had reigned.

But these weren't entirely black days. Between 200BC and 700AD some of the most impressive civilisations in Peruvian history thrived, creating some of the country's finest art, hence the name 'Mastercraftsmen period'. In the south, the **Huarpa** built sophisticated clay-lined irrigation canals, metres wide and kilometres long. In the Callejón de Huaylas the Recuay made fine polychrome pots and squat statues, and on the coast the oracle of Pachacamac was founded by people of the Rimac river. However, the high-water marks of this period were left by two of the most significant of Peru's civilisations who created some of the finest and most intriguing works of art: the Moche and the Nazca.

The Moche

The Moche conquered the territory from the Piura river in the north of Peru to the Huarmey in the south. They were a bloodthirsty lot: there are many representations on their ceramics of prisoners and battles, but the lack of defensive buildings within the Moche empire suggests that once they conquered a race there was peace. Judging from the structures they left behind, they organised their empire in quite a complex way. In the north they ruled through local puppet lords leaving very few large buildings of their own while in the south they ruled directly, building monumental administrative centres in each valley. The Moche state lasted about 1000 years, but their legacies lasted longer still: they were great craftsmen in metallurgy, in architecture but most importantly in clay.

❏ **El Señor de Sípan – a hoard missed by the Spaniards**
As well as producing portrait pots, the Moche also decorated their ceramics with line drawings, in a style rather like that of the ancient Greeks. It's thought that these line drawings illustrate about 25 different stories from the mythology of the Moche. In one scene captives are paraded before an important person, then killed with their fresh spurting blood being caught in a cup. The cup is then handed to the VIP, who wears quite unmistakable clothing. Archaeologists call this person the Warrior Priest. He was the subject of one of the most amazing archaeological finds of the century.

In 1987, the body of a Warrior Priest was discovered, encrusted and surrounded by his unmistakable ornaments of office. *El Señor de Sípan* (Lord of Sípan), as he's been called, had evaded the greed of the Spaniards. Before his body was found, he'd only been known through representations on thousand-year-old pottery. The story of the discovery is fascinating in itself. A local man called Ernil Bernal and his friends dug a small tunnel into an adobe pyramid of Huaca Rajada. After a night of pillaging the tomb, they were looking for a way out. Ernil's walking stick went into the roof above him. He pulled it out, and the roof began to give way. First some dust fell on him, then some clods of earth. And then, suddenly, a torrent of gold collapsed through the roof and he was buried in treasure. Sadly, it was a week before the curator of the local museum was told of the find, and by then much of value had been lost, ultimately to find its way into the hands of rich collectors in the USA. Only 123 objects from the tombs were ever returned to Peru.

Much of the remaining treasure of El Señor de Sípan can be seen today in the Museo de la Nación (see p117), along with a mock-up of his tomb.

Moche ceramics One of the great highlights of pre-Hispanic Andean art is Moche portrait pots, the naturalism of which is breathtaking. The high points are the portraits of men: looking on the finest of these is like looking into the eyes of a still breathing Moche noble. However, Moche artists could represent many other things, from buildings to demons, from human pregnancy to a llama with her young, and in the fired clay you can read things like happiness, serenity, surprise and even disease and disfigurement: there is a pot of a woman with leishmaniasis (a disease that rots the nose and lips) and a pot of a man with a cleft palate.

The Moche also made pornographic ceramics, quite astounding in their graphic representation of various sexual acts, small copies of which can be found in just about all the tourist markets of Peru. Scholars are divided as to why the Moche took such pains to represent such diversity of sexual acts (including bestiality and sex with skeletons), and theories range from the suggestion that these are a celebration of life, to the idea that they may be religious artefacts.

Moche buildings The Moche's main temple was the huge **Huaca del Sol** (Sun Temple) complex, which, in its time, was the largest adobe structure in the Americas. It was massive. What remains is a mere fragment of what was built because of the greed of the Spaniards, who developed a novel way of pillaging these old tombs. Tunnels were dug under the structure and then a nearby river diverted to wash away the adobe. With the temple dissolved, gold and treasure could be either picked from the ruins or fished out of the river.

The Nazca

The barren desert pampa by the Nazca river was the workplace of German mathematician, Maria Reiche, for many decades. The whole pampa is criss-crossed by a multitude of lines, patterns, polygons and designs, discovered when the area was first surveyed from the air in 1926. There is a hummingbird that is five times the length of a jumbo jet, an enormous monkey with a whirl of a tail, a killer whale and a bird the size of a house. How? Why?

'How' is the easy question. The dry dusty surface is a natural blackboard – the dark surface conceals a light sandy base, and clearing the dark surface reveals the lighter sand underneath. The Nazca did this to create their patterns, and the desert is so stable that these have lasted through the centuries.

'Why' is more difficult. Theories range from the frankly incredible (Erich von Däniken in his book, *Chariots of the Gods*, said that the Nazca lines are runways for extraterrestrial spacecraft) to the sensible (Maria Reiche thought that there were astronomical and calendrical reasons for the lines). The current favourite comes from the observation that many of the lines are orientated towards water sources, suggesting that they are likely to be processional routes designed to be walked upon as part of the ritual worship of water.

Nazca pottery The Nazca did not only leave their perplexing lines behind them. They also created some very fine polychrome pottery, drawing on pots with a palette of 13 slip colours, sometimes using the same icons as appear in the lines. The pots themselves are beautiful in their combination of colours, and in a similar way to the Moche portrait pots, appeal to today's aesthetic tastes.

TIAHUANACO-HUARI (700 TO 1000AD)

The coast of Peru was again united at the end of the first millennium. Two related but distinct peoples dominated the Andes: the Tiahuanaco (or Tiwanaku) and the Huari (or Wari). The two were united by an icon that has been called the Gateway God, the Staff God or Viracocha.

Legendary Tiahuanaco

Tiahuanaco has been the site of legend for centuries. In some Incas myths, it was the place of giants, and Viracocha came here to make humanity out of mud. For today's mystics it's still a place of enduring mystery: HS Bellamy in *Built before the Flood* insisted that Tiahuanaco was built thousands of years ago and destroyed when one of earth's moons (he thought we had more than one) hit the surface of the earth. In early 1998 John Bashford-Snell, accompanied by a team from the Explorers' Club of New York, began searching in the area around Titicaca for Plato's lost city of Atlantis. More recently it was suggested that Tiahuanaco was the capital of a sophisticated worldwide civilisation that was destroyed over 10,000 years ago.

The **Gateway God** (or Staff God), fundamental icon of the Huari and the Tiahuanaco people. The figure was carved on the Gateway of the Sun, a monumental doorway that's still standing at the extensive site of Tiahuanaco, now in Bolivia.

The site of Tiahuanaco Tiahuanaco is on the south side of Lake Titicaca, in Bolivia. It was first settled from 400BC, but it wasn't until about 500AD that stone buildings and high pyramids were constructed.

The whole site is very reminiscent of the Inca (with its giant blocks linked together without mortar), but it was built by people who flourished just under 1000 years before their rise. Old accounts say that Pachacutec (see p80) modelled Cuzco on this site, which was already ancient by the time of the Incas.

The empire of Tiahuanaco Like the Inca empire, at its peak Tiahuanaco spread its wings over vast tracts of what is now Chile and Bolivia. The Tiahuanaco traded with peoples as far to the south as the oasis of San Pedro de Atacama and the peoples of the Azapa valley, both of which are now in Chile. In cemeteries in these areas, amongst the dead buried in the local style, there are the graves of people buried surrounded by Tiahuanaco finery: wood carvings, gold, textiles. These artefacts are sufficiently small and light to be portable over long distances, and it's likely that they were carried by llama caravans across the desert, sent from Tiahuanaco to reward local agents of the Tiahuanaco empire, or perhaps local regents who ruled in the name of the far away capital.

Closer to home, the Tiahuanaco ruled more directly. The major colony was a very large site called Omo in the Moquegua valley. Omo was occupied quite early on before it was suddenly abandoned, only to be re-inhabited later. This odd pattern might be explained by the fact that the Tiahuanaco felt threatened by the sudden establishment of the Huari citadel of Cerro Baul, just 20km away.

Tiahuanaco life Like most great Andean peoples, the Tiahuanaco were skilled farmers. They developed a way of preparing the land that produced twice the yield of crops as the techniques of today. They built ridged fields: a field in which trenches are dug and the earth excavated is piled in a ridge between the channels, which are then filled with water. Tiahuanaco ridged fields have imported rock bases and have high quality imported soil on top, indicating that much work was involved in their construction. They are more fertile than other fields, but they're difficult to build and maintain. When the Tiahuanaco culture declined, these field systems declined and were ultimately replaced by the terraced hillsides of the Inca, but the land around Titicaca has never again been as productive as it was in the days of the Tiahuanaco.

In 562AD there was a great drought in the whole of Peru which lasted thirty years. We know this from analysing samples taken from glaciers, samples that indicate the weather patterns of Peru throughout the centuries. This drought was a contributing factor to the decline of the Moche – about this time the Huaca del Sol was abandoned. (Moche civilisation was dealt a double blow by the drought killing crops and then the advance of sand dunes burying the ancient capital.) However, the Tiahuanaco survived, and even thrived; an icon of the Gateway God has been found painted on a Moche pyramid, indicating that the Tiahuanaco cult stretched as far to the north as the river Piura.

The demise of the Tiahuanaco Eventually the great civilisation of Tiahuanaco suffered the fate of all peoples, and by 1000AD the fields lay fallow, the distribution of high grade Tiahuanaco pottery had stopped, and the empire had fragmented. Why this happened isn't known – like so many things in Andean pre-history it is a mystery – but the creators of the earliest great Andean stone city lived on, spiritually in the myths of the Incas, and physically in the silent remains of their architecture.

The Huari

The Huari and Tiahuanaco knew of each other but it seems they didn't like each other. Near the river Moquegua the Huari built the fort of Cerro Baul within a short distance of the Tiahuanaco settlement of Omo, in what looks like a directly confrontational act. Nevertheless there's no doubt that the Huari were influenced by them: the Gateway God and other Tiahuanaco icons appear painted in many pieces of Huari pottery and tapestry. However, the way the Huari depicted the Gateway God illustrates that there were differences between the two cultures: the Tiahuanaco representations of the god has sun rays emanating from behind his head, while those of the Huari can be more abstract and often appear with different accoutrements, sometimes, for example, bearing cobs of maize not wielding rods of power.

Who the Huari were is one of these things about which scholars can't agree. Some say that they were an empire, that expanded by force, but there is little evidence of military conquest about the time of their expansion. Others say that their style and icons were present in client states because of the influences of trade. Still others suggest the icon was dispersed throughout Peru because the Gateway God was a religious symbol of their shared Peruvian religion like the fanged cat of the Chavín.

The heritage of the Huari In a similar way to the Tiahuanaco, it's likely that the Huari survived so long and were so successful because of their agricultural technology: in their case a system of irrigation that involved long canals, high-altitude water sources and extensive irrigated terraces (probably derived from the Huarpa see p72). This was a labour-intensive technique, but it was fruitful so they survived the days of drought. Their methods were later adopted by the Incas.

THE DAYS BEFORE THE INCA (1000 TO 1450AD)

The Chimú (Chimor) culture from the northern coast dominated the period before the rise of the Incas. Other civilisations also flourished, such as the Aymara kingdoms who stepped into the void left by the decline of Tiahuanaco (the Aymara still thrive today). Around Cuzco, the Killke replaced the Huari and were probably descended from the Huari who lived in a settlement called Pikillacta, and on the south coast the Ica carried on the ceramic and textile traditions of the Nazca and the Paracas. To the north of the Rimac, where Lima is now, the Chancay thrived. The Rimac itself was inhabited by the Ichma.

Chimú stirrup-spout vessel

The Chimú
The great rival of the Inca empire was the northern empire of Chimú. At its height, this nation encompassed two-thirds of the Peruvian coast, stretching from Tumbes in the north to just above Lima in the south. It was not con-

quered by the Incas until 1470AD, and when the Spanish arrived there were still people alive that remembered the old traditions.

The Chimú were not the only people on the north coast. At first, it seems they lived peacefully with their neighbours, irrigating the barren desert with extensive canal systems, but in about 1100AD there was a great flood caused by El Niño which altered the water system. No amount of careful rebuilding could repair the canals, so the Chimú began to take other peoples' agricultural land by conquest.

Chimú and Sican One of their more significant northern neighbours were the Sican, who lived near the site of the modern city of Lambayeque. The Chimú conquered the Sican in about 1370AD.

The Sican had an ancient history and are responsible for the production of much beautiful art, one of their main sites called Batan Grande yielding up thousands of golden artefacts. (Interestingly, the Sican manufactured a type of money in the form of small copper axes, which they buried with their dead.)

The origin myths of the Chimú and Sican are remarkably similar, and consequently there have been attempts to link these with archaeological discoveries. Sadly it's not really been possible. In both traditions, society was begun by a man who arrived from the sea saying that he had been sent to take control. In the Sican tradition this man was called Naymlap. On his death, his court and 12 children spread the story that he had sprouted wings and flown away, and then each founded one of the 12 cities of the Sican people. For the Chimú, the man was called Taycanamu, and he settled in the lower Moche valley. When he died, his children did not found cities but extended the territory of his people by conquest, including, in the end, the Sican.

Chan-Chan The centre of the culture was the great Chimú city, Chan-Chan which covers six square km and consists of 12 great palaces or *ciadadelas* built by communal (*mit'a*) labour (see p83). Ciadadelas are enclosures surrounded by a large wall, inside which there are labyrinths of storage rooms, a large platform (which doubles as a burial place) and audience rooms called *audiencias*. The outsides of the audiencias are decorated with adobe friezes of the sea, and they are often U-shaped – an architectural feature dating back to the Initial Period (see p69).

The ciadadelas were probably a ruler's residence and, when he died, his tomb. It's likely that as with the Incas (see p86), a ruler's estate was preserved for his living relatives and his successors had to make their own way in the world. Chan-Chan has been responsible for some of the greatest treasure found in Peru, and at one stage the Spanish formed a mining company to exploit these ruins. Chimú metalwork is some of the most sophisticated in ancient Peru, and if the Chimú were such craftsmen imagine what wonders the Incas must have produced.

Conquest of the Chimú The last Chimú ruler was Minchancamon. According to oral history, he was single-handedly responsible for the extension of the Chimú empire from the river Chillon to the river Tumbes in the far north. According to archaeology, which has dated the Chimú settlements in these regions, this is unlikely; more probably he took the credit for the victories of his forefathers. When he was conquered by the Inca he was taken to Cuzco with his best artisans, a puppet monarch was left to rule in his place and the Chimú empire was broken up. Loyal Inca settlers took over Chimú land, and the Chimú themselves were exiled to other places within the Incas' territory. So ended the last great empire before the Incas.

Days of the Inca

PIECING TOGETHER THE JIGSAW

The Incas did not have writing, and so a caste of oral historians (*amautas*) arose to keep alive the legends and stories of the past. Much of the information that these people carried died with them but some was recorded by early Spanish writers. Fitting together these oral histories with the facts that can be deduced from archaeology is one way we can get a picture of what life was like under the Incas.

Oral history is inevitably unreliable: the Incas simply air-brushed awkward or embarrassing facts from their past. However, the nearer to the Spanish conquest you get, the clearer the picture becomes because there are other sources of information. The conquistadors wrote accounts which they published on their return to Europe, and some of the Incas left their side of the story; a mestizo called Garcilasco de la Vega wrote an early history of Peru, and an account dictated by the rebel Inca Titu Cusi himself (see p99) has survived the years.

There are many other documents too, and new discoveries are still being made. The historians, Luis Miguel Glave, María Remy and John Rowe recently uncovered in the library of a Cuzco monastery some papers which cast light on the mystery of Machu Picchu (see p213). Our knowledge of what life was like under the Incas, and what happened during their fall has been pieced together like a jigsaw.

THE ORIGINS OF THE INCAS
Myth

There are two different myths about the creation of the Incas. According to the first, the primordial Inca called Manco Capac emerged from the depths of Lake Titicaca and travelled underground with his brothers and their sister-wives to a place near Cuzco called Pacaritambo. There they all emerged from the ground and made their way to Cuzco. Manco's three brothers were either turned to stone or grew wings and flew away, while Manco himself pressed on. When he arrived in the Cuzco valley he thrust his golden staff into the fertile soil and it disappeared. This he took as a sign from his father, the Sun, that the valley was good and there he stayed, naming the place Qosqo, which meant 'navel of the earth'. There, too, he built the first *Coricancha* (Sun Temple).

The second myth is also set near Lake Titicaca. In Tiahuanaco, the creator god, Viracocha, ruled over a shadowy people whose name has been forgotten (see p75). They angered him and so he arose from the waters of the lake and turned them all to stone, replacing them with the sun, the moon and with humanity. These new people were sent out from Titicaca to the four corners of the earth, and the Incas were sent to Cuzco.

Archaeology

The myths might be true when they say that the Incas aren't native to the Cuzco region: there's archaeological evidence that a people called the Killke inhabited the area before the Incas (see p122) and were displaced by them. But there's also a lot of archaeological evidence suggesting that the Incas were a local people whose ceramics and architecture evolved from the arts of local populations like the Killke.

ORAL HISTORY

Inca is properly the title of the monarch and according to ancient lore (and the scholar, John Rowe), the first eight Incas were Manco Capac, Sinchi Roca, Lloque Yupanqui, Mayta Capac, Capca Yupanqui, Inca Roca, Yahuar Huaca and Viracocha Inca. Little is known about any of them apart from Viracocha Inca. Stories exist about him because he was the father of one of the great folk heroes of Inca history, Pachacutec.

Pachacutec (c1438-1463)

Viracocha Inca's bitter enemy were the Canchas, a tribe who attacked Cuzco. He and his anointed heir, Urco, fled but his younger son, Pachacutec, remained to destroy the Canchas. It was said that such was the support for him that even the stones of the field grew legs to fight on his side. Once his victory was complete he allowed his father back to Cuzco, but usurped the throne for himself and exiled his brother, erasing him from the roll of history.

Pachacutec rebuilt Cuzco and transformed it into a stone city from a much more meagre settlement, based on the ruins he'd seen at Tiahuanaco. He also ordered Sacsayhuaman to be built, (although the size of this place makes one suspect that it was the product of more than one

The Inca and his wife. An attendant holds a feather sunshade. This is one of a series of somewhat fanciful engravings by the 19th century traveller, Paul Marcoy.

Inca's rule) and he began the expansion of the Inca empire. Pachacutec was an important figure in Inca history, but it may be that he usurped not only the throne but also the glories of his forefathers. The stories about his taking power differ; some leave out Urco, some credit Viracocha Inca with a much more dynamic rule – but also such great feats are attributed to him that doubt is cast on his historicity. Was he superhuman or a composite man?

Tupac Yupanqui (or Topa Inca: c1463-1493)

Pachacutec may have shared the latter days of his rule with his son, Tupac Yupanqui, as there may have been a greater and a lesser Inca ruling at the same time (see 'Clans' below). When Pachacutec died, Tupac Yupanqui succeeded him. He was a great conqueror and has been called the Alexander the Great of the Americas. He extended the empire so that the Incas ruled a territory that ran from Ecuador to the river Maule in Chile, extending from the shores of the Pacific into modern-day Argentina. This was an empire that stretched the same distance as Cyprus is from London, or Minneapolis from New York.

One of Tupac Yupanqui's greatest achievements was the conquest of Chimú, the desert empire that at one stage rivalled the Incas' own in size and sophistication (see p79). Sadly the Incas themselves left very little information about this conquest, even though it must have been a significant undertaking – an example, perhaps, of the Incas airbrushing their rivals from the record of history. The oral history we do have comes from accounts collected by the Spanish from old Chimú people who remembered the days before the coming of the Incas.

Tupac Yupanqui didn't do quite as well in the east. The Incas never extended their empire far into the Amazon, finding the heat, humidity and disease too much for their mountain troops.

Huayna-Capac (c1493-1525)

Huayna-Capac was Tupac Yupanqui's chosen successor, but he almost never made it to be Inca when his brother challenged the succession. However Huayna-Capac managed to beat off his sibling and took over the empire.

He started his rule by campaigning in the south, in Chile. After a year, he moved to the north of the empire where he spent the rest of his life fighting. He died shortly before the arrival of the first Europeans on Peru's shores, and was the last in the line of the great independent Incas.

CLASS AND CLANS

The Inca was the sovereign, the head of the state religion and the son of the Sun. He was a general too, and he led his forces into battle. He was the distillation of all power, the focus of all respect and the icon of his people. The state was governed by the Inca, supported by his nobles who were called *orejones* (big ears) by the Spanish because they extended their earlobes as a mark of rank. Positions of greatest responsibility were reserved for true Incas by blood, people of the same royal family or tribe as the Inca. In time the empire grew too large for these positions to be filled solely by his relatives so the Inca created a caste of Incas by privilege from the people who lived around Cuzco in the Sacred Valley of the river Urubamba and allowed them to hold office.

Clans An important facet of Inca society was its division into two clans: *Hanan* and *Hurin*, which roughly mean upper and lower. You can see the physical expression of this division in the way that the Incas divided their cities into two parts: in Machu Picchu, for example, and in old Cuzco.

Scholars disagree over the significance of this division. Some think it was simply tribal town planning, a way of making sure that there was a fundamental rift within Inca society, which reduced any risk of united opposition to central rule – on the principle of divide and rule. Others believe that these were two great clan groups that divided the whole of Inca society from top to bottom, even to the extent of having a greater and lesser Inca ruling at the same time. The senior Inca, drawn from the Hanan, was called the Sapa Inca.

INCA GOVERNMENT

Administration

At its height, the Inca empire – Tahuantinsuyu – was 5500km (3400 miles) long, longer than the full extent of the Roman empire. Tahuantinsuyu means place of the four quarters, (or *suyu*). The four suyu were: Collasuyu (to the far south), Cuntisuyu (to the south-west), Chinchaysuyu (the northern quarter), and Antisuyu (to the east: the forested lower slopes of the Andes). The word Andes is a derivation of this Quechua word Antisuyu. Four principal roads led from the centre of Cuzco to these provinces.

Tahuantinsuyu was profoundly hierarchical – the Inca himself at the top, with his orejones below him, and below them men who were in charge of successively smaller clan groups called *ayllus*.

Land and labour

The lands of each ayllu were divided into three parts: the produce of one part went to the community, the priests had the rights to a second part and the produce of the last third was the state's. This maintained the state religion, the administration and fed the people. The members of the ayllu were also subject to a tax called *mit'a*, payable in food, cloth or labour. Mit'a labour built canals, walls, road and cities, and Sacsayhuaman, for example, the great fortress temple that overlooks Cuzco.

AGOSTO
CHACRAIAPVI

August – a time of planting
FELIPE HUAMÁN POMA DE AYALA (c1590)

When the Spanish came they greedily incorporated this system of taxation to their own ends, stating that a vast proportion of each Indian's yearly labour was to be for the benefit of the Spaniard who owned the encomienda on which the Indian lived. The Spanish argued that they were simply continuing the ancient system, but changing the beneficiary from heathen to Christian. This was, of course, complete cant. In the days of the Incas, the people could expect to benefit from mit'a labour by being fed from the state's storehouses (*qollqa*) in times of famine, or being protected by a fort (*pucara*) in times of war. The burden of mit'a labour was relieved by the benefit of shared wealth and responsibility, but in the days of the Spanish mit'a labour was nothing more than exploitation.

The system wasn't bad for all the Indians, and the native middlemen, called *caciques* (originally a Caribbean word) or *curacas* (the Quechua word), generally did rather well. Some Incas went so far as to become Hispanicised, most importantly Don Cristóbal Paullu Inca, Atahualpa's brother. Paullu was baptised, took a Spanish name, built a church in Cuzco (see p141) and lead armies against the independent Inca state of Vilcabamba (see p99).

The system of ayllus survives to this day, and campesino society is founded on the notion of reciprocal obligations. If you need a roof putting on your house, then your neighbours are obliged to come and help, but in return you must help them with their harvest, say, next year. The ayllu structure is a pan-Andean thing, with the Aymara who live in Bolivia and northern Chile having the same basic attitude to communal work.

Expansion

The Incas were well versed in conquest by many means, from ethnic-cleansing and resettlement, to indoctrination, to the menace of total war; but they preferred to conquer by threat rather than use of force.

When the Incas conquered a new nation they sent a group of loyal settlers (*mitimaes*) to the occupied territories. By planting loyal citizens the Inca could ensure a concentration of local support as the isolated settlers banded together in a hostile country. In the meantime the leaders and chiefs of the newly conquered people were taken to Cuzco, educated and indoctrinated into Inca civilisation. The idols of the conquered were brought to Cuzco, too, and were placed in minor shrines in the Coricancha (see p139). Should there be a revolt, despite all these precautions, the idols were brought out, befouled and thrown into the sewers, and the Incas would attack with ruthless violence.

HOW THEY RAN THE EMPIRE

Record keeping

The Incas never invented writing. Yet without writing, they managed to govern a vast territory and make provision to feed and provide work for the population who lived there. They had to keep records to be able to achieve this – records of how much food they had in storage, of how many people there were in this village, of how long it would take to get from that place to the next on the road. To record this information, the

Quipucamayoc (record keeper)
FELIPE HUAMÁN POMA DE AYALA (c1590)

Incas used a system of knots on strings, called *quipus*. The secrets of reading quipus were entrusted to a class called the *quipucamayoc*, but the basic principles of quipu reading are still known. The Incas counted in base ten, as we do, and they placed knots in different places on the string to indicate whether they were counting one unit, ten units, a hundred units and so on. Different coloured strings signified different things, and so a roll of strings with knots could contain a large amount of information about provisions, populations and wealth. Many of these rolls of knotted string survive and you can see them in museums today.

Some people think that this wasn't the only form of record-keeping that the Incas devised and that there's a lost form of communication hidden in Inca cloth. Many of the designs you'll see woven into Quechua fabrics today have a significance: this one represents a condor, that represents a llama. The theory suggests that in the days of the Incas similar cloth designs were a system of communication.

Inca roads

The Incas had a famous system of roads that led to every corner of the empire. It was said that the Inca in Cuzco could breakfast on fresh seafish every morning, so efficient were the roads and the system of relay-runners (*chasquis*) that ran on them.

The road network was extensive; there were two main north-south trunk roads, one following the cordillera, one the coast, with numerous east-west link roads. Within this framework there were many smaller roads leading to sacred or important places: The Inca Trail to Machu Picchu is one of these. In total there were about 33,000km (20,000 miles) of roads covering the empire, enough to circle the earth two and a half times.

Travel was permitted only on official business, and the average campesino was not allowed to travel unless, for example, he was required for mit'a labour. Guardians of the roads were appointed to check on traffic, and overseers of royal bridges looked after the many twine suspension bridges that traversed the deep canyons that fracture the Andes. Messages were carried by runners in relays, and there were *tambos* (inns, or way-stations) where travellers could rest and expect to find food and a place to sleep for the night.

Many roads still exist today, and if you visit Chile's Atacama desert to the east of Chañaral, for example, or the nearby Parque National Tres Cruces, you'll still see the faint outlines of implausibly straight roads heading off into the dust and heat, leading now to nowhere.

SPIRITUAL LIFE OF THE INCAS

The Incas worshipped a wide variety of gods. The main deities were Inti the sun, thunder, lightning, the rainbow, the Pleiades, Viracocha (the creator) and Pachamama (the earth-mother).

The Inca – Son of the Sun

The Inca was the son of the Sun, and therefore was a living emanation of a god. Religion and the state were so closely entwined that our separation of the two would have been incomprehensible to the Incas. As a living god the Inca was the head of the state religion, but he was more than just a figurehead. His religious standing was the well-spring from which he drew his political power.

He wasn't an abstract figure. He was linked to everyday life by a complicated system of festivals and ceremonies. For example, no one was allowed to sow seed until they had been told that the Inca had broken the ground in Cuzco (the information was sent out from Cuzco by chasquis). Some of these festivals, such as Inti Raymi are still celebrated.

The Inca's power after death

The Inca's importance didn't end with his death. His estate was maintained (a system called *panaca*), and at every important ceremony his mummified body was brought out and placed on a sacred dais (*usno*) to participate with the living Inca and all the other dead ones. The dead were ritually fed and given drink, which was burnt on an altar beside them, before they were returned to the darkness of their living palaces.

A special class of people looked after his lands and preserved his wealth. Machu Picchu itself may have been such an estate, once owned by Pachacutec, and maintained for the benefit of his mummy. This system of fossilising an Inca's possessions forced each new Inca to forge his own way and create his own heritage from newly conquered lands. It was a spur to conquest.

Priests and spiritual places

The state religion had a caste of priests, the chief of which was the *Villac Umu*. He was a very powerful man in the empire: he acted as a military adviser in the days of the Spanish conquest. The centre of religion was Cuzco, the capital of the state. The centre of the centre was the Coricancha, the Sun Temple, from which sacred lines (*ceques*) radiated to sacred places (*huacas*), rather like the physical roads that ran from the main square to the four suyus. Modern scholars think that this is no accident, and that the huacas and ceques were orientated along the same sacred axes as the geographical quarters.

Despite the centre being in Cuzco, religion wasn't centralised and each place had its own spirits and huacas that were worshipped. Some huacas were carved stones, like Cuquipalta, a carved white stone near Vitcos, or Qenko near Cuzco (see p146). Others were simply geographical features like waterfalls or springs, and some were shrines like the Intihuatana at Machu Picchu (see p222). Still others were supposed to be the fossilised remains of the magnificent dead, the hill overlooking Cuzco's airport being those of one of Manco Capac's brothers. As the Inca empire expanded, it absorbed new gods, spirits and huacas, some of which – like Pachacamac on the coast – became major shrines for the Incas themselves.

The Spanish destroyed huacas when they found them, and prohibited their worship, claiming that they were possessed by the devil. Intihuatanas were smashed, and places like Cuquipalta were exorcised. It didn't work. To this day the Quechua find such places sacred, believing mountains, for example, to be inhabited by spirits called *apus*. Old huacas are still worshipped, and ceremonies like Qoyllur Riti (see p45) incorporate elements of the old religion into Christianity.

Sacred women

Women were very important to Inca spirituality. One of the major deities was the female Pachamama (who inevitably got confused with the Virgin Mary); and the Inca's wife, the *coya* (who, as with the Pharaohs of ancient Egypt, was also his sister) was a person of high status and nobility.

Women were tightly bound into religious and profane life. There were convents of Inca nuns (*acllas*), drawn from the most beautiful maidens in the empire. They were headed by mother superiors (*mamaconas*), and their mission in life was to serve the Inca. They wove his fabric and looked after

The Coya, the Inca's wife
<small>FELIPE HUAMÁN POMA DE AYALA (c1590)</small>

Inca stonemasons
FELIPE HUAMÁN POMA DE AYALA (c1590)

him, brewing his sacred *chicha* (maize beer) and preparing his food. The most beautiful acllas were awarded to high-status men as rewards for distinguished acts, whilst other acllas confined themselves to a life in his service. Some, indeed, confined themselves to a death in his service on the rare occasions when a situation demanded human sacrifice.

INCA CULTURE

Architecture

The Incas are of course most famous for their architecture. They built in a number of different styles, all of which seem to be characteristically Inca. Some of these characteristics are in fact Andean rather than Inca, such as mortarless walls derived from the Tiahuanaco, the trapezoidal arch (first seen in Kotosh) and terracing (derived from the Huari). Others are strikingly Inca, such as the way that their architecture incorporates a natural form, perhaps as a rock outcrop or a hillside, and enhances it with the structures that are built around it. Machu Picchu itself is a classic and perfect example of this, situated as it is astride a ridge and emphasising the outcrop that is the Intihuatana, and surrounded by the terracing that forms and reflects the shape of the living rock.

Types of Inca building One type of Inca building is the imposing stone fortress-like Sacsayhuaman (see p144), whose walls are made from blocks the size of large cars, locked together without mortar but immovable because of the perfect fit.

Another type is the regular fine-bricked buildings such as Coricancha (see p139), whose delicate brickwork was reserved for the highest status buildings. Again these walls have no mortar, just accurately carved blocks in walls that taper inwards as they get higher to resist earth movements. In the famous circular wall in Coricancha you can see that these bricks aren't really rectangular blocks but are carved so their inside faces fit together in a three-dimensional jigsaw.

The Incas also built using simpler techniques. A method of fitting rough stone together with adobe (mud) was called *pirka*, and some pirka structures still remain. The most basic construction technique was to build a simple adobe wall on a fieldstone foundation, but most of these haven't survived the passage of time.

How did they do it? It isn't known how the Incas managed to achieve such a snug fit in their ceremonial structures using the few tools they had

– river stones and small bronze crowbars (they hadn't discovered iron). There are many theories. One suggests that after one row of stones was laid it was dusted with a small film of fine sand, and when a new course was placed on top and removed, marks in the sand would indicate where the base layer needed to be carved. The top layer was then hoisted up on wooden props, the lower level was carved, and then the new course was lowered into its newly made slots. However, this theory doesn't explain how the Incas managed to get their vertical joints as good as their horizontal ones. Another plausible theory suggests that the Incas used a tool a little like a builder's scribe to score a guideline on the rock to be cut.

Predictably, this question has attracted the usual outlandish theories: it's been seriously suggested that the Incas achieved their masterful masonry by melting the rocks, focusing the sun's rays into the corners using parabolic mirrors.

Textiles

It's difficult to overstate how important woven cloth was to the Incas. It was a statement of rank, an object of value and even a medium of exchange. It's said that when the Spanish first arrived they were handed not gold and silver but fabric. What you wore was an indication of your rank. The acllas wove the finest fabric for the Inca, called *qompi,* some of which he gave away as an honour to the most worthy of his subjects. The tunics he wore were of magnificent patterning and were made from such

---

❑ **Inca technology in modern use**

After the conquest, the highlands became depopulated as the Spanish removed its inhabitants to purpose-built villages. The terraces and canals fell into decline and the land has never again been as fertile as it was in the days of the Incas.

But recently, a project run by the Inca expert, Dr Ann Kendall, has started to reverse that. Dr Kendall is an archaeologist who excavated in the Cusichaca valley (see p170), paying close attention to the old Inca canals that transect these hills. She realised that these old watercourses could be repaired, using only ancient technology, and irrigate the dry terraces of the Cusichaca valley, increasing the area's agricultural productivity and benefiting the impoverished local community. So, in a practical spin-off from her archaeological excavations, she began to help the campesinos to repair the old Inca water channels. The project worked, and the fertility of the area increased massively.

Dr Kendall is now bringing these skills to other parts of Peru, breathing life into the dead old water channels. If you'd like more information about this fascinating blending of archaeology and development, or to contribute to the **Cusichaca Trust**, the development charity that's associated with this project, write to The Cusichaca Trust, Springfields, 62 High St, Belbroughton, West Midlands DY9 9SU, UK.

varied fabric as vicuña wool and vampire-bat skin (see Fabrics, p58). Soldiers had their own uniforms, and the reports of the first sight the Spanish had of the Incas describe the royal vanguard being dressed in black and white checked cloth. Everyday cloth was also made, called *awaska*, and was worn by the vast majority of people.

Ceramics

The Incas made pottery, but they never reached the aesthetic heights of their ancestors, the Moche and the Nazca. The characteristic Inca pot form is the large *urpu*, which has a fat belly, a curved base and long spout. It was generally a vessel for storage and transport of food: chicha, maize and chuño (freeze-dried potato).

It was carried slung over the back, tied to the body by a band of cloth that passed through the little eyes on the pot's side. Porters on the Inca Trail still carry baggage in this way today.

Metalwork

The melting down of Inca metalwork is one of the Spaniards' greatest crimes. Hardly any gold or silver escaped the furnaces; most of it reduced from dazzlingly-worked artefacts to lump-gold. A few objects remain but they're only things that were small enough to escape the flames of Spanish greed. We can only dream about what Inca metalwork must have been like, prompted by descriptions left by the conquistadors.

> ❑ **Inca gold**
> 'In one cave they discovered twelve sentries of gold and silver, of the size and appearance of those of this country, extraordinarily realistic. There were pitchers half of pottery and half gold, with the gold so well set into the pottery that no drop of water escaped when they were filled, and beautifully made. A golden effigy was also discovered. This greatly distressed the Indians, for they said that it was a figure of the first lord who conquered this land. They found shoes made of gold, of the type that women wore, like half-boots. They found golden crayfish such as live in the sea, and many vases, on which were sculpted in relief all the birds and snakes that they knew, even down to spiders, caterpillars and other insects.' **Pedro Pizarro** *Discovery and Conquest of the Kingdoms of Peru*, 1571.

Hunting

Royal Hunts (*chacos*) were a great sacred event. Beaters encircled a large area and started to walk inwards; and inside the circle, the animals would be herded closer and closer together. Such was the scale of the hunt that it would take many days for the circle to tighten. When the beaters stood almost shoulder to shoulder, hunters entered the circle and killed or sheared the animals it contained: guanaco and vicuña (types of llama), puma, foxes, deer and bears. The hunt provided the locals with much meat and wool, and the nobles with sport.

Warfare

The Spaniards weren't very impressed with the Incas' weapons, and that's not surprising since the Incas hadn't progressed beyond the slings, clubs (*chambis* and *macanas*) and bronze-headed javelins that the Moche had used centuries before. At close quarters a Spaniard's lightning-fast rapier would usually make short work of an Inca armed only with a club or javelin. Despite its effectiveness the rapier wasn't the greatest advantage the Spaniards had over the Incas nor, given the amount of time it took to load and fire, was the arquebus (gun). It was the horse.

The Incas had never seen horses before, and didn't know how to fight them. They must have felt rather like the Romans when faced with the elephants of Hannibal. The Spanish were, of course, excellent fighters, renowned in Europe for their prowess in war but it's unlikely that this alone would have been sufficient to take the Inca empire. Just the sight of an armoured Spaniard on the back of his beast, thundering towards the massed ranks of Inca warriors would have sent fear into the hearts of the bravest. Only by avoiding confrontations on flat ground were the Incas successful against the invaders. The native Americans who mastered the horse themselves, such as the Mapuches of southern Chile and the Apaches of North America, managed to check the Spanish advance.

How, then, were the Incas so successful in building their empire before the arrival of the Europeans? This is one of those questions to

❑ The Incas and Easter Island

Thor Heyerdahl, the Norwegian explorer and writer, has been convinced for many years that the ancient Peruvians colonised Easter Island, the tiny speck of land 3700km west of Peru in the Pacific Ocean. He's based his theory on a number of things: a wall on Easter Island which bears a striking resemblance to Inca masonry; the fact that the dominant tribe of Easter Island had elongated ears like the Inca Orejones (see p83); and the discovery of the sweet potato on Easter Island, a plant that's a species native to South America. Heyerdahl also points out that the predominant currents in the Pacific Ocean lead from Peru to Easter Island, a fact which, he says, makes the colonisation of Easter Island from Peru likely. (Heyerdahl spectacularly proved that it is possible to float from Peru to Easter Island on a raft when in 1948 he did just that aboard his reed raft, *Kon Tiki*.)

It's a seductive idea, and it's backed up by oral history. On the coast of Peru, there's a myth that a king, defeated in battle, called Kon Tiki, sailed off into the sunset and was never seen again. There's a complementary myth that both Easter Island and its near neighbour the Marquesas Islands, were colonised by a man from a country far away to the east who arrived by sea, and this man is called Tiki in some myths.

Sadly for Heyerdahl, his theories have never been accepted by the academic community, not least because there's no evidence of any Peruvian language, ceramics or textiles on these islands. Still, it's a intriguing possibility.

which there's no easy answer, but it's likely that the efficient road network was the key, allowing reinforcements to be brought up to support an Inca fighting column in times of need. The Incas could then overwhelm their adversaries by sheer force of numbers.

This fits with the fact that the Incas found it extremely difficult to subdue the peoples in the extreme north and south of their empire. The Chronicles tell how hard pressed the Incas were in the north, against local tribes who protected themselves with strings of forts, and in the south, the Incas never managed to conquer the Mapuche. Their lines of communication were stretched too far, and they couldn't bring up their support easily – they had literally reached the end of the road, even for their extremely efficient infrastructure.

The fall of the Incas

On 24 September 1532 Francisco Pizarro marched into the lands of the Inca empire with 62 horsemen and 106 infantry. How he managed to subdue and rape the greatest empire of its day is a fascinating story of greed and cunning.

PLAGUE AND CIVIL WAR

Some years before Pizarro marched out the old Inca Huayna-Capac had retired to Quito, the northern city of the Inca empire. Huayna-Capac was in the north subduing local tribes. One of his legitimate sons, Huascar, had remained in the imperial capital Cuzco. The bastard son, Atahualpa, was with Huayna-Capac in Quito.

Generally, these were times of peace, the empire was secure and life was luxurious. But it was not to last. Disaster struck in the form of a plague of biblical proportions which spread over the land, and Huayna-Capac himself died as did his heir, Ninan Cuyuchi. Modern historians think that the plague was smallpox, or some other disease brought to the New World by the Europeans, freshly arrived in the hemisphere. The vanguard of conquest, it killed off the Inca, his heir and many of his court and brought the country to civil war.

Huascar coveted the throne, as did his natural brother Atahualpa. Huascar had the support of the Cuzco nobility and the trappings of traditional empire. Atahualpa was in the north, with the seasoned, battle-hardened generals of the Ecuadorian campaign. Civil war erupted. After a long, bitter struggle Atahualpa was the victor.

And so the scene was set for the arrival of Pizarro and his Spanish adventurers. Had they arrived two years before or two years later they would have discovered a stronger, united empire with armies well able to push them back into the sea. As it is, when they arrived they were lucky enough to march into a country ravaged by disease and broken by civil war.

PIZARRO AND ALMAGRO

Pizarro was born in Extremadura in rural Spain. He knew hardship in his youth: he was a swine-herd in the poorest part of a country still recovering from centuries-long occupation by the Moors. He was illiterate, a poor horseman but a machiavellian judge of human character and a ruthless military genius.

Pizarro and Almagro set sail
FELIPE HUAMÁN POMA DE AYALA (c1590)

By middle age he found himself a prosperous burgher in the new Spanish colony of Panama. This would have been enough for many: he had climbed far from his lowly beginnings. But it wasn't enough. He wanted more.

The search for El Dorado

Rumours reached Panama of a great, rich country to the south, a country where there were vast treasures of gold and hoards of silver. There had been attempts to reach it – one man had got as far as a river called the Biru (hence the country's name), but had to turn back. Pizarro and his partner, Diego de Almagro, decided to fit out an expedition and go and see for themselves. News was breaking of how dashing Cortés had defeated the infidel Aztecs and secured Mexico for Spain, and these stories confirmed the possibility that there was another great kingdom filled with riches hidden in the undiscovered lands to the south.

First expeditions

Pizarro's and Almagro's first expeditions weren't successful. It's true that they met an ocean-going raft, filled with Inca cloth, which indicated that there was some truth to the rumours of developed lands, but Pizarro and his men became near-shipwrecked on a desert island in the bitter winter of 1527. The conquest of Peru almost foundered at that point, and would have done had Pizarro not drawn a line in the sand with his sword and challenged his men to cross the line to greatness and riches. Thirteen crossed, and thirteen became the richest and most powerful men in all the Americas. Of that thirteen, how many died in their beds? Pizarro was murdered. Almagro was murdered. All but one of Pizarro's brothers met gruesome ends. Such is the price of greed.

In 1528 Pizarro returned to Spain to beg the indulgence of the crown. He got it, and with it the title of Governor and Captain-General of Peru. He secured for Almagro the title of Commandant of Tumbes, a little port on the coast. Almagro was to prove unhappy with this. He only agreed to continue with the venture if he was given all the land beyond Pizarro's claim.

Pizarro then returned to Peru at the head of a small army. They landed on the coast at Tumbes, and found a ruined town, a result of the civil war that had been raging in the old Inca empire.

FIRST CONTACT

Pizarro and his men marched up into the hills. They were impressed with what they saw: well-maintained roads, stone towns, orderly people, warehouses filled with food. This was obviously no land of barbarians. They, on the other hand, could not earn such praise. When they saw food they ate it and when they saw women, they took them.

News of the strange new arrivals reached the Inca's ear. Atahualpa was resting near Cajamarca taking his time over his triumphal return to Cuzco, seeking to heal the country of the wounds inflicted by a fratricidal civil war – or if he couldn't heal the wounds, to cut them out of the body of the state. He heard mention from his chasquis that a group of men, accompanied by strange beasts a little like llamas, had landed on the coast and were walking on the roads without imperial permission. They were breaching all of the Incas' laws: stealing from imperial storehouses and even taking acllas, the sacred nuns, for their pleasure.

The Inca was with an army, numbered in the thousands. These weren't just any old soldiers; they were used to battle and were strong, fit and fierce. The Inca could have wiped away the Spanish with a flick of his wrist. Why he didn't is a fascinating question that has been asked and asked again over the years.

Fatally the Inca allowed the Spaniards to advance. They came to Cajamarca, and were stunned when they saw the hills alight with the camp-fires of the Inca's army, and they were afraid. A Spaniard described the sight: 'The Indians' camp looked like a very beautiful city … So many tents were visible that we were truly filled with great apprehension. We never thought that Indians could maintain such a proud estate nor have so many tents in good order'. The Spanish sent emissaries to the Inca, asking him to come and meet them in the main square of the town, to talk. That night, they laid a trap.

THE TRAP

The main square had one exit only, and was surrounded by buildings. The small cannon that the Spaniards possessed was set up on a high point. At a certain sign, it was to be fired and the Spanish cavalry was to pour out of its hiding places around the square and attack the natives, who had never seen horses or guns. This would give the Spanish a chance. Despite the plan, and despite their horses and their guns, the Spaniards spent a fearful night.

The next day it looked as if the Inca wasn't going to come. The Spaniards posted as lookouts could see his camp and could see that there was no movement. Things got even more tense in the Spanish camp. Then, in the afternoon, the Inca and his army moved.

The chroniclers described the scene: the Incas wore gold and silver crowns, dressed in fine clothing and sang 'graceful' songs. The townspeople swept the road before the procession, which was led by a squadron of men in chequered tunics. The Spanish urinated out of pure terror.

Atahualpa made his way into the main square. The Spaniard's priest, Vincente de Valverde, approached the monarch as he sat on his litter, and said 'I have come to teach you the word of God'. Atahualpa seized the priest's breviary, and leafed through it, admiring the writing. He then, so the story goes, put it to his ear, then threw it to the ground in irritation. The priest cried out, cursing the Indian devils and letting slip the dogs of war.

It was a massacre. The Indians who bore the Inca's litter were his nobles and not his fighting men. They were amongst the first to fall. The cavalry butchered the rest of the Inca's escort, riding them down through the small, orderly streets or slaughtering them where they stood, dumfounded by these strange charging half-beasts. It did not last long.

A chronicler describes Pizarro's reaching Atuhualpa's litter and grabbing at the unarmed Inca 'with great bravery'. Atahualpa was captured. As John Hemming has said in *The Conquest of the Incas*, the conquest of Peru began with a great checkmate.

THE GREAT CHECKMATE

Atahualpa's troops, still for the most part massed outside the town gates, didn't mount a rescue attempt. The Inca sent word that they were to disband. Why?

Atahualpa had attempted a bargain for his life. He expected to be killed, and when he saw the Spaniards' lust for precious metal offered to fill a room with gold and two more rooms with silver for good measure in exchange for his life. (The Spanish could speak to him because they'd trained up an interpreter whom they'd captured from the ocean-going raft, see p93). The Spanish agreed to the bargain, and as a gesture of good faith, Atahualpa sent word that his army should disband. Power in the Inca state was so distilled in the Inca himself, that without him at their head the people could not act. He was a god, a king, and a general. When he ordered something, they obeyed. So when he ordered that they should not attack the Spanish, they did not. There has seldom been a more crucial and catastrophic misjudgment by one man in the history of his race, or a less trustworthy set of people in whom a captive has placed his faith. The Spaniards were after the Inca's whole country, nothing less, and by ordering his people not to destroy them he destroyed his country.

Messengers were sent to the four suyus of the empire, and told to bring back gold and silver. In time the llama trains arrived – first little by little, then in small bands, then in floods. The room began to fill with gold.

A king's murder

The Spaniards became jumpy. What would happen when the room was full? Wouldn't the Inca go off and raise an army to return and annihilate every last foreigner in his land? They couldn't let him go. Happily

The death of Atahualpa
FELIPE HUAMÁN POMA DE AYALA (c1590)

enough for them, there were reports that a large Indian army was massing a couple of days' march from Cajarmarca. Charges were laid against Atahualpa that he was planning a rebellion, and he was tried, found guilty and sentenced to death by burning. As an Inca, it was crucially important to him that his body should survive intact so it could be mummified and partake of future rituals, as tradition dictated. Burning was literally a fate worse than death. The Spanish told him that he could avoid the fire by converting to Christianity. So this he did.

Atahualpa, the last undisputed Inca, was garroted on 26 July 1533. In a particularly cynical piece of treachery, even for the Spanish, they burnt his body anyway. He was buried a Christian, and they say that Pizarro, in an act of superhuman hypocrisy, cried at his funeral.

The first puppet Inca

Pizarro realised the importance of maintaining a puppet monarch, through whom he could exercise power with the minimum of force. He therefore selected an Inca to succeed Atahualpa from one of the princelings in Atahualpa's retinue; he chose Huascar's brother, Tupac

(Opposite) Top left: Sacsayhuaman (see p144). Top right: The terraces of Machu Picchu, looking up to the Watchman's Hut (see p220). Bottom: The sites of Patallacta and Pulpituyoc (see p170), near the start of the hike from Km88.

Huallpa (Huascar had died mysteriously, probably murdered on Atahualpa's orders, during the time of Atahualpa's imprisonment.) This was a masterstroke. Pizarro set himself and the Spanish up as protectors of Huascar's line, and thus bought themselves support from the defeated side in the recent civil war.

Then the Spaniards began the march on Cuzco.

THE MARCH ON CUZCO

The march on Cuzco was long and hard, and each step of the way the Spanish were fearful of their own shadows and of an Inca army waiting to bar their way.

The army that awaited them consisted of the remains of the army of the north, the army of Quito. However, as the Spanish marched they found friends: many tribes, only recently come under the Incas' yoke, gave them support and encouragement and the Huascar faction inevitably preferred the foreigners to the Quitan army. So the Spanish weren't as entirely bereft of support as their more vainglorious accounts would have us believe, and on their march on Cuzco they picked up supplies, willing helpers and auxiliaries.

About half-way to Cuzco the young Tupac Huallpa died, probably of natural causes but there were many in Atahualpa's camp who wished him dead. Pizarro exploited the situation by playing off those who wanted the successor to be of Atahualpa's line against those who preferred Huascar's children. When the Spaniards were nearing Cuzco, Manco Inca, a young prince of Huascar's line, came forward. With Pizarro's approval he was made Inca.

A desperate defence

The Quitan army did oppose the march on Cuzco – but they did not have the weapons nor the tactics to oppose the full force of the Spanish cavalry. Every encounter, save one, resulted in a crushing rout of the Incas. The glorious exception was partly brought on by the arrogance of a dashing Spanish conquistador, Hernando de Soto. De Soto wanted to be the first into Cuzco, wanted the glory and the money, and he was leading the advance guard of the Spanish column. He came to the Apurímac river. The Indians had burnt the bridge, but the Spanish were lucky enough to find the river at low water and they forded it. As they were making their way up the other side, the horizon blackened with Inca soldiers. The Spanish tried to form up into a defensive line, but the Incas had let loose

---

(**Opposite**) **Top:** Coricancha in Cuzco (see p139) was the Incas' Temple of the Sun. The Dominicans grafted their monastery, Santo Domingo, onto its foundations. **Bottom:** Impressive mortarless Inca walls can still be seen in parts of Cuzco.

the mountainside at them, and stones, rocks and boulders crashed into their unprotected ranks, followed by a tidal wave of warriors.

The Spanish made for the top, but their horses were exhausted and five conquistadors fell from the saddle. Once off their horses, they were quickly despatched by the Incas that surrounded them. The remaining Spaniards then retreated and camped for the night, a night that they feared would be their last. However, with the morning light came reinforcements presciently sent forward by Pizarro, and the disheartened Incas faded into the morning mist.

CUZCO – CAPITAL OF THE EMPIRE

The Spanish rode into Cuzco, and set up Manco Inca as their puppet. They took control of the city in an arrogant re-founding ceremony on 23 March 1534, and ruled the empire for a couple of years, in relative harmony, Manco was satisfied because he had status, the Spanish were satisfied because they had power. Many conquistadors went home and published accounts of the expedition, but others stayed on and were awarded plots of land, encomiendas, from which they could derive an income. All Spaniards had to live in Cuzco, however, to establish a firm, secure and defensible concentration of men.

The northern part of the empire, of course, had yet to be subdued, and the Quitan army still posed a threat to the Spanish, but it was just a matter of time now before that fell. The Spaniards now had a power base, access to the sea, and the loyalty of many of the subjects of the old empire. The Inca generals, Rumñavi, Zope-Zopahua and Quisquis deserve more of a mention than I can give them in these pages, but they were all conquered by 1535.

SOW THE WIND

That could have been the end of the story but it was just the start of another chapter. The first seed of discontent which was sowed related to Diego de Almagro, the short-changed partner of Pizarro. In 1535 he rather grumpily set off to inspect the territory he'd been awarded, and he discovered northern Chile, a vast tract of land as barren as the Sahara. Almagro was to come back, a cloud on his brow and envy in his heart at the riches of Cuzco.

That was to prove a problem but a more immediate problem was caused by Francisco Pizarro's brothers. Francisco Pizarro had gone to the coast to found Lima, and the city of Cuzco was left under the control of hot-headed and vulgar Juan and Gonzalo Pizarro. They began to insult Manco Inca and abuse his subjects.

REAP THE WHIRLWIND

At Easter in 1536, the announcement was made to the citizens of Cuzco that Manco Inca had rebelled and headed for the hills. The conquistadors did what conquistadors do best – they rode out to meet the rebellion head-on. In the valley of Yucay, they came across it: 100,000 to 200,000 Inca soldiers bent on their death. The Spaniards only just made it back to Cuzco alive.

The siege of Cuzco

And so began the siege of Cuzco. These were grim times for the Spanish, all 180 of them, only a half of whom had horses. On an early foray the Mayor had his head cut off. On 6 May the Incas entered Cuzco and beat back the Spanish who holed-up in buildings, so the Incas set fire to the city.

Manco Inca himself was directing the siege from Sacsayhuaman (see p144), a site that overlooks Cuzco. The Spanish realised that dislodging him from this fortress-temple was the only solution. They rode out, around the obstacles that had been placed to trip up their horses, and took possession of the Rodadero. There they faced the massive, three-tiered walls of Sacsayhuaman, which in those days were topped by three castles.

It was a long, savage fight. Juan Pizarro was hit on the head by a sling-shot and killed, but Gonzalo Pizarro and the Spanish, fighting with a desperation borne of terror and a courage that was their wont, took the citadel. They say that in the days that followed condors feasted on the piles of the dead Incas lying around the walls of Sacsayhuaman. The arms of the city of Cuzco, granted in 1540, show a castle surrounded by condors that represents this terrible day.

Vilcabamba – the last city of the Incas

Manco Inca escaped. He was pursued, and retreated – from Pisac, from Ollantaytambo, and then deep into the jungle where he founded a new city called Vilcabamba. It was here that he carved out a new Inca state, a mere rump of the glories of the past, but a state where there were no Spanish. It was from here that he harassed the invaders, and here that he died, murdered by Spanish renegades to whom he'd given sanctuary – yet another example of the cynical lack of honour that characterised the conquistadors.

For the next 30 years his sons ruled this last scrap of Inca empire, lost in the uncongenial humid jungles of the east – first Sayri-Tupac Inca, then Titu Cusi Inca until the last Inca Tupac Amaru was finally crushed by the Viceroy Toledo in 1572.

After his city of Vilcabamba was sacked, Tupac Amaru fled into the jungle. With him, he took the *Punchao*, the sacred Idol of the Sun, the icon that had stood in happier days at the heart of the Coricancha in Cuzco. Tupac Amaru was eventually captured, preferring to trust in his Spanish pursuers than in the jungle tribes that were his native bodyguards. It was trust that was yet again to prove misplaced, and he was publicly executed in Cuzco's Plaza de Armas after a sham trial.

His last words, perhaps testament to the tortures that had been inflicted on him, amounted to a betrayal of his Inca past. He said: 'Lords, you are here from all the four suyus. Be it known to you that I am a Christian, they have baptised me and I wish to die under the law of God. And I have to die. All that I and my ancestors the Incas have told you up to now – that you should worship the sun Punchao and the huacas, idols, stones, rivers, mountains and vilcas – is completely false. When we told you that we were entering in to speak to the sun that it advised you to do what we told you, and that it spoke, this was false. It did not speak, we alone did; for it is an object of gold and cannot speak.'

Punchao, a gold figure the size of a small boy, was recovered by the Spanish but has never been seen again.

REAP ANOTHER WHIRLWIND

The other seed that was sown, that of Almagro's discontent, also grew and blossomed. Almagro returned from his gruelling Chilean venture in 1537, disappointed at the thin pickings of the place. He marched on Cuzco, and took it, but his victory was short lived as the Pizarrists would not let go that easily. In 1538 when the Almagrists controlled the sierra and Pizarrists controlled the coast, confrontation was inevitable, and the matter was finally settled at the battle of Las Salinas in April. Diego de Almagro was captured, put on trial and executed.

He had his revenge from beyond the grave. On 26 June 1541 Francisco Pizarro, was murdered by supporters of the dead Almagro. One story says that with his dying breath, Pizarro drew the sign of the cross on the floor with his blood. Another story says that his murderers crushed his hands as he was trying to make absolution and cried that he would have to confess his sins in Hell. So died the conqueror of Peru, murderer of Atahualpa and scourge of the Incas.

❏ **Epitaph**
'OLD MARTIN: So fell Peru. We gave her greed, hunger and the Cross: three gifts for the civilised life. The family groups that sang on the terraces are gone. In their place slaves shuffle underground and they don't sing there. Peru is a silent country, frozen in avarice. So fell Spain, gorged with gold; distended; now dying'. **Peter Shaffer** *Royal Hunt of the Sun*, Act 2 Scene 12.

PART 4: LIMA

Lima

'Lima the Horrible' was the rallying cry of a band of 1950s Peruvian intellectuals, and after a day or two in this smog-smothered city you may well end up agreeing with them. Certainly the noise, pollution and chaos, added to the need to be on constant alert against muggings, make Peru's capital a stressful place. But it would be harsh to write it off completely, and while it's unlikely anyone would come to Peru just to see Lima, there's enough here to keep you entertained as you prepare to head up to Cuzco and Machu Picchu.

Cloaked in the thick, grey *garúa* (sea fog) that engulfs the city for most of the year are still some fine colonial buildings, informative, well laid-out museums and excellent seafood restaurants. The Limeños themselves are a good advertisement for their city, and most are wonderfully welcoming.

HISTORY

Origins
People have lived here at the mouth of the Rímac river for the past 7000 years. When you fly into Jorge Chávez airport, you'll see from the aeroplane window some of the large adobe pyramids that these early Limeños built, now surrounded by Lima's urban sprawl. These date from about 3000BC, long before the arrival of the Spanish, long, even, before the Incas. They were built in the U-shaped style that's characteristic of the temples on this part of the Peruvian coast (see p69).

By the fifteenth century when the Incas arrived, the local shrine and oracle called Pachacamac was already ancient, having been established about 900 years earlier. The Incas absorbed it into their religion, building an acllahuasi (convent) at the site. They then occupied the district, and by the time the Spanish arrived there were about 400 temples along the river supported by a network of peaceful communities.

The days of conquest
In 1535 the city of Lima was founded on the banks of the river Rímac by Francisco Pizarro, shortly after he'd captured Cuzco. He wanted to build his capital close to the sea because this provided the Spaniards with contact to the motherland, and here was a good harbour with a reliable water

supply. The city was called *Ciudad de los Reyes* (City of the Kings) after the Magi and the kings of Spain but the name didn't stick, and by the sixteenth century the place was called Lima, a corruption of Rímac.

Only a year after it was founded, the city was almost destroyed and the Spaniards pitched into the ocean during the revolt of Manco Inca (see p99). The Inca general, Quizo Yupanqui, besieged Lima but was destroyed by the power of the Spanish cavalry riding on flat ground. The failure to take Lima meant that the Incas could not cut the Spanish off from their lifeline to the sea, and the whole Inca rebellion was doomed.

Capital of Spanish Peru

The Viceroy of Spanish South America lived in Lima, and the city attracted the trappings of power. It became a rich place. The University of San Marcos, the continent's oldest, was founded in 1551, and in 1569 the city became the seat of the Spanish Inquisition. An account survives of the entry of a new viceroy into the city in the eighteenth century that illustrates the wealth of the municipality. It describes streets hung with tapestries, the local officials decked out in crimson velvet and brocade, and celebrations involving days of bullfights and banquets. This evidence of riches attracted the attentions of less welcome visitors, and Sir Francis Drake was the first of many privateers (pirates) to raid Lima when he attacked the port in 1579. The city walls were built as a result.

In 1746 there was a catastrophic earthquake that shook most of the glorious old colonial buildings to dust, and 16,000 people died from the quake and its ensuing plagues. A vivid eye-witness account runs: 'Monday 31st [three days later] there was a suffocating smell coming, not only from the countless corpses, but also from the dead horses, dogs and donkeys. The bodies were taken in cartloads to the cemetery where they were buried in large trenches.'

Capital of independent Peru

San Martín liberated Lima from the Spanish in 1821. He was criticised for delaying but said that he felt that the Limeños didn't want to be liberated: they were so plump with the opulence of Spain. San Martín waited until the locals discovered that there was to be no help from the mother country, at which they turned their loyalty to him. The Viceroy escaped to the mountains with an army (see p39).

Charles Darwin visited in 1830 on his voyage aboard *The Beagle*, and provided a description of Lima post-independence: 'The city of Lima is now in a wretched state of decay: the streets are nearly unpaved, and heaps of filth are piled up in all directions; where the black gallinazos, [vultures] tame as poultry, pick up bits of carrion. The houses have generally an upper story, built, on account of the earthquakes, of plastered woodwork; but some of the old ones, which are now used by several families, are immensely large, and would rival in suites of apartments the most magnificent in any place. Lima, the City of the Kings, must formerly have been a splendid town.' (*The Voyage of the Beagle*).

The city walls were torn down in 1870 as Lima expanded. Although the land was needed for houses, the demolition of the walls was a mistake because in 1881 the city was occupied by the Chileans during the War of the Pacific (see p40). They didn't leave for two years.

More recent times

In 1920 there was a huge influx of poor, unskilled labour and the city's population grew to 170,000. President Leguía worked hard to rejuvenate the city, constructing sewers and building open places like the Plaza San Martín, but the sheer number of people here has been a problem ever since. The population is now 8,000,000.

Many live in *pueblos jóvenes* (shanty towns) which aren't as bad as others in South America but are still pretty dismal places; unemployment and underemployment are rife. You'll no doubt be driven around by university graduates who work as taxistas because it's the only work there is, and for many from the pueblos jóvenes, the only work is on the street. As with other capitals, there is another side to Lima, a face decorated with the wealth and opulence of the wealthy neighbourhoods of San Isidro and Miraflores, inhabited by people who can afford to shop for groceries in Miami. Lima is a city of extremes.

ARRIVAL

A note of caution

Lima has a crime problem, and you need to be careful – see p59.

By air

There's a cambio in the arrivals terminal, a glass box of a building, and ATMs and another next door in the departures area. To get to the departures area, go through the doors at the end of the arrivals' hall, try to brush away the touts you will inevitably attract, turn left into the next door building. The cambio is on the right and the ATMs a little further on.

The centre of town is to the east of the airport. Most people stay in either **Lima Centro** or **Miraflores**, and to take you there the taxistas will ask for half as much again as you should be paying – they quote s/20 to take you the 12km to Lima Centro but you should only pay about s/10 to s/15. A taxi to Miraflores should cost about s/5 more.

By bus

Many buses come in near to the Hotel Sheraton near the Parque Universitario, very near Lima Centro, but there isn't a central bus terminal in Lima, so the place at which you'll arrive will depend on which company you're travelling with and from where. It's best to take a taxi from the terminus to your hotel, as bus stops are a magnet for thieves.

GETTING AROUND

Taxi

Most taxis in Lima are currently unregulated: they're just private cars displaying a 'Taxi' sticker but this is changing. If you see a cab with a number painted on the side of the door it's been registered with the authorities. Yellow cabs with numbers on the door are one stage further on; they're regulated. Both are less likely to try to cheat you.

Bus

The bus network in Lima is a mess. Apparently it all used to be better: buses that ran on particular routes were painted the same colour, and there were timetables but nowadays the colours mean nothing and there's no real timetable. They do have their route number and destination written on their front and sides; your hotel will tell you which bus you need to get and from where. **Beware of pickpockets and bag-slashers**.

The main bus thoroughfares in Lima Centro are Av Alfonso Ugarte and Av Tacna, and in Miraflores it's Av Arequipa.

Tours

Lima Vision (☎ 447 7710), Malecón Balta 870, 1st Floor, Miraflores offer tours of the museums, the city and Pachacamac, costing US$20-35 for a half-day. **Expediciones Viento Sur** (☎ 429 1414), Av Grau, La Punta, Callao, do cruises around the bay of Lima out towards San Lorenzo Island for US$30. Abimael Guzman (see p43) is imprisoned on San Lorenzo Island. There are many other companies.

Car rental

Avis (☎ 434 1111), Av Javier Prado 5235, Camacho; **Budget** (☎ 442 8703, 🖹 441 4174), Av La Paz 522, Miraflores; **Hertz** (☎ 442 4509); **Localiza** (☎ 242 3939); **Mitsui** (☎ 470 9040), Av Canadá. Prices are variable but range from US$25 to US$50 a day.

ORIENTATION

Lima is built on a flat plain above a large arc of a bay. It's a big place with many different neighbourhoods, and the distances between them are too great for walking.

Lima Centro is the ancient centre of the city on the banks of the Rímac, a good few miles inland from the sea. The Plaza de Armas is here, as is the cathedral, the statues of Bolívar and San Martín, a pedestrian zone and many cheap hotels. To the south-west, close by, is the more residential district of **Breña**. To the north are the poorer suburbs. To the south-east is the industrial-commercial area of **La Victoria** and the suburbs of **San Luís** and **San Borja** where the Museo de la Nacíon is (see p117). Further out is the plusher **Monterrico** and the Museo de Oro del Peru (see p117).

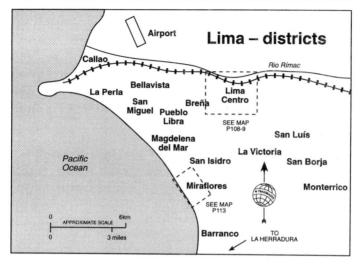

Driving west from Lima Centro, you'll come to **Bellavista**, the sea and **Callao**, the port of Lima. There's a fort, a good view of the sea and some excellent cheap *cevicherías* (seafood restaurants selling the dish ceviche). Callao is really not as dangerous as some guidebooks make out, although it's wiser to be out of here by night.

Down the coast from Callao you'll pass through **San Miguel** where the zoo is; **Magdalena del Mar**; the posh embassy district of **San Isidro**; residential **Miraflores** with its more expensive hotels and North American airs, and bohemian **Barranco** with bars and night-life. You'll end up climbing El Morro, the hill which provides a first-class view of the coast and the city. Beyond El Morro is **La Herradura** – the name means 'horseshoe' because that's what the bay looks like.

Unless otherwise noted, addresses in this chapter are for Lima Centro.

SERVICES

Banks and cambios

The following banks have branches all over Lima: **Banco Latino** (MasterCard), Carabaya 341; **Telebanco** (Visa), Jr de la Unión 790; **Banco Mercantil** (AMEX), Carabaya and Ucayali, **Citibank** (Citicorp), Ribeira Naearrete 857, San Isidro. For cambios try Boulevard Tarata at 248 Miraflores (☎ 444 3381), and many others, for example **Interbanc** Jr de la Unión 600, which is quick and gives good rates. **Western Unión** (☎ 422 0014), is at Miró Quesada 198 and Petit Thouars 3595, San Isidro.

❏ South American Explorers' Club (SAEC)

This useful club for travellers in South America provides a wide range of assistance to members – everything from storing equipment to helping to find a trekking partner; from reconfirming flights to holding mail, faxes and email. There's a good library of books in English and reports, written by other travellers, on just about every corner of Peru. The people who run the place are a fount of helpful information on everything from train times to more complex issues like the current political situation in the highlands. There's a comfortable lounge where you can escape Lima's bustle, and the place contains what is probably the only Arsenal football club shirt in the whole of the continent. There are branches of the club in Quito, Ecuador, and in the USA.

SAEC (☎ 425 0142, email: montague@amauta.rcp.net.pe) is at Avenida Republica de Portugal 146, Breña (postal address: Casilla 3714, Lima 100, Peru). They're open Monday to Friday, 9.30am-5pm. Membership costs US$40 per year (US$70 for couples).

Books (English)

For books in English try the **American Bookstore Center** (☎ 442 2900), Benavides 455, Miraflores; or the **British Cultural Library** (☎ 221 7550), Av Arequipa 3495, San Isidro. The **SAEC** (see above) has a book exchange for members.

Communications

● **Telephone and fax** The code for Lima is 01. **Telefónica del Peru** (☎ 433 1616), is at Jr Carabaya 933, Plaza San Martin, but they're expensive and you'd be better off direct dialling from a pay phone in the street.

● **Post** The main **correo** (post office), is on the block on the north-west corner of the Plaza de Armas, open Monday to Saturday 8am-10pm, Sunday 8am-2pm. There's a poste restante here. For **American Express** client mail go to **Lima Tours** (☎ 427 6624), Belén 1040. The **SAEC** also holds mail for members.

● **Email Dragonfans** (☎ 444 9325) is a cybercafé at Calle Tarata 230, Miraflores; they charge s/8 an hour. There's another in Lima Centro – up the stairs in the arcade on the right, Office 210, Jirón de la Unión 853. The **SAEC** allows members to use its computers to send and receive email.

Emergencies and medical services

● **Ambulance** Alerta Médica (☎ 470 5000); Cruz Roja (☎ 265 8783, 222 0222), or take a taxi.

● **Doctor** Dr Alejandro Rivera (☎ 471 2238) at the Instiuto Médico Lince, León Velarde 221, speaks English.

● **Hospitals Anglo-American** (☎ 221 3656), San Isidro; **Maison de Santé**, (☎ 467 0753), Chorrillos.

● **Pharmacy** Botica Inglés, Jr Cailloma 336, is well stocked.

● **Rabies** Anti-rabies centre (☎ 425 6313).

❑ **Embassies and consulates**
Argentina (☎ 433 5704), Pablo Bermudez 143, 2nd Floor; **Austria** (☎ 442 0503, 442 1807), Av Central 643, 5th Floor, San Isidro; **Australia** (☎ 221 7020); **Bolivia** (☎ 422 8231), Los Castaños 235, San Isidro; **Brazil** (☎ 421 5650), José Pardo 850, Miraflores; **Canada** (☎ 444 4015), Jr F Gerdes (or Libertad) 130, Miraflores; **Colombia** (☎ 441 0530), Av Jorge Basadre 1580, San Isidro; **Chile** (☎ 221 2817), Javier Prado Oeste 790, San Isidro; **Ecuador** (☎ 442 4184), Las Palmeras 356, San Isidro; **France** (☎ 221 0273), Arequipa 3415, San Isidro; **Germany** (☎ 442 9919), Arequipa 4201, Miraflores; **Ireland** (☎ 445 6813), Santiago Acuña 135, Urb Aurora, Miraflores; **Italy** (☎ 463 2727), Gregorio Escobedo 298, Jesus María; **Israel** Natalio Sánchez 125, 6th Floor (☎ 433 4431); **New Zealand** (☎ 221 2833); **Spain** (☎ 221 7704), Jorge Basadre 498, San Isidro; **United Kingdom** (☎ 433 4839), Natalio Sánchez 125, 4th Floor; **USA** (☎ 434 3000), Av la Encalada Cda 17, Monterrico.

Laundry

There aren't many laundries in Lima Centro, but most hotels will do laundry for a price. In Miraflores, try **Laverap** Schell 601.

Maps

● **Lima** Maps of the city can be bought at kiosks and tourist shops, but there's a full map with index of streets in the back of the *Páginas Amarillas* (Yellow Pages) which you'll find at your hotel.

● **Hiking maps** The **Instituto Geográfico Nacional** (☎ 475 9960, 475 3090, 🖹 475 9810), Av Aramburú 1198, Surquillo (take a taxi there), open Monday to Friday 8am-12pm, 1-5.30pm sells good 1:100,000 maps of the hikes in this book. You can also pick these up at the **SAEC**.

Police

Tourist police (☎ 471 4313 and 423 7225) or toll free from a private phone (☎ 0800-42579).

Tourist information

The very helpful tourist information office, **Infotur Peru** (☎ 431 0117), open Monday to Friday 9.30am-5pm, Saturday 10am-1pm, is through an archway off Jirón Belén 1066 (almost opposite the Hostal La Estrella de Belén).

There are lots of other places offering tourist information but they're generally trying to sell you something.

Visa extension

Direccion General de Migraciones y Naturalizacion (DIGEMIN) (☎ 330 4020), Av España 700-734, Breña.

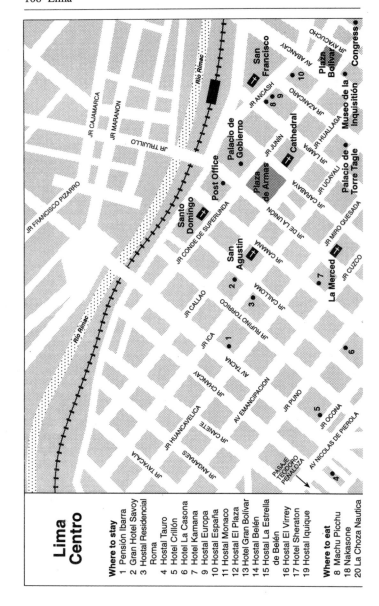

Lima Centro

Where to stay
1 Pensión Ibarra
2 Gran Hotel Savoy
3 Hostal Residencial Roma
4 Hostal Tauro
5 Hotel Crillón
6 Hotel La Casona
7 Hotel Kamana
9 Hostal Europa
10 Hostal España
11 Hostal Monaco
12 Hostal El Plaza
13 Hotel Gran Bolívar
14 Hostal Belén
15 Hostal La Estrella de Belén
16 Hostal El Virrey
17 Hotel Sheraton
19 Hostal Iquique

Where to eat
8 Machu Picchu
18 Nakasone
20 La Choza Nautica

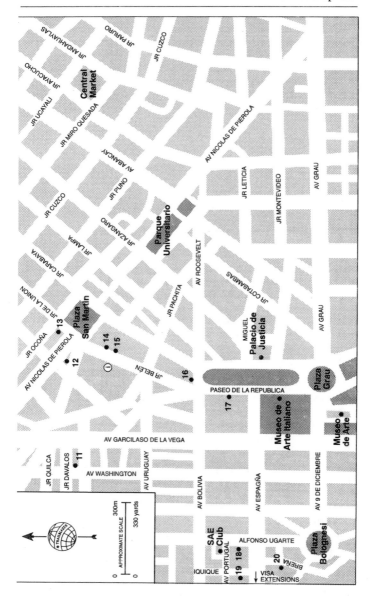

WHERE TO STAY

You can stay in districts other than Lima Centro and Miraflores but these areas have the highest concentration of hotels and services for tourists. Of the two, Lima Centro is dirtier, noisier and has greater crime problem but is more central and cheaper.

Note: the following abbreviations are used here: **com = room with common bathroom; att = bathroom attached**.

Lima Centro

● **Budget accommodation** The first mention has to be the *Hostal España* (☎ 427 9196/428 5546), Azangaro 105, close to the Church of San Francisco. Top of the list of places to stay in some guidebooks, this has inevitably become gringo central. It's an old building with an interior courtyard; it's friendly, has lockers, and costs s/23 (double, com). Breakfast's good in the café downstairs. If it's full, there's the *Hostal Europa* (☎ 427 3351), Ancash 376, around the corner, which costs the same, and offers a similar package but not to the same standard.

I prefer the *Pensión Ibarra* (☎ 427 8603/427 1035), Avenida Tacna 359, 14th and 15th floors, flat No 2, a place where your mother would be happy for you to stay. There's no sign outside, and it's in a tower block, but it's spotless, safe, has a fridge and cooker and good views. The women who run it are helpful and do laundry. It costs s/26 (double, com). If tower blocks turn you off, try *Hotel La Casona* (☎ 426 6552), Moquega 289, a wonderful old tiled-building. The beds are a bit soft and the rooms a bit tatty, but it's well priced at s/28 (double, com). It is, however, less secure than other hotels.

If you're after the **lowest prices**, there's a road of cheap hostals in Pasaje Teodoro Peñaloza (off Nicolas de Pierola), charging s/8 a night (single, com). Don't expect much, and be careful. Around the corner, there's the *Hostal Atenas* (☎ 330 5149), Nicolas de Pierola 370, which is s/20 (double, com), gringo-free, pretty clean with a lovely painted lobby and the *Hostal Monaco* (☎ 424 9181), Washington 949 – the same kind of thing without the interior decoration at s/26 (double, com).

● **Mid-range hotels** The *Hostal Iquique* (☎ 433 4724, 423 3699), Jr Iquique 758, Breña, is recommended as it's safe, very helpful, friendly and light and clean – though the ground floor rooms smell musty. It costs s/40 (double, att), and there are discounts if you're a member of the SAEC.

A similar type of place in a building with more character is the good *Hostal Residencial Roma* (☎ 427 7576, 426 0533, email: resroma@peru. itete.com.pe), Jr Ica 326. The people who run the Roma are helpful and polyglot, and charge s/58 (double, att, cable TV extra), which is a little too much.

The *Hostal Belén* (☎ 427 8995), Jr Unión/Bélen 1049, is also in a rambling old building, and has clean lavatories but soft beds in rooms that some people will find poky. The communal areas are light and airy, and there's a wonderful old marble staircase. It costs s/32 (double, com). Next door is the *Hostal La Estrella de Belén* (☎ 428 6462), Jr Unión/Belén 1051. This is a good place; it's modern and seems clean though the owner was not very friendly; it's s/45 (double, att). Also worth mentioning is *Hostal Tauro* (☎ 427 5541), Av Tacua 768, where s/32 will get you a double room with cable TV, fans and linen sheets.

At the more expensive end is the recommended *Hotel Kamana* (☎ 426 7204, email: kamana@ amauta.rcp.net.pe), Jr Camana 547, used by tour companies. It's well run if a little antiseptic; a double (att) costs US$46. The *Hostal El Virrey* (☎ 428 5905/426 8305), Av F Roosevelt 115 – don't confuse it with the Hostal los Virreyes – is also good at US$38 (double, att), and you're getting the same views you get at the Sheraton. You could try the *Gran Hotel Savoy* (☎ 428 3520), Jr Cailloma 224, where a stay in a genuine 1950s hotel room will cost you US$50 (double, att, includes breakfast), or finally the *Hostal El Plaza* (☎ 428 6270/5–9), Nicolás de Piérola 850, which is better decorated than its neighbour and charges s/60 (double, att).

● **Expensive hotels** If you're going to splurge on an expensive hotel don't stay in Lima Centro, go to Miraflores. If you must be based here the best hotel is the *Lima Sheraton* (☎ 433 3320, 🖹 433 5844), Paseo de la Republica 170, where you can stay in a standard Sheraton room tinged with Lima shabbiness for US$230 (double, att).

The *Gran Hotel Bolívar* (☎ 426 7438, 428 7672/3/5), Plaza San Martín, has a beautiful lobby and much more class than the Sheraton and is considerably cheaper at US$115 (double, att, breakfast), but the rooms are disappointing.

There's also the Swiss-run *Hotel Crillón*, (☎ 428 3290), Casilla 2981, Nicolás de Piérola 589, who were much too exclusive to show me around. It's about US$120 for a double here.

Miraflores
● **Budget accommodation** There are very few places to stay at this price in Miraflores. The welcoming *Albergue Juvenil* or youth hostel (☎ 446 5488/242 3070, 🖹 444 8187), Av Casimiro Ulloa 328, Miraflores, is the best deal with clean, spacious rooms, lockers, and a travel agency; it costs US$10 (discount for members). Also try the *Pensión Yolanda* (☎ 445 7565), Domingo Elias 230, Miraflores, where a double costs US$30, it's friendly and safe but a little dingy.

Lima area code: ☎ 01. If phoning from outside Peru dial +51-1.

KEY TO MIRAFLORES MAP (OPPOSITE)

● **Mid-range hotels** Most of these hotels have cable TV, fan and phone in the room. At the lower end of the scale is *Hostal Bellavista de Miraflores* (☎ 444 2938), Jr Bellavista 215, Miraflores, centrally located with a pleasant courtyard at US$35 (double, com, breakfast, att extra). The *Hostal el Carmelo* (☎ 241 3652, ▤ 441 7786), Bolognesi 749, Miraflores, is trying hard, and has a good location close to the sea-front Parque al Amor. Doubles (att) are US$45 but you can probably bargain them down.

The *Hostal Lucerna* (☎ 445 7321, ▤ 446 6050), Las Dalias 276, Miraflores, is a good, clean hotel with a lovely garden and costs US$53 (double, com). The recommended *Suites Eucalyptus* (☎ 445 8594, ▤ 444 3071), San Martín 511, is more imaginative, with studies of famous artworks in the rooms. Most rooms are suites, but there's no garden here – rates start at US$55 (all att).

At the top end of this price bracket is the *Hostel Señorial* (☎ 444 5755/445 9724), José Gonzáles 567, Miraflores, a colonial house with a lovely courtyard, good rooms and parking. They charge US$60 (double, att, breakfast included).

Worth considering is the *Hotel las Palmas* (☎ 444 6033, ▤ 444 6036, email: hpalmas@amauta.rcp.net.pe), Bellavista 320, Miraflores. It's central, adequate but lacks charm; rooms are US$60 (double, att). Also recommended is *Hotel San Antonio Abad* (☎ 447 6766, ▤ 446 4208, email: gfer@amatua.rcp.net.pe, website: www.ascinsa.com/sanantonioabad), Ramón Ribeyro 301, Miraflores, run by a helpful, polyglot manager (he even speaks Japanese), a good, safe, clean place costing US$60 (double, att, breakfast).

● **Expensive hotels** The best value in this group is the understated *Miramar Ischia* (☎ 446 6969, ▤ 445 0851), Malecón Cisneros 1244, Miraflores. The hotel's a seafront villa with good views, and is very professionally run with a personal touch. A double is US$85 (double, att, breakfast). You can park here.

If you want something more flashy, then stay at the other end of the scale: the *Hotel Las Americas* (☎ 241 2820, 444 7272, ▤ 444 1137), Benavides 415, a five-star hotel with everything you'd expect for US$190 (double, att). If you haven't got that sort of money, you could try

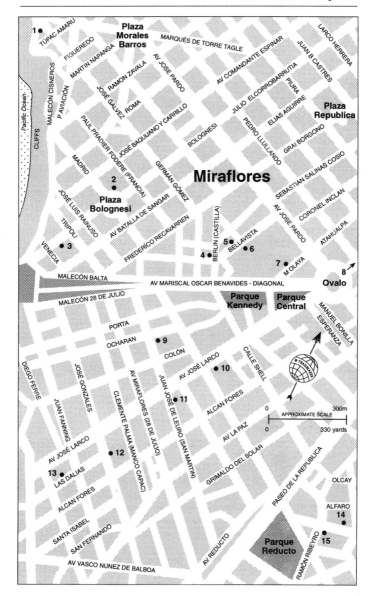

their other establishment the ***Residencial Las Americas*** (☎ 242 6600, 🖹 242 5976, email: amerires@chavin.rcp. net.pe.), Bellavista 216. Suites here cost US$102. Also worth a splurge is the ***Sol de Oro*** (☎ 446 9876, 🖹 447 0967), San Martín 305, an aparthotel, where a suite costs US$166.

WHERE TO EAT AND DRINK

Lima caters for every palate and pocket. You may not be here for long, but there's no reason to suffer at mealtimes.

Budget food

There are lots of cheap eating places in **Lima Centro**. The restaurant without a name under the ***Hostal Europa*** (see p110) is a fine for breakfasts; try the Americano (egg, bread, jam, tea/coffee, juice) at s/3.50. Just along the road are some good places for lunch: the ***Bar-Restaurant Machu Picchu*** (Ancash 312) and the ***Restaurant Chessman*** (Ancash 273). Around the corner from the SAEC on Ugarte between España and Portugal the fried chicken at ***Nakasone*** is recommended. Nearby on Av Breña 204 you'll find a good cevichería, ***La Choza Nautica***.

There's a string of cevicherías by La Puenta in **Callao**. It's a shame to pick any one of them out; they're all excellent, and the fish is so light it almost floats off the plate but try the ***Chifa Marina***. There are other good cheap cevicherías by the fish market on the south of the bay near the Playa Aqua Dulce, underneath El Morro.

In **Miraflores** you can still get a good s/2 lunch in the restaurants in the side roads around Larco and Benavides: try the *causa rellena* (spiced potato cake) if you see it. In **Barranco**, you can get an excellent traditional dinner in the restaurants under the Puente de Sospiros; walk down towards the sea, they're on your left. Try the *jalea* (fried whitebait) or the *chupe de camarones (*prawn chowder). If you're brave have *anticucho* (beef heart kebabs), which are surprisingly tender and taste a little like roast liver.

Mid-priced restaurants

For a traditional meal with a song, try the ***Peña Huascaran*** at 779 Camaná, or ***Brisas del Titicaca***, Jr Walkuski 168, or ***Manos Morenas*** Av Pedro de Osma 409, Barranco. Shows generally start at about 10pm.

There's decent, if a little overpriced, international food (sea bass, filet mignon) with a Peruvian touch in a relaxing dining-room, at ***La Ermita***, Bajada de Baños 340, Barranco. If you're a confirmed carnivore and fancy a challenge, try to get through the parilladas (mixed grill) at ***La Carreta,*** Av Rivera Navarrete 740, San Isidro.

There are pizza restaurants around Parque Kennedy by the Diagonal; they're overpriced, boring and safe. ***McDonald's*** and ***Burger King*** are also on Parque Kennedy.

Expensive restaurants

The *Sky Room* restaurant on the top floor of the Hotel Crillón (see p111) has breathtaking views but the food is overpriced, decently prepared but typically 1970s. A couple of courses will cost around s/100. The *Gran Hotel Bolívar* (see p111) is better, cheaper and has friendlier service. For the same sort of price as the Crillón, you can sample some of the best cuisine in Lima. The food at *Brujas de Cachiche* Bolognesi 460, Miraflores, who specialise in preparing traditional dishes, is excellent – try *ceviche* here if you're not going to risk it anywhere else.

Another top-rate restaurant is the *La Rosa Nautica* at Costa Verde, on the end of the pier off the beach below Miraflores. Its location is unrivalled in the whole of Lima, and the food's really good.

Cafés and bars

Café Café, Matir Olaya 250, Miraflores, serves large portions of well-cooked, unchallenging dishes (lomo cordon bleu and milanesa) in a jazzy café with good music, and claims to have a hundred different blends of coffee. If you're after a French-style café there's the French-run *Café de Paris* (Jr Diez Canseco 180, Miraflores – near Larco, just south of Parque Kennedy), where the brasserie-style food is good.

A good place to sit and watch the sun set over the Pacific is the *La Posada del Mirador*, Calle Ermita 104, Barranco. Head over the Puente de los Suspiros from the Plaza, turn left and walk towards the viewpoint. Pick up some picarones (doughnuts with honey) from one of the small cafés on the way. If you want live music, *La Estación*, Av Pedro de Osma 112, Barranco, usually has a Latin singer accompanied on guitar. For dancing, there's the *Mamut Club,* Berlin 438, (the old Cine Colina) Miraflores, with three floors of music and a small brewery. There are also many discos in the Diagonal in Miraflores.

WHAT TO SEE

You'll probably want to spend as little time in Lima as possible while you sort out your transport to Cuzco, but there's lots you could see and do here. Some of it you may not consider seeing unless you are really interested in pre-Hispanic South American ceramics or 18th century colonial Spanish church architecture, so what follows is a short guide to the best of Lima's sights tailored for the person heading out to Machu Picchu.

Lima Centro

● **Plaza de Armas** The Plaza de Armas is a nobly proportioned plaza built on the site of an ancient Inca square. Behind high metal railings, the **Government Palace** (Palacio de Gobierno: irregular opening hours, free) takes up the whole of one side of the Plaza, and red and purple-uniformed guards parade in the courtyard every morning, usually at 8am. On the right of this building is the **Cathedral** (changeable opening hours Monday to Saturday, 10am-1pm and 2-5pm, entrance s/4), the construction of which first began in 1535. It's been rebuilt a number of times since, and was completely flattened in the 1746 earthquake. The structure you see dates from 1758. Francisco Pizarro's remains lie in the imposing interior. Set between the Government Palace and the cathedral is the **Archbishop's Palace**, with its delicate carved wooden balcony.

On the opposite side of the square, running away from the Rímac is **Jíron de la Unión**, a pedestrian precinct lined with cheap shops and fried chicken restaurants.

● **Torre Tagle** Now occupied by the Foreign Ministry, this eighteenth-century mansion is one of Lima's colonial pearls. You can poke your head into the patio during office hours and relish the fine balcony and intricate carvings. There's a sixteenth century carriage sitting in the main courtyard with a built-in lavatory.

● **Church of San Francisco** (9.30am-5.30pm, entrance s/5) One of the few large buildings to survive Lima's earthquakes, this church was consecrated in 1673. It's a very pretty building, but the greatest attractions are the recently discovered catacombs of the monastery, piled with the bones of 70,000 of the city's dead (entrance another s/5).

● **La Merced** (7am-1pm, 4pm-8pm, free). There's been a church here since Lima's first mass was celebrated on this spot. It's such an important place that the Virgin of La Merced, the patroness of the religious order that lives here, has been made a marshal in the Peruvian military. The building itself has a façade of dauntingly ornate baroque, a frontage worthy of its importance, constructed from white Panamanian granite which made its way to Lima as ballast in cargo galleons. It's been rebuilt several times.

Other districts

Callao La Puenta (the Point) is refreshingly exposed to the sea breeze and can make a pleasant change from the claustrophobic atmosphere of Lima Centro.

Nearby there's **Castle of Real Felipe** (open daily, 8am-12pm, 1-6pm, s/3 entrance), a squat, solid piece of military architecture, completed in 1767. Inside you'll find the **Military Museum** (same hours, no further charge) and around the corner is the **Naval Museum** (Avenida Jorge Chavez 121, Monday to Friday 9am-5pm, Saturday and Sunday 9am-4pm, entrance s/3). Both of these museums yield an interesting insight into the minds of the Peruvian military, and a lot of space is devoted to explaining why they lost the War of the Pacific to Chile (see p40).

Barranco Definitely worth a visit, this is a great place to relax over a chilled beer while you watch the sun go down over the Pacific. Barranco is where Lima's artists and musicians gather, and during the day the pace of life is more gentle here than in the rest of the city. Courting couples frequent the Puente de los Suspiros (Bridge of Sighs). At night, this is a place for dancing and drinking.

Miraflores Miraflores is Lima's modern suburb with good views over the sea, North American franchise restaurants and high-rise hotels. It's a pleasant enough place if you like these kinds of things, but it's rather anaemic. It gets a bit more lively in the evenings, and the place has a thriving night-life. The central Parque Kennedy (also called 7 de Junio – the name changes often but it's the same park) has a very good weekend **art and craft market** at lunchtime, especially on Sundays. The standard of work for sale is, on the whole, very high, not your usual tacky watercolours; it's expensive though.

San Miguel San Miguel contains the zoo (☎ 452 6913, usually 9am-5pm) in the **Parque de las Leyendas**. Even if you don't like zoos, this is a better place to catch up on your Peruvian wildlife than the **Natural History Museum** (☎ 471 0117 Arenales 1256, Jesús María) – at least the animals are alive. There's also an ancient adobe pyramid in the grounds.

Recommended museums
● **Museo de la Nación** (☎ 476 9875; Av Javier Prado Este 2465, San Borja) open Tuesday to Sunday, 9am-9pm, entrance s/1. A splendid, new museum, well laid out and informative. This is an ideal place to put in context all the ancient things you're going to see in Peru. Don't miss the treasures of the Señor de Sípan – see p73 – well worth another s/10. The gold- and gem-work is tremendously impressive.

● **Museo Nacional de Antropología y Arqueología** (☎ 463 5070, Place Bolívar, Pueblo Libre) open Monday to Saturday 9.15am-5pm, Sunday and holidays 10am-5pm, entrance s/5. This is a bit of a prim maiden aunt compared to the flashy Museo de la Nación, but it's a good place: it contains the original objects of which the Nación only has copies. Look for the icons of Chavín (see p70): the Raimondi Stela (if you look at it upside down the image reads completely differently, see p70) and the Tello Obelisk (a sculpture of a male and female cayman), and the Paracas mummies looking rather shocked at having been dug up after centuries under the sands. The model of Machu Picchu will clarify the lay-out of the original when you get there. On the corner of the square you can quench your thirst at the friendly café.

● **Museo de Oro del Peru** The Gold Museum (☎ 435 2917; Calle Alonso de Molina 1100, Monterrico) is open daily, 12pm-7pm, entrance s/15. This private collection contains a staggering display of pre-Hispanic gold, Paracas textiles and ceramics including Moche erotic pots. It's wise to have some idea about Peru's pre-history before you come here – go to the Mueso de la Nación first as the Museo de Oro won't teach you much:

everything is just stuffed in cupboards or laid on tables without explanation. There's also an excellent bookshop, and a large display of military objects connected with important people from South American history.

● **Museo del Tribunal de la Santa Inquisición** (Plaza Bolívar, Calle Junín 548, open Monday to Friday 9am-8pm, Saturday 9am-5pm). The headquarters of the South American Spanish Inquisition. The tribunal room is beautiful with its carved wooden ceiling, and the dungeons show the unbelievable tortures that went on downstairs.

Pachacamac

Thirty kilometres south of Lima is the ancient shrine and oracle of Pachacamac (daily 9am-5pm s/5); you can get here on one of the buses which leave every couple of hours from Avenida Abancay. The pyramids are on the whole badly preserved, and to the untrained eye tend to look like piles of dry mud but some, like the acllahuasi (see p100), have been reconstructed.

The Spaniards would have looted Pachacamac to collect Atahualpa's ransom (see p95) but it had been stripped by the priests before they arrived. There's a description of what the main shrine looked like in those times, written by the conquistador, Miguel de Estete: 'Its locked door was closely studded with a variety of objects – corals, turquoises, crystals and other things. This was eventually opened, and we were certain that the interior would be as curious as the door. But it was quite the contrary. It certainly seemed to be the devil's chamber, for he always lives in filthy places… It was very dark and did not smell very pleasant'.

SHOPPING

Centro Artesenal, Camino Real 485, San Isidro, is a rather bland Peruvian crafts market. For a more challenging experience and a larger choice, go to the massive **Artesanaria** between 600 and 1000 on Avenida de la Marina out towards Pueblo Libre. A taxi here from Lima Centro will cost you s/5 or s/6. There's also a weekend arts market in **Parque Kennedy** in Miraflores.

MOVING ON

By air to Cuzco

Lima to Cuzco takes about an hour and a one-way ticket costs US$80. Since AeroPeru went out out of business you'll need to book well in advance. Currently, only AeroContinente makes the flight.

Overland to Cuzco (see map p121)

Travelling overland by bus (or by bus and train) is by far the more scenic way to get to Cuzco, even if it does take a lot longer. There are two main routes, via **the highlands** and via **Arequipa**. The most travelled route is

---

❏ AIRLINE INFORMATION

Airline offices in Lima

AeroContinente (☎ 242 4260), Av Pardo 651, Miraflores; **Aerolineas Argentinas** (☎ 444 0810), José Pardo 805, 3rd Floor, Miraflores; **AeroPeru** (not currently flying: ☎ 241 0606), José Pardo 601, Miraflores; **Air France** (☎ 442 9285), Av José Pardo 601, Office 601, Miraflores; **Alitalia** (☎ 442 8506), Camino Real 497, 3rd Floor, San Isidro; **American Airlines** (☎ 442 8555), Juan de Arona 830, 14th Floor, San Isidro; **British Airways** (☎ 422 6600), Andalucía (between 42 and 43 Av Arequipa); **Continental** (☎ 221 4340), Victor Andrés Belaúnde 147, V Principal 110, Office 101, San Isidro; **Iberia** (☎ 421 4622, 421 4633), Av Camino Real No 390, Central Tower, 9th Floor, Office 902, San Isidro; **KLM** (☎ 242 1240), José Pardo 805, 6th Floor, Miraflores; **Lan Chile** (☎ 241 5522), José Pardo 805, 5th Floor, Miraflores; **Lloyd Aero Boliviana** (☎ 241 5510), José Pardo 805, 2nd Floor, Miraflores; **Lufthansa** (☎ 442 4466), Av Jorge Basadre 1330, San Isidro; **United Airlines** (☎ 421 3334), Camino Real 390, Central Tower, 9th Floor.

Lima airport

General enquiries (☎ 575 1434, 575 0912), **national flights** (☎ 574 5529), **international flights** (☎ 575 1712).

---

via Arequipa because it's shorter and the roads are better; in the rainy season the highland roads can become completely washed away. For details of bus companies, see p120.

Highland routes The **northern** route goes from Lima inland to La Oroya, turns south-east to Huancayo and Ayacucho, and then heads to Abancay and Cuzco. There's no direct **bus** – you take one from Lima to Huancayo and then change. It takes about 50 hours and costs about US$30. The passenger **train** to Huancayo is running again and it departs Friday/Saturday 7.40am returning Sunday/Monday 7am. It takes $10^1/_2$ hours (s/60 return).

The **southern** route follows the coast, visiting Pisco before heading inland to Ayacucho and then passing through Abancay to reach Cuzco. This takes about 35 to 40 hours and costs about US$25. Catch the bus from Lima to Ayacucho where you change to the Abancay or Cuzco bus.

There's a third route via Nazca, but at the moment it's not safe because of banditry – check with the SAEC for the latest details.

All these routes were closed to travellers for many years, but are now opening up again. Don't, as I did, read Mario Vargas Llosa's novel *Death in the Andes* on the bus to Cuzco, as it starts with a description of two French tourists taking the highland bus and getting held up and murdered by the Sendero Luminoso.

Arequipa route The other way to travel to Cuzco is via Arequipa. It looks like a terrible detour on the map, but in fact it's the quickest overland route. Anyway, Arequipa is a very pretty city and you might be able to fit in a climb up the volcano El Misti or a trek down the Colca Canyon. There are direct buses from Lima to Arequipa. To get from Arequipa to Cuzco, you can take a bus or the train.

● **Lima to Arequipa (bus)** Direct buses on this route cost s/30-55; journey time is about 14 hours.

● **Arequipa to Cuzco (bus)** The bus can either go via Juliaca (a reasonable road) or straight to Sicuani (a less good road); both take about 15 to 20 hours and cost around s/25. Travelling by night is not really recommended because you'll miss the view.

● **Arequipa to Cuzco (train)** It will take 25 to 30 hours to get to Cuzco from Arequipa if you opt to take the train. It's more comfortable and reliable than the bus but check the timetable before you leave (Enafer ☎ 054-222003) or you'll risk being stuck in Arequipa for a couple of days. At the time of writing, trains leave Arequipa for Juliaca/Puno on Sunday and Wednesday at 9pm and arrive at Juliaca at 5.50am. Trains from Juliaca leave for Cuzco on Monday, Wednesday, Thursday and Saturday at 9.30am and reach Cuzco at 7pm.

As with the trains from Cuzco to Machu Picchu, there are a number of different classes on offer. **Inka**, which only goes from Puno/Juliaca to Cuzco, costs US$24, is a plush service with attendants. **Pullman** or **Turismo**, which costs s/30 from Arequipa to Puno/Juliaca and another US$19 to Cuzco, has reclining seats and secure carriages. **Económico** costs s/18.50 from Arequipa to Puno/Juliaca, and s/25 more to Cuzco, is basic and crowded and vendors are allowed on.

Puno is an hour down the railway from Juliaca, at the end of the line. If you want to break your journey between Arequipa and Cuzco, this is a pleasant place to do it as Puno is on the shores of Lake Titicaca. On all the trains, you'll probably meet touts selling rooms in some of Cuzco's cheap hotels and tickets for travel agencies – don't part with your money until you've seen what they're offering.

❏ Bus companies
There are many companies. **Ormeño** (☎ 427 5679), Carlos Zavala 177, are recommended to most destinations; **Mariscal Caceres** (☎ 427 2844), Av Carlos Zavala 211, are good to Huancayo; **Cruz del Sur** (☎ 424 1005), Jr Quilca 531, the biggest company, are also recommended to most destinations; **Carhuamayo** (☎ 426 0785), Montevideo 766 and Av 28 de Julio 1758, have a 'direct' service (via Arequipa), to Cuzco; **Civa** (☎ 428 5649); **Empressa de Transportes Ica** (☎ 428 0630), Av Abancay 1167, specialise in travel to Ica and Nazca; **Flores** (☎ 431 0485), Paseo de la República 627, go to all destinations along the southern coast.

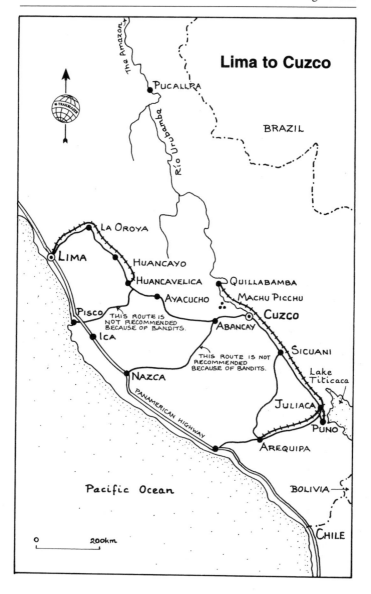

PART 5: CUZCO AND AROUND

Cuzco
(Qosqo)

What remains with you is the sense of a great outrage, magnificent but unforgiv-
able. The Spaniards tore down the Inca temples and grafted splendid churches and
mansions onto their foundations. This is one of the most beautiful monuments to
bigotry and sheer stupid brutality in the whole world. **Christopher Isherwood**,
The Condor and the Cows, 1948.

Cuzco was the capital of the Incas, the cultural and religious focus of the
empire. Today it's the focus for almost all visitors to Peru but it's much
more than a tourist town. With a population of almost 300,000 inhabitants
it's a large commercial centre and the administrative capital of Cuzco
department.

Cuzco is 3360m (11,000ft) above sea level, and the air is thin here.
When you first arrive, don't do anything too energetic: take a couple of
days to acclimatise.

HISTORY

It's difficult to know much for certain about Cuzco's origins because
there is no written record of Peruvian history before the arrival of the
Spanish, and there are very few recorded oral histories of the times before
the rise of the Incas.

The Huari and the Killke

What *is* known is that before the Incas the great culture known as Huari
dominated the Cuzco valley. The area around Cuzco and the sacred valley of the Urubamba were part of the highland frontier of the Huari state.
The Huari declined and withdrew to their capital west of Cuzco. The local
people, the Killke, were left to their own devices, building hilltop
defences throughout the area.

One place where the Killke did not build their forts was in the Cuzco
valley itself. This makes archaeologists think that it wasn't necessary to
build fortifications around Cuzco, suggesting that by about the twelfth
century there were settlements in Cuzco already stable, secure and strong
enough to deter attacks from outsiders. The Incas had taken them over by
about the thirteenth century.

The capital of the Incas

Cuzco in the days of its glory as the capital of the Incas must have been a magnificent sight. The seat of the god-king, the Inca, it was a city constructed to reflect the might of the empire. Walls were sheathed in gold, something which was imposing enough to impress even the Spanish thugs sent by Pizarro to search for loot for Atahualpa's ransom (see p95). One was sufficiently moved to write to the king: 'The city is the greatest and finest seen in either this country or anywhere in the Indies. We can assure Your Majesty that it is so beautiful and has such fine buildings that it would be worthy of notice even in Spain.'

Cuzco was impressive not only because it was built from fine dressed stone and covered in precious metals. It had also been built with an understanding of the infrastructure a city needs and boasted channels providing running water and sewerage making it cleaner and more healthy than any European city. Such cleanliness did not survive the conquest, and another Spaniard wrote: 'now there are large piles of garbage on the banks [of the river Huatanay]. It is full of dung and filth. It was not like this in the days of the Incas, when it was clean and the water ran over stones. The Incas sometimes went there to bathe with their women.'

The city was not only the seat of political power, but also the cultural and religious centre of the empire. The cardinal roads to each suyu of the Inca empire led out from the main square, and sacred religious lines from spiritual places converged on the Coricancha. All roads led to Cuzco, and the ceques pointed towards Cuzco.

Construction and destruction

Despite the vast amount of work that clearly went into Cuzco's construction, legend has it that the city was built on the orders of one man alone: the Inca Pachacutec (see p80). He tore down Cuzco's old humble buildings shortly after seizing power, and ordered them to be replaced with a stone city. Some say that Pachacutec designed Cuzco to look like a puma, a sacred animal of the Incas. The river Tullumayo formed the spine of the puma, the river Huatanay the belly, and the fortress or temple mound of Sacsayhuaman made the puma's head.

But the Cuzco of Pachacutec has been lost to us although you can still make out the puma, and we see only a pale imitation of past splendours. The magnificent gold was torn off by the greedy hands of the Spanish, and in the siege of Cuzco the whole city was burnt when rebel Incas put it to the torch in a desperate attempt to smoke out the Spanish invaders (see p99).

Cuzco after the conquest

After the conquistadors secured Peru for the king of Spain, they needed to found a capital. They were dependant on the sea for communications and reinforcements and so Cuzco was not a suitable place to set up government. Francisco Pizarro therefore founded his capital on the coast, in 1535. From this point, Cuzco's influence began to wane.

The town itself was largely rebuilt by the Spanish on old Inca foundations, re-using the snug Inca stonework pillaged from many sites including the massive Sacsayhuaman. The Spanish work is less strong than that of the Incas, as shown by the occasional serious earthquake that shakes colonial buildings to the ground leaving their Inca foundations standing. The monastery of Santo Domingo (which is built over Coricancha) has pictures showing that exactly this happened in the 1950 earthquake.

Throughout the following centuries Cuzco was overshadowed by Lima, but it did enjoy brief flashes of its former importance. It was the centre of rebellion in 1780 when José Gabriel Condorcanqui, also called Tupac Amaru II, rose against the Spanish, and again in 1825 when Bolívar himself arrived and set up camp. The royal oath of independence was sworn by Peru's first Prefect, Garmarra, before the cathedral's *Señor de los Tremblores* (see p138), and in the seventeenth and eighteenth centuries, the city's artists distinguished themselves in creating the famous Cuzco School of painting.

With the rebirth of interest in the ancient civilisations of Peru, the discovery of Machu Picchu in 1911 and the development of the subsequent tourist trade Cuzco re-emerged as one of Peru's principal cities.

ARRIVAL

Take a couple of days to acclimatise when you first arrive. Acclimatisation is easier if you don't overeat and avoid smoking and alcohol.

A note of caution

Cuzco has a bad but deserved reputation for robbery, and the area around San Pedro station and the market can be a hot spot, as is the San Blas district. Be careful when you walk around, especially when arriving and leaving. See p59 for more details.

By air

The airport is about a five-minute taxi ride from the Plaza de Armas. A taxi to the Plaza will cost s/5 from the airport car park, and s/3 from the road outside, because there is a fee *taxistas* (taxi drivers) have to pay to get into the compound. Walking to the Plaza would take you about 40 minutes, but I wouldn't recommend it (see 'A note of caution' above).

By rail

The train from Puno arrives at **Huanchac station**, which is at the southeastern end of Avenida del Sol, 20 minutes' walk from the centre of town.

The train from Machu Picchu and the jungle arrives at **San Pedro station** (also called Machu Picchu station) which is just by the church of San Pedro, 10 minutes' walk from the south-west of the Plaza.

By bus

There are plans to build a bus terminal, but they haven't come to anything yet, so where you arrive depends on where you've come from and what bus you took to get to Cuzco.

If you're coming from Lima or Arequipa, you'll probably arrive at Avenida Pachacutec, which is just by Huanchac railway station, or Plaza Tupac Amaru, a 10-15-minute taxi ride out of town to the east.

If you've come along the Abancay route, you should arrive in either Calle Arcopata 10 minutes' ride to the west of the Plaza de Armas, or in Calle Granada which is one block west of the Plaza Regocijo.

Sacred Valley (Ollantaytambo, Pisac, Urubamba, Urcos etc) buses go to Calle Huascar, just north of Huanchac station, or the side street of Inticahuarina one block west of Huascar. Both are a 10-minute walk from the Plaza de Armas.

GETTING AROUND

Taxis in Cuzco are much better than those in other Peruvian cities, and they should charge a flat fare of s/2 for a trip anywhere in the centre (except the airport), though if they see you've just arrived, they might just forget this. You can flag them down on just about any street, or find them around the Plaza de Armas. Other forms of transport are the communal **colectivos** which are cheaper if much less comfortable than taxis.

If you're on a bigger budget you may want to hire a **car**. Two companies are **Localisa** (☎ 242285/263448, email: localiz@mail.cosapida-ta.com.pe), Avenida del Sol 1089; and **Mitsui** (☎ 221980), Cuesta del Almirante 269. You've got to be over 25 to drive a hire car, and the daily rates vary from around US$25 to US$70. Petrol's extra.

ORIENTATION

Central Cuzco is small and set out almost on a grid, with the Plaza de Armas pretty much in the middle. If you stand by the fountain in the Plaza and look up at the figure of Jesus (north), the hill to Jesus' right is the hill of Sacsayhuaman (north-west). Between Sacsayhuaman and the Plaza is a district of steep streets and cheap hotels. Between Jesus and you is the cathedral and the district of San Blas, while behind you (east and south) is the Compañía and the Avenida del Sol which leads to Huanchac station and the airport. Jesus is looking almost to the south-west, towards the market and San Pedro station.

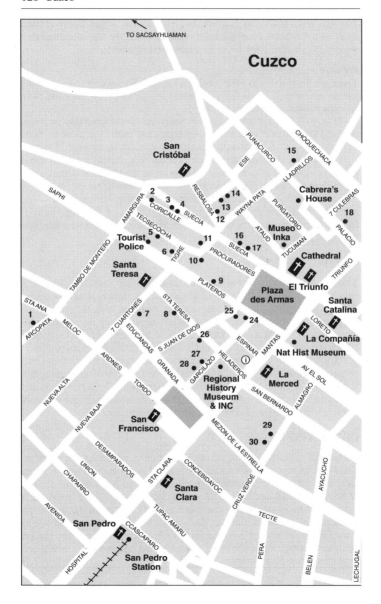

TO SACSAYHUAMAN

Cuzco

San Cristóbal

Cabrera's House

San
Cristóbal

15

2
3 4
13
14
12

11
16
17

Museo
Inka

Tourist
Police

5

6

10

Cathedral

Santa
Teresa

9

El Triunfo

Plaza
des Armas

Santa
Catalina

1

7
8

25
24

La Compañía

26

Nat Hist Museum

27
28

La
Merced

Regional
History
Museum
& INC

San
Francisco

29
30

Santa
Clara

San Pedro

San Pedro
Station

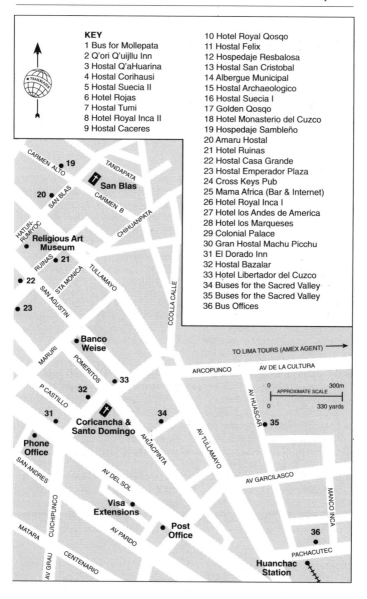

KEY
1 Bus for Mollepata
2 Q'ori Q'uijllu Inn
3 Hostal Q'aHuarina
4 Hostal Corihausi
5 Hostal Suecia II
6 Hotel Rojas
7 Hostal Tumi
8 Hotel Royal Inca II
9 Hostal Caceres
10 Hotel Royal Qosqo
11 Hostal Felix
12 Hospedaje Resbalosa
13 Hostal San Cristobal
14 Albergue Municipal
15 Hostal Archaeologico
16 Hostal Suecia I
17 Golden Qosqo
18 Hotel Monasterio del Cuzco
19 Hospedaje Sambleño
20 Amaru Hostal
21 Hotel Ruinas
22 Hostal Casa Grande
23 Hostal Emperador Plaza
24 Cross Keys Pub
25 Mama Africa (Bar & Internet)
26 Hotel Royal Inca I
27 Hotel los Andes de America
28 Hotel los Marqueses
29 Colonial Palace
30 Gran Hostal Machu Picchu
31 El Dorado Inn
32 Hostal Bazalar
33 Hotel Libertador del Cuzco
34 Buses for the Sacred Valley
35 Buses for the Sacred Valley
36 Bus Offices

☐ **Embassies and consulates**
Belgium and Holland (☎ 221146/098), Avenida del Sol 954; **France** (☎ 233610), Avenida Micaela Bastidas 101, Edif, Diagonal, 4th Floor, Huanchac; **Germany** (☎ 235459), San Augustin 307; **Italy** (☎ 233192), Avenida Garcilasco 700, Huanchac; **UK** (☎ 226671, 🖥 236706), Barry Walker (landlord of the Cross Keys Pub), find him at the pub or Casillo 606; **USA** (☎ 224112), Instituto Cultural Peruano Nort Americano (ICPNA), Avenida Tullumayo 127.

SERVICES

Banks and cambios
Banco de Crédito (Visa): Av del Sol 189; **Banco Latino** (MasterCard): Av Almagro 125–127, but there is an ATM in the wall of the El Dorado Inn on Av del Sol 395; **Banco Weise**, Calle Maruri 315, charges the lowest bank commission when changing travellers' cheques but is slow.

There are **cambios** are all over Cuzco, and it's difficult to pick out any one over the other, but **Multitours**, Av del Sol 314 (☎ 236946), exchange Visa, Thomas Cook and AMEX travellers' cheques. The AMEX agent in Cuzco, Lima Tours (see Tour Agencies), does not deal with travellers' cheques. **Western Union** (☎ 224167) is at Av del Sol 627A.

Bookshops
Many of the tourist shops on Portal de Comercio and Portal de Confituría sell books, and **Los Andes** (☎ 234231), Portal Comercio 125 specialises in them, but the best bookshop is the **Libreria Jerusalen**, Heladeros 143.

Communications
● **Telephone and fax** Cuzco's telephone code is 84. There are public pay phones everywhere, and it's easy to ring abroad, or you can get someone else to do it for you at **Telser** (☎ 242424; also does faxes), Calle de Medio 117, or the central **Telephonica del Peru** on Av del Sol 382.
● **Post** For letters, the **correo** (Monday to Saturday 8am-6pm, Sunday 8am-12pm), is on the west side of Avenida del Sol, on the sixth block downhill from the Plaza de Armas, and **AMEX** client mail is at Lima Tours (see Tour Agencies).
● **Email** There are places to send and receive email at **Mama Africa** bar (see Where to eat), **Telser**, and **Internet Cuzco** (☎ 238173), Galerías UNSAAC, down a side-street off the eastern side of Av del Sol, one block down from the Plaza de Armas. They all cost s/5-6 an hour. Check the website: www.cybercaptive.com to see if any others have sprung up.

(Opposite): During the festival of Corpus Christi (ninth Thursday after Easter, usually in June), statues and silver from the cathedral (see p136) are paraded around Cuzco's Plaza de Armas. **(Following pages):** Across Cuzco's Plaza de Armas.

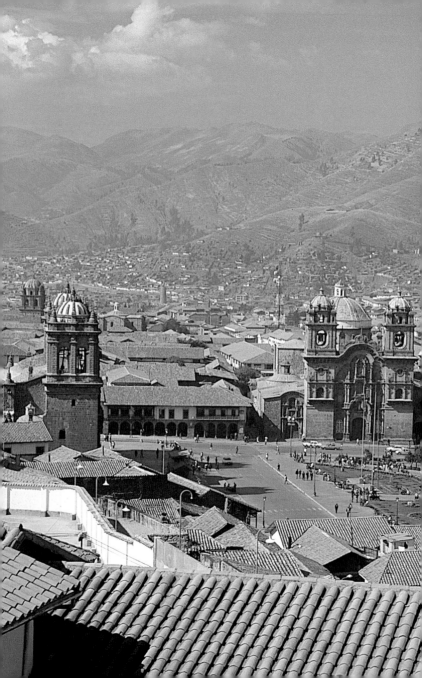

❏ Tour agencies

You won't have any trouble finding tour agencies – they'll come and find you as you sit in the sunshine in the Plaza de Armas, but if you want to find them, they're centred around Procuradores and Plateros.

The most common tours on offer are: the Inca Trail (with some variations), the Ausangate circuit, white-water rafting on the Urubamba and Apurímac rivers, a tour of the sites of Cuzco, a tour of the Sacred Valley and a trip to the jungle in the Manu National Park.

Remember that the cheapest price is not necessarily the best value, so find out exactly what's on offer. Rock bottom agencies are often not the bargain they seem, as all they do is bus you in and out of an area, leaving you with half-a-dozen other groups and an ill-informed guide who hardly speaks Spanish, let alone English. These companies also have a reputation for exploiting their porters, leaving rubbish on the trails and generally not caring at all for the environment.

At the cheaper end of the market are **United Mice** (☎ 21139), Plateros 351, recommended, and **Luzma Tours** (☎ 261327), Santa Teresa 399, **Rikuni Tours** (☎ 241700), Plateros 341. **Inca Explorers** (☎ 239669), Calle Suecia 339, is mid-priced and recommended, and **Mistyc Inca Trail** (☎ 221358, 🖹 221348, email: ivanndp@mail.cosapidata.com.pe), Unidad Vecinal, Santiago, Bloque 9, dpto 301, who run a tour that recreates 'an Inca rite of spiritual initiation', which sounds interesting. **Instinct** (☎ 233451/238366, email: instinct@mail.cosapidata.com.pe), Procuradores 50, organise mid-priced white-water rafting excursions. For the jungle, **Manu Nature Tours** (☎ 252721, 🖹 234793), Avenida Pardo 1046 email: mnt@amatua.rcp.pet.pe have a good reputation. For just about everything, there's **Expediciones Vilca** (☎ 251872, email: manuvilca@protelsa.com.pe), Amargura 101.

One of the more expensive companies is **Peruvian Andean Treks** (☎ 225701, 🖹 838911), who also do tailor-made itineraries, recommended, and there's **Lima Tours** (☎ 228431, 🖹 221266), Calle Machu Picchu D-24, Urb Manuel Prado, Avenida Cultura, the AMEX agent who has moved a ten-minute taxi-ride away from the centre.

Disabled travellers should contact **Apumayo Expeditions** (☎ 246018, email: apumayo@mail.cosapidata.com.pe), Calle Garcilasco 265, Interior 3, who run special tours.

Emergencies and medical services

Fire ☎ 103; **Police**: ☎ 105; **Tourist Police**: ☎ 321961 (24 hours), Saphi 510, and an office on the Plaza de Armas 9am-6pm, very helpful; **Hospitals**: Regional ☎ 231131, IPSS ☎ 221581, Lorena ☎ 226511; **Tourist Medical Assistance** ☎ 222644/621838 (24 hours).

Doctor: Ramon Figueroa at the Regional Hospital (☎ 231131), or Mantara 410, Office 201 (☎ 244019), speaks English and French. **Pharmacy** (☎ 245351), Calle Heladeros 109, (24 hours).

(Opposite): Sacsayhuaman (see p144), a 20-minute walk from Cuzco centre, is the dramatic setting for Inti Raymi, an Inca pageant performed annually on 24 June.

Equipment rental

Camping equipment can be hired at most of the tour agencies on Plateros and Procuradores, but do check the quality because some of it is pretty ropy. Butane and butane-propane gas cylinders can also be obtained at these places, or at one of the tourist shops on Portal de Comercio. However, the best place for all of this is **Soqllaq'asa** (☎ 252560), Calle Plateros 359, where they will also buy equipment you no longer need.

Hiking provisions

There's a good supermarket on the corner of Almagro and Avenida del Sol, another at Plateros 346 and, of course, the market opposite San Pedro station. Camera and film shops are not recommended. It would be much wiser to bring out your films to be developed at home. If you can't wait there is a string of film shops that also do developing on the first block of Avenida del Sol down from the Plaza de Armas, on the west side of the road. If you have to buy, check the use-by date and avoid film that looks as if it might have been kept in the sun.

Laundry

There are many on Procuràdores but try **Lavarapido,** Pampa del Castillo 427, because it's cheaper at s/3 per kg.

Language courses

Amatua (☎ 241422), Procuradores 50, Casilla Postal 1164; **Excel** (☎ 232272), Calle Cruz Verde 336; **Milla Tourism** (☎ 231710, 🖹 231388, email: andinos@wayna.rcp.net.pe), Avenida Pardo 689, who also provide seminars on Andean culture and history.

Shopping

Alpaca III, Plaza Regocijo, has good quality alpaca woollens in Frank Bough designs, but note that there's a cheaper branch of the same shop in the departure lounge of the airport and **Etno Artesania** Triunfo 118, has more modern styles. For local craftwork, try **Feria Artesanal Inca**, Corner of Q'era and San Andrés, or **Tresors del Inca** (craft market), Plateros 334, or anywhere in San Blas. Other places to buy traditional goods are the markets at Pisac and Chinchero (see p148).

Tourist information

There is one very helpful tourist office in the arrivals hall of the airport, and one less helpful and reliable one at Portal Mantas 188 in the arcade opposite the Merced (☎ 252974/263176). They both hand out free maps and provide information.

Visa extension

Ministerio del Interior Avenida del Sol 620 (☎ 222741), open Monday to Friday, 9am-1pm, 3-6pm.

WHERE TO STAY

Hot water is a problem in Cuzco, whatever the people at the hotel may tell you. Water supply is unpredictable and vanishes completely at certain times of day. Try to talk to someone already staying in the hotel to get an idea of whether you are going to get a shower for your money. As for the cost of your room, Cuzco prices are highly negotiable and depend on the usual laws of supply and demand. If you find yourself in Cuzco in low season, you'll be able to find plenty of bargains.

An organisation has recently been set up to help find rooms for visitors with a traditional Cusqueño family. Contact the **Asociacion de Micro y Pequeñas Empresas de Establecimientos de Hospedaje** (Small Business Association of Family Lodgings), Calle San Augustín 415 (☎ 244036, 🖹 233912, email: ititoss@mail.cosapidata.com.pe).

Note: the following abbreviations are used here: **com = room with common bathroom; att = bathroom attached**.

Budget accommodation

The best place to find cheap hotels is in the hilly streets that lead from the Plaza de Armas up to Sacsayhuaman. Recommended are *Hospedaje Resbalosa* (☎ 224839/240461), Calle Resbalosa 494, and *Hostal San Cristobal* (☎ 223922), Kiskapata 244, each of which is family-run. Resbalosa has a bright friendly courtyard, beautiful 180° views over the town towards Mount Ausangate, a communal kitchen and costs s/20 (double, com). Cristobal is a much smaller place; it, too, has good views but is a little grubby and is s/8 per person (com). Another good value place is the *Hotel Rojas* (☎ 228184), Tigre 129, with a pleasant green courtyard behind enormous front doors, s/26 (double, com). Try to get the top floor rooms, which have a view.

Other options in this district are the slightly poky *Golden Qosqo* (☎ 223112), Calle Suecia 368, which is s/15 (double, com), an old house with Inca stonework and a fluffy dog that could be a golden retriever, or the *Q'ori Q'uijllu Inn* (☎ 263683), Coricalle 537, an excellent little place with a big gate at the front, splendid views but only six rooms, s/20 (double, com).

Worth looking at are the *Hotel Royal Qosqo* (☎ 226221), Tecsecocha 406, which is well maintained and costs s/25 (double, com), and the *Hostal Felix* (☎ 241949), Tecsecocha 171, a real gringo dive s/20 (double, com) – as is the *Hostal Tumi*, Siete Cuartones 245, s/20 (double, com). Also worth considering is the *Hostal Caceres* (☎ 232616/228012), Plateros 368, an old house with blue creaking woodwork and a friendly welcome; s/24 (double, com).

In other areas, there are the highly recommended *Gran Hostal Machu Picchu* (☎ 231111), Calle Q'era 282, with its two colonial courtyards and talkative parrots ('¡Hola gringo!'), s/25 (double, com), or at the other end of town in San Blas the recommended *Hospedaje Sambleño* (☎ 221452), Carmen Alta 114, which has cable TV in the lobby and is a bargain at s/10 (double, lavatory), though prices are bound to go up. There are many other little hospedajes tucked away around here in Calle Tarapata.

South of San Blas there is the recommended *Hostal Casa Grande* (☎/🖥 243784), Santa Catalina Ancha 353, an old house as yet pretty much undiscovered by gringos, a good value s/25 (double, com), or s/30 (double, att). Opposite Santo Domingo you'll find the cheap *Hostal Bazalar* (☎ 226265), Plazoleta de San Domingo 260, s/30 (double, com), a warren-like hotel. They weren't particularly friendly when I called but all its bizarre fittings and religious paraphernalia are certainly worth seeing.

Other places worth looking at are the two Hostals Suecia which are run by the same people who are friendly and popular with foreigners. *Hostal Suecia I* (☎ 233282), is at Calle Suecia 332, and *Hostal Suecia II* (☎ 239757) at Tecescocha 465. Both cost s/30 (double, com), and Suecia II has some doubles with attached bathroom for s/40.

Also recommended but completely different is the youth hostel: *Albergue Municipal* (☎ 252506), Kiskapata 240, which is spanking clean, has a café and good views from a sunny concrete balcony. It costs US$5.90 a person with a discount for members and is a great place to stay if you're in a group.

Finally, there are cheap hotels around both train stations (the *El Imperio* by San Pedro has been recommended), but they are a little out of the way and in unsavoury areas.

Mid-range hotels

Hotels in this category are spread throughout Cuzco, and usually set their room rates in US dollars, but be careful to check whether the price includes taxes and service. Budget hotels tend to forget about taxes and service, and expensive hotels slap the extra percentage on top but you can never be sure with the mid-range places.

A little expensive for what you get but with great character is the recommended *Hotel los Marqueses* (☎ 227028), Garcilasco 256, an old house with ancient carved doors, antique chairs, old paintings in the lobby and a very pretty courtyard. They charge US$35 (double, att, breakfast).

Closer to Sacsayhuaman than the Albergue Municipal are two other recommended hotels which are on the same street as each other. The first is *Q'aHuarina* (☎ 228130), Calle Suecia 575, which is efficient, clean, modern and friendly and offers free coca tea throughout the day. It has only six rooms and is good value for Cuzco at US$26 (double, att, breakfast). Just down from Q'aHuarina is **Hostal Corihausi** (☎ 232233, email: corihausi@amatua.rcp.net.pe), Calle Suecia 561, Casilla Postal 157, which charges US$35 (double, att, breakfast), a larger hotel favoured by some adventure tour companies. Try to get the room directly above reception which has the best view in all Cuzco.

If you fancy something a little more central there's the new **Hostal Emperador Plaza** (☎ 261733/227412, 📧 263581), Santa Catalina Ancha 377 Izq. It's clean as a new pin, has cable TV in the rooms and costs from US$38 (double, att, breakfast); the balcony rooms are best. Also central but much older is the aptly named and rather splendid **Colonial Palace** (☎ 232329), Calle Q'era 270, US$25 (double, att, breakfast).

The **Hostal Loretto** (☎ 226352), Loretto 115, deserves a mention because some rooms have genuine Inca walls, but it's overpriced at US$30 (double, att, costs more in high season). If you want to stay in San Blas, try the **Amaru Hostal** (☎ 225933), Cuesta San Blas 541, an old house with a green courtyard filled with geraniums in rusty cans. It also has a book exchange and piano, and they charge s/40 (double, att – less for a com). Finally, the **Hostal Archaeologico** (☎ 232569, 📧 235126), Ladrillos 405, is a favourite with the French. It's pleasant enough but at US$24 (double, com) you can do better for the money.

Expensive hotels

More than others, these hotels jack up their prices in high season and are willing to give away bargains when the rooms are empty. The prices quoted can go up by about 20% in June/July.

The two best hotels in Cuzco are the Hotel Monasterio del Cuzco and the Hotel Libertador del Cuzco. **Hotel Monasterio del Cuzco** (☎ 241777, 📧 237111, email: reserlima@peruhotel.com, www.peruhotel.com), Calle Palacio 140, is a sensitive conversion of the old Seminary of San Antonio Abad, and along with everything you'd expect from an international five-star hotel it also has a gilded chapel. It's not cheap at US$165 (double, att, breakfast), but you can knock the prices down. The **Hotel Libertador del Cuzco** (☎ 231961), Plazoleta Santo Domingo 259, is a converted colonial building, once a palace called the Casa de Los Cuatro Bustos. Again this hotel has the full 5-star package but is a little more welcoming to dirty trekkers than the Monasterio. It costs US$180 (double, att, breakfast).

Down from the first rank but still very good is the **Hotel Ruinas** (☎ 260644/245920, 📧 236391, email: ruinas@mail.interplace.com.pe), Calle Ruinas 472. This is a new place but it has character and the rooms with outside views are the best. It is well run and costs US$89 (double, att).

The **Hotel San Augustin International** (☎ 221169/231001, 📧 221174), Calle Maruri 390 deserves a mention because of its adobe-style interior decoration; it costs US$102 (double, att, breakfast). If you can't afford the San Augustin International, the **El Dorado Inn** (☎

231232/231135, 📱 240993, website: www.cosapidata.com.pe/empre ssa/doratur/doratur. htm), Avenida del Sol 395, has a similar quirky interior with aerial walkways. Rooms are US$80 (double, att, breakfast).

The *Hotel Royal Inca I* (☎ 222284/131067), Plaza Regocijo 299, US$78 (double, att, breakfast), is built on the foundations of Pachacutec's palace. It's slightly better than its more expensive sister, the *Hotel Royal Inca II,* which is just up the road. Also good is the new and efficient *Hotel los Andes de America* (☎ 222253, 📱 223058), Garcilasco 236, US$76 (double, att, breakfast).

WHERE TO EAT AND DRINK

Cuzco is overflowing with places to eat and drink, from cheap steaming anticucho barrows on the street to exclusive restaurants, from back-street bars with sticky plastic tablecloths to loud, brash, young clubs where the music hits you like a fist. If you're looking for food or drink, just wander around Calle Procuradores or Calle Plateros and you are bound to find something that takes your fancy. The following is only a small selection of what's on offer:

Budget food

La Tertulia, Procuradores 44–50, has really good breakfasts with as much fresh fruit juice as you can drink, pitta bread, and lashings of jam but it's expensive at s/10. It also has a book exchange. *Frutos*, Calle Triunfo 393/201, serves a good veggie lunch for s/7, has fine views and doubles as an esoteric bookshop but the service is miserable. You could try the Krishna-run *Govinda*, 130 Espaderos, for better service but the food's not so good. *Tiziano*, Tecsecocha 418, is famous for its fresh, melt-in-the-mouth pastas, and you can pick up a cheap lunch here for around s/3.

If you fancy trying traditional Cusqueño food, go to *El Tronquito*, Plateros 327, or any of the restaurants on Pampa del Castillo; or the highly recommended, very friendly *Quinta Eulalia*, Choquechaca 384, with its enormous portions of roast meat. For between s/5 and s/10, these places will fill you up so completely you won't want to eat for the rest of the day. A basic lunch will cost around s/2.

Mid-price restaurants

Many of the mid-price and expensive restaurants offer a folk-music show included in the price of the meal. The food is pretty standard fare: lomo milanese, pollo dorado (roast chicken), suprema de pollo and the like, everything coming with papas fritas (chips). *Paititi*, Poral de Carrizos 270 (on the Plaza de Armas), does a good job with this food, and has decent Peruvian dishes and folk music; around s/50 for two people. *Mesón de Espaderos,* Espaderos 105, has a wider range which includes cuy (guinea pig), anticucho, trout, and fine parilladas. *Café Restaurant Roma*, Portal de Panes 105 is pretty much the same as the rest, but it does extend to ceviche. It has Inca walls inside. For Chinese cooking, try the restaurant on Calle Q'era on the other side of the road from the Colonial Palace.

If you're after one of Cuzco's famous pizzas, walk down Calle Plateros. *Chez Maggy,* Plateros 339, always gets a mention in guidebooks and it deserves it: the pizzas here are good, cooked in a real wood-fired oven but the bases are a bit crispy for me. For more imaginative Italian food and real risotto (which takes ages to prepare because of Cuzco's altitude) there's *Da Giorgio,* Calle Suecia 308. *Trattoria Adriano*, Calle Mantas 105, serves a Peruvian version of Italian food (more pollo dorado than parmigiano Reggiano) at s/46 for two.

Expensive restaurants

The top end spread in Cuzco is a little disappointing, but there are a few very good restaurants. *El Truco*, Plaza Regocijo, is stylish and has good service and if you're lucky they'll put a flag on your table to remind you of your nationality. *La Retama*, Portal de Panes 123, can cook fish meunière and steak béarnaise (dinner for two s/99 with wine) but it's often booked up.

My favourite restaurant in Cuzco is the *Inka Grill*, Portal de Panes 115, (on the Plaza de Armas) which is more modern and imaginative than its competitors as regards food and décor. They try to give Peruvian dishes a contemporary twist, so you could have pollo relleno prosciutto (chicken stuffed with prosciutto ham), or a good (but very expensive at s/20) aji de gallina, or mouth-watering langostinos (like Dublin Bay prawns – which one diner recommended as the best she'd had anywhere). It's not cheap, though, and a meal for two with wine will cost about s/150.

Don't forget that expensive restaurants will add 28% tax and service on to your bill.

Cafés

The Plaza de Armas is virtually lined with cafés, and sitting in them sipping coffee and gazing out over the square can be really addictive. All the cafés in Cuzco are indoors; you don't get tables set out on the pavement. These two are just examples of what's on offer: *Trotmundos*, Portal de Comercio 177 (overlooks the Plaza de Armas), has a laid-back atmosphere, board games, good breakfasts and real toast. *Los Perros*, Tecsecocha 238, has the best cappuccino in Cuzco (perhaps that's not saying much), and is a good place to relax because it has sofas.

Bars

The *Cross Keys,* Portal Confiturías 233, is almost a British pub just as *Paddy O'Flaterty's*, Triunfo 124, is almost an Irish pub, and *Norton's Tavern,* entrance same as the Hostal Loretto, is almost a North American bar. *Mama Africa,* Espaderos 135, 2nd Floor, is good and loud and stuffed with gringos (entrance with a pass you can pick up on the Plaza outside), and the cellar-like *Kamikaze* on the Plaza Regocijo is slightly less loud but good. For Abba, the Gypsy Kings and the company of gringos go to *Ukuku's*, Plateros·316.

WHAT TO SEE

Plaza de Armas

Just as it is today, the main square was a focal point for the people of Cuzco in the time of the Incas, but it used to be twice as big. The Plaza de Armas was once called Aucaypata and was a ceremonial area enclosed on three sides by the imposing mansions of the Inca. The other side of the river Huatanay, which ran down one side of Aucaypata in a stone ditch, was Cusipata where the Plaza Regocijo and its surrounding buildings now stand. Cusipata was the square of celebration, and a Spaniard described being there on a feast day when so much chicha (corn beer) was drunk that the drainage ditch overflowed with pure urine; to this day, the gutters and flagstones of the Plaza de Armas are regularly awash on festival days.

Cathedral

(Monday to Saturday 2-6pm, entrance with Visitor's Ticket.) Built from 1556 to 1669 in the Renaissance style, the cathedral nestles between the church of **Jesús María** (1733) on its right and on its left **El Triunfo** (1536), the site of Cuzco's first church and the resting place of the historian, El Inca Garcilasco de la Vega. The cathedral is probably built on the

---

❏ **Boleto Turístico Unico (BTU) – Visitor's Ticket**

There's an entrance fee of about US$2 at most of Cuzco's museums and archaeological sites. Many of these can also be visited using the Boleto Turístico Unico (BTU or Visitor's Ticket), which costs US$10, is valid for five or ten days and is sold at the **Instituto Nacional de Cultura** (INC) on the corner of Garcilasco and the Plaza Regocijo and some of the sites. The ticket allows only one entrance to each of the sites it covers – tiresome if you want to go back – but if you paid entrance fees for all the sites separately it would cost much more than US$10. Note that, contrary to what is said in many guidebooks, the ticket does not cover the Coricancha-Santo Domingo complex. The Visitor's Ticket allows you entry to these sites:

Sacsayhuaman	Cuzco Cathedral
Pikillacta	Religious Art Museum
Tipón	Church of San Blas
Ollantaytambo	Regional History Museum
Pisac	Chinchero ruins
Qenko	Santa Catalina Museum
Puca Pucara	Palacio Museum
Tambomachay	Coricancha Museum (not the ruins)

❑ CUZCO – WALKING TOURS

West

Start your tour in the **Plaza de Armas**, and face south-west. Walk down the small alley (Medio) towards the Plaza Regocijo. To your right is the **Town Hall**, and the road which leads uphill (north or right) from the square leads to the church of **Santa Teresa** (see p140). On the opposite corner of the square (downhill, left and south) there's the **Regional History Museum** (see p140) in the reconstructed house of Garcilasco de la Vega.

Carry on heading south-west, down Garcilasco, the street that leads away from the square directly opposite the road on which you entered the square. Walk one block further down here and you'll reach the Plaza San Francisco, with the **Monastery of San Francisco** on the opposite side (see p140). The bottom corner of this square (south) is **Santa Clara** leading to the convent of the same name (see p140), and ultimately the **market** and **railway station** for Machu Picchu. Be careful around here, as the area is notorious for muggings and bag slashings.

Return to the Plaza de Armas along Santa Clara.

South and east

Start in the **Plaza de Armas** and face La Compañía. Walk south-east (downhill) through **Calle Loreto** (see p140), and turn left at the end when you arrive in Maruri. Visit the **Banco Weise** (see p140), and turn right and the end of the block down Pomeritos until you reach a little square where the **Hotel Libertador** is situated. In front of you, slightly to your right, is the **Coricancha and Santo Domingo monastery**. (see p139).

From Coricancha, go back up Pomeritos to Maruri, then turn right and then left again up San Agustin. The fourth road on your right is **Hatun Rumliyoc** (see p140-1), and on the corner is the **Religious Art Museum**.

Turning right, and walking down Hatun Rumliyoc will take you up to **San Blas** (see p141), and walking the other way back towards the Plaza de Armas leads past the road in which there's the **Convent and Museum of Santa Catalina** (see p141).

North

Stand in the **Plaza de Armas** and face Sacayhuaman. Walk up the little alley of Procuradores (also known as Gringo Alley or Pizza St) to the north-west. At the end, turn left then right again and climb up Coricalle. At the end of Coricalle turn right, and you'll soon be on a large paved road. Walk to the right up hill on the road, and you'll pass the church of **San Cristobal** (see p141) on your left. Just after the church, turn right and walk downhill, down Rebalosa, savouring the view down towards Cuzco. Turn left at the junction of Resbalosa and Waynapata, and continue along to Punacuro (which means 'puma's spine', a reference to the fact that the street-plan of Cuzco was originally designed to resemble a puma). Soon you'll arrive at a small square, the sides of which are graced by the **House of the Serpents**, **Cabrera's House** and the **Seminary of San Antonio Abad** (see p141).

If you turn right, heading back towards the Plaza de Armas, you'll walk down a street called Tucuman, past the **Museo Inka** (see p141) and end up back on the Plaza.

Mary douses the flames
FELIPE HUAMÁN POMA DE AYALA (c1590)

❏ **The Virgin saves the Spanish**

During the siege of Cuzco, the Spanish were at one stage cornered in the Suntur Huasi or round house (where the Triunfo church is now). The roof of this building was thatched, and the Incas aimed a hail of red-hot stones from their slings at the straw until the roof caught fire.

What happened next depends on who you want to believe. The Spanish said that they were protected by divine intervention. The Virgin Mary appeared, joined by St James (the patron of the Spanish Army) and sprinkled water on the flames to douse the fire, and save the Spaniards. The Incas, on the other hand, remarked that the Spanish had positioned some of their black auxiliaries on the roof to beat out the fire.

site of Inca Viracocha's palace, and the next-door Triunfo (currently closed for restoration) is built on the site of the Suntur Huasi, where the Spaniards hid during the siege of Cuzco (see above).

The floor plan of the cathedral is a Latin cross with added processional isles and ambulatories. It's filled with wonders, from the carvings of alder and cedarwood by Martin Torres and Melchor Huamán (don't miss the minute detail on the choir), to the sacristy, filled with portraits of past bishops of Cuzco. The blackened crucifix, generally kept halfway down on the right, is the *Señor de los Tremblores* (Lord of the Earthquakes), which was paraded around Cuzco to stop the 1650 quake. It worked and this example of particularly Andean religiosity is commemorated in a painting kept at the very end of the nave on the left.

The Compañía (Jesuits' Church)

(No set opening hours; admission free). This is the other massive church on the Plaza de Armas. The Jesuits wanted it to be more imposing than the cathedral, but the Pope stopped them just before they finished, and the two buildings are so very similar it's a close-run thing. Work began in 1578, but the structure was practically demolished by the 1650 earthquake, and the church wasn't finished until 1668. It is a single nave design and was built on the palace of the Inca Huayna Capac, described by chronicler Pedro Sancho as the greatest of the Incas' palaces on the square with its red and white gateway ornamented with precious metal.

One of its most interesting paintings, which hangs by the door, represents the marriage of Martín García de Loyola to Ñusta (Princess) Beatriz. Loyola was the nephew of the Jesuits' founder, St Ignatius, but he was also the gallant captain who hunted down the last Inca Tupac Amaru. Beatriz was of royal Inca blood, and the marriage of the two was highly significant for the Jesuits because it associated them with this symbolic union of Spain and Peru, and so Loyola's and Beatriz's noble forbears look on approvingly at the union.

Loyola captures Tupac Amaru
FELIPE HUAMÁN POMA DE AYALA (c1590)

Other sights around the Plaza de Armas
● **Museum of Natural History** (Monday to Friday 8am-1pm, 3-6pm, s/2). The museum is housed in a little building to the right of the Compañía. It's not very informative, but is worth a visit if only to see the horrors it contains: a two-headed alpaca, a two-headed guinea pig, a six-legged goat and a frog the size of two clenched fists.

● **Inca walls** The wall on the north-western side of the Plaza is probably the remains of the Inca Pachacutec's palace, and the northern corner of the square is the site of the palace of the Inca Sinchi Roca.

Coricancha (Temple of the Sun) and Santo Domingo
(About 500m south-east of the Plaza de Armas; open Monday to Saturday 8am-5pm, Sunday 2-4pm s/2). The Coricancha was the centre of Incan religion. It was lavishly decorated, even by the standards of ancient Cuzco. One Spaniard tells of the 700 plates of gold, each three quarters of a metre long ($2^1/2$ ft), that were prised from its walls.

It consisted of a number of chapels dedicated to different deities: the Rainbow, Thunder and, of course, the Sun himself. The kidnapped idols of subdued tribes were kept hostage in the temple and if the tribe stepped out of line the idols were ridiculed and then destroyed. Outside the temple was the garden, in which the Incas displayed some of the most astounding of their goldwork. The historian, Garcilasco, describes large and small plants and birds, various animals both wild and domesticated, butterflies, snakes and lizards all made from gold. Most of course did not escape the greedy Spanish furnaces. After the Spaniards' triumphant entry into Cuzco, Coricancha was given to Juan Pizarro but he didn't have long to enjoy it. He was mortally wounded at the siege of Sacsayhuaman and on his deathbed gave it to the Dominicans (the priest Vincente Valverde who accompanied the Pizarros was a Dominican).

The monastery of Santo Domingo is worth a visit too, with a splendid carving of Santo Domingo by Melchor Huamán and the graves of the rebel Incas Sairi Tupac and Tupac Amaru and of Juan Pizarro himself. There is a Coricancha museum in the grounds (entrance via Av del Sol).

West and south of the Plaza de Armas

This is the area south of Plateros, and north of the Avenida del Sol behind the Portales de Comercio and Confituría.

● **La Merced** (8am-12pm, 2-4.30pm s/3) Built in 1534 and then rebuilt after the 1650 earthquake, La Merced rivals the cathedral in its riches, and has particularly beautiful cloisters. It faces the old Indian market, which allowed the clergy inside the church to preach to the milling crowds outside. Both Almagros are buried here, as is Gonzalo Pizarro.

● **San Francisco Church** (daily 6.30-8am, 6-8pm) Austere and with rather bloodthirsty decoration, this church and monastery dominates the square outside.

● **Santa Clara Church** (free). The church isn't often open, but if you're lucky enough to get inside you'll find wall-to-ceiling angled mirrors which multiply a hundredfold the candlelight. When I visited a woman was singing in a mournful, high-pitched, mesmeric wail which made the whole place feel like another world.

● **Regional History Museum and House of Garcilasco** (8am-6pm, entrance by Visitor's Ticket). The museum has an overview of Peruvian history with some interesting exhibits such as a Nazca mummy, and a collection of paintings of the Cuzco School. Look for St Michael armed with a gun. The house itself was rebuilt by the famous Peruvian architect, Víctor Pimentel, after it almost collapsed in the 1986 earthquake.

● **Market** Bustling, smelly, noisy, and filled with fat women in large hats carving dripping hunks of meat or spooning multi-coloured beans from huge sacks. All the world's goods are here, such as living frogs and skinned dead ones being sold amongst the piles of fresh fruit. A must but be careful of your wallet and watch out for bag slashers.

● **Santa Teresa** (unpredictable opening hours, free). A pleasant church with illustrations of Saint Teresa's life inside, but the outside of the building gets used as a public toilet, so hold your nose. The square in front of the church is pretty, and the wall bordering Calle Sapphi is a marvellous example of polygonal field-stone masonry.

East of the Plaza de Armas

This is the arc of streets south of Triunfo and north of the Avenida del Sol, behind the Compañía.

● **Calle Loreto** Another famous Inca alley, leading off the Plaza de Armas, the left-hand wall of which used to be the Acllahuasi (see p87).

● **Banco Weise, Calle Maruri** (free, open when the bank is). The bank occupies the palace of Tupac Inca Yupanqui, with its wonderful Inca walls. There's a little museum inside telling you about the history of the building and exhibiting some of the artifacts found here.

● **Religious Art Museum and Archbishop's Palace** (Monday to Saturday 8.30am-12pm, 3-5.30pm, entrance with Visitor's Ticket). This building is in **Hatun Rumliyoc,** an alley which was originally the side of the palace of the Inca Roca. The wall contains the famous twelve-angled stone which you can see on every bottle of Cusqueña beer. The museum has a fine collection of religious paintings with accurate period detail, and the colonial building founded on Inca remains is impressive.

● **Convent and Museum of Santa Catalina** (Monday to Thursday, Saturday 8am-6pm, Friday 8am-7pm, Visitor's Ticket) The museum is small and a little uninspiring, filled with some religious art and a couple of interesting models. However, the proportions of the interior of the building are quite beautiful, especially by the stairs up to the first floor internal balcony.

● **San Blas** (Monday to Saturday 2-5.30pm) is a simple church, but it contains a breathtaking carved cedar wood pulpit, believed to contain the skull of the man who made it. The area around is the ancient district of Cuzco's artisans.

North of the Plaza de Armas

This covers the arc of streets between Plateros and Triunfo, under the shadow of Sacsayhuaman.

● **San Cristobal Church** (free, no set opening times) stands proudly high above Cuzco, its grounds enclosed by a massive Inca wall that is possibly the remains of the palace of the first Inca Manco Capac. The church was built by the quisling, Inca Paullu, as a demonstration of his Christian faith.

● **Museo Inka (Archaeology)** and **Admiral's Palace** This is at Cuesta del Almirante 103 (Monday to Saturday 9am-5pm, s/5). The museum's collection is well displayed and informative with leaflets in English. They also have some Incan gold though you might have to ask to see it, and some paintings. A particularly gory *Execution of Atahualpa* shows his head being cut off, (it wasn't, he was garrotted and then partly burnt). The impressive buildings belonged to Admiral Don Francisco Maldonado.

● **House of the Serpents** Legend has it that this house was owned by the man who stole the golden disc of the Sun from the Coricancha, then gambled it away playing cards. It's called the House of the Serpents because of the carved snakes on its stones, and such ornamentation indicates it's a Spanish construction not an Inca one.

● **Cabrera's House** Cabrera founded Ica on the coast and also Cordoba in Argentina, and his house is an interesting colonial mansion with his coat of arms on the façade, its large salons and spacious interior patio graced with arches.

● **Seminary of San Antonio Abad** This is now the Hotel Monasterio (see p133), which makes it easy to visit if you put on your clean clothes and are prepared to pay their prices for a beer. The open courtyards are spoilt by glassed-in cloisters, but it's a splendid building.

MOVING ON

Air

The airport is five minutes by taxi from the Plaza de Armas, whence you can fly to most major Peruvian towns. The helicopter company **HeliCuzco** will fly you to Machu Picchu and back by 24-seat helicopter for US$150 (US$80 one way). The flight takes 25 minutes and leaves Cuzco at 8.45am.

● **Airlines   Aero Continente** (☎ 235660/666), Portal de Harinas 182; **AeroPeru** (not currently flying – ☎ 240013/233051), Avenida del Sol 319; **American Airlines** (☎ 225961/226605), Avenida del Sol 603-A; **Groupo Ocho** Avenida del Sol 507 (they also have a desk at the airport); **HeliCuzco** (☎ 227283), Calle Triunfo 379; **Lloyd Aero Boliviano** (☎ 222990), 675-A Av El Pardo.

Bus

See the Arrival section on p125 for where the buses arrive and leave. If you want to hitch, trucks can often be picked up at the same places from which the buses leave, but check in your hotel.

● **Bus companies** There are literally hundreds of companies. Some of the main inter-city ones are: **Carhuamayo** (☎ 264159), Pachacutec 510, recommended; **Christo Rey**: (☎ 222277), Pachacutec 227; **Civa** (☎ 227662), Pachacutec 420; **Cruz del Sur** (☎ 233383), Pachacutec 510, recommended; **Empressa Transporte Colca** (☎ 240422), Pachacutec 504; **Ormeño** (☎ 228712), Pachacutec 501, recommended. For local trips to the Sacred Valley, there are ticket offices at the places where the buses stop (see Arrival p125).

Rail

The station for the Puno line is **Huanchac** and the station for Machu Picchu and the jungle beyond is **San Pedro**. Tickets for the Puno line can only be bought at Huanchac, which is also the place to buy tickets for the expensive Machu Picchu trains. Tickets for the cheaper Machu Picchu trains are available only from San Pedro. Check the train timetable, the times when the stations are open to sell tickets and the ticket prices as everything changes often. Note that the stations won't sell tickets or reserve seats earlier than the day before you want to travel. The train station for Machu Picchu is called Puente Ruinas and was out of action at the time of writing, with trains stopping at Aguas Calientes instead, and buses running up to the ruins.

● **Buying tickets Huanchac station** (☎ 233592/238722) is open for tickets to Puno Monday to Friday 7am-12pm, 2-5pm and for expensive tickets to Machu Picchu Monday to Friday 9am-4pm and on Saturday and Sunday 9-11am. **San Pedro station** (☎ 221352/235201), is open for Express tickets Monday to Friday 3-5pm, Sunday 8-10am, and for local

Tickets Monday to Friday 3-4pm (for the next day's morning train) and Monday to Friday 8-11am for that day's lunchtime train). If you haven't booked in advance, it's worth going along an hour before the train leaves to see if there are any tickets left.

● **Classes** For the Puno run, see p120. On the Machu Picchu run there are three basic classes: Autovagon is the best, the tourist train next, while the local train is the most basic.

● **Prices** **Autovagon**, return ticket US$55, clean toilets and service from attendants; **Pullman**, return ticket US$34, not often crowded and reserved seating; **Express**, return s/55, a pretty basic standard, but not as bad as the **local train**, first class s/15, second class s/8.50 (both one way) which is a South American train red in tooth and claw. Having a reserved seat means nothing unless you're prepared to fight for your rights.

● **Timetables** Trains to **Puno** leave on Monday, Wednesday, Thursday, and Saturday at 8am and arrive at Juliaca at 5.30 pm and at Puno at 7pm. Trains to **Machu Picchu** leave at various times. The Autovagon leaves Cuzco at 6am and arrives at Aguas Calientes at 9.10am, Monday to Sunday. The Pullman and Express leave Cuzco at 6.25am and reach Aguas Calientes at 10.15am, and don't run on Sunday. Neither does the local train, which leaves Cuzco at 6.45am and reaches Aguas Calientes at 10.40am. For return times see p227. Note that timetables often change.

Around Cuzco

RUINS NEAR CUZCO (DAY HIKE)

There are lots of small but interesting sites within walking distance of Cuzco's Plaza de Armas. You could probably cover many in half a day if you wanted to but you'd miss so much; it's worth spending a little time exploring each one, and anyway walking through the rolling grassland around Cuzco is a pleasant way to acclimatise to the altitude.

The route described here is the most commonly walked day hike, and visits Sacsayhuaman, Qenko, Salapunco, Puca Pucara and Tambo Machay – take a packed lunch. If you don't feel like a walk, you can always take a tour (p129), take the bus (Pisac bus – ask to be dropped off at Tambo Machay), or hire a horse. Horses are readily available at Sacsayhuaman; just ask around. If your Spanish isn't good enough to do this, one of the tour agencies will be able to sort it out.

Sadly there have been muggings in the ruins close to Cuzco and some attempted rapes (at Sacsayhuaman and Qenko). Leave valuables at the hotel, don't go to these places on your own, and at dawn or dusk.

Sacsayhuaman

(7am to 5.30pm, Visitor's Ticket). It takes about 20 to 30 minutes to walk to Sacsayhuaman from the Plaza de Armas. There are several routes but the easiest way is to head up one of the streets by the cathedral to Pumacurco, also called Palacio and Herrajes, turn left and walk uphill. After some stairs you'll reach a main, tarred road and a signpost to Sacsayhuaman, which points up a path on the left (west) of a gully. Follow the stairs (you can go either way around the large hillock that blocks the way) until you reach the massive stones of Sacsayhuaman on your left.

❑ 'This was the greatest and most superb of the edifices that the Incas raised to demonstrate their majesty and power. Its greatness is incredible to those who have not seen it; and those who have seen it, and studied it with attention, will be led not alone to imagine, but to believe, that it was reared by enchantment – by demons, and not by men, because of the number and size of the stones placed in the three walls, which are rather cliffs than walls, and which it is impossible to believe were cut out of quarries, since the Indians had neither iron nor steel wherewith to extract or shape them. And how they were brought together is a thing equally wonderful, since the Indians had neither carts nor oxen nor ropes, wherewith to drag them by main force. Nor were there level road over which to transport them, but, on the contrary, steep mountains and abrupt declivities, to be overcome by the simple force of men. ... It passes the power of imagination to conceive how so many and so great stones could be so accurately fitted together as scarcely to admit the insertion of the point of a knife between them'. **Garcilasco de la Vega**. *Comentarios reales que tratan del origen de los Incas* (1609).

No one knows for sure what Sacsayhuaman was. It was called 'the Fortress' by the Spanish, but current research suggests that it was more likely to be a temple, and Inca tombs have been discovered in the area. Whether or not it was designed to be a temple, it was certainly used as a fort by the armies of Manco Inca when they attempted to dislodge the Spaniards from Cuzco (see p97), and the Spanish chronicler, Pedro Sancho, estimated that it was large enough to hold a garrison of 5000 Spanish soldiers. He went on to say that the widely-travelled Spaniards he was with commented 'that they have never seen a building to compare with this fortress, nor a stronger castle'.

It was topped by three towers and riddled with tunnels, in which the historian, Garcilasco de la Vega, remembers playing when he was a child. The towers were called Salla Marca, Paunca Marca and Muyu Marca. The concentric rings of foundations of the last remain, but the stones of the others were pillaged in the days when Cusqueños used Sacsayhuaman as an unofficial quarry. Some tunnels remain in the northern amphitheatre – bring a torch.

The mound opposite the zigzag walls is called the Inca's Throne or

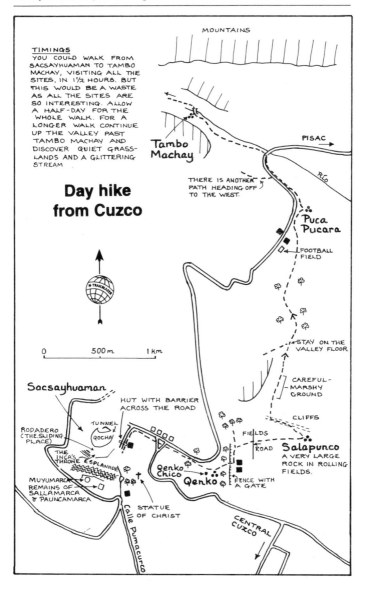

MOUNTAINS

TIMINGS
YOU COULD WALK FROM SACSAYHUAMAN TO TAMBO MACHAY, VISITING ALL THE SITES, IN 1½ HOURS. BUT THIS WOULD BE A WASTE AS ALL THE SITES ARE SO INTERESTING. ALLOW A HALF-DAY FOR THE WHOLE WALK. FOR A LONGER WALK CONTINUE UP THE VALLEY PAST TAMBO MACHAY AND DISCOVER QUIET GRASS-LANDS AND A GLITTERING STREAM

Day hike from Cuzco

Tambo Machay

PISAC

RÍO

THERE IS ANOTHER PATH HEADING OFF TO THE WEST.

Puca Pucara

FOOTBALL FIELD

STAY ON THE VALLEY FLOOR

CAREFUL-MARSHY GROUND

0   500 m   1 Km

Sacsayhuaman

HUT WITH BARRIER ACROSS THE ROAD

CLIFFS

RODADERO (THE SLIDING PLACE)

TUNNEL

QOCHA

FIELDS

ROAD

Salapunco
A VERY LARGE ROCK IN ROLLING FIELDS.

THE INCA'S THRONE ESPLANADE

Qenko Chico

Qenko

FENCE WITH A GATE

MUYUMARCA REMAINS OF SALLAMARCA & PAUNCAMARCA

STATUE OF CHRIST

Calle Pumacurco

CENTRAL CUZCO

the *rodadero* (sliding place). It was probably where a high-ranking person supervised sacred ceremonies, but nowadays the deep polished grooves in the rock are used by children as a slide. The green meadow between the Inca's Throne and the tiered walls is called the Esplanade.

Qenko

From Sacsayhuaman, the path leads to Qenko (7am-5.30pm, Visitor's Ticket), which is further to the east beyond the statue of Christ. If you stand in the Esplanade and look away from Cuzco you'll see a path heading uphill towards a barrier with a hut beside it. Walk up there, turn right (east) beyond the hut and follow the road past some souvenir sellers into a small wood. The road turns to the left (north), and on your right there is the stone mound of Qenko Chico (little Qenko), at the bottom of which there is a wall containing a block carved with twenty-one angles. A little further on, by a car park on the right-hand side of the road, is Qenko.

Qenko – the name means 'zigzag' or 'labyrinth' – is a huaca (sacred site). There is a monolith in front called the Seated Puma which is enclosed by a niched wall of fine masonry.

There are carvings everywhere, but some are a little indistinct: a llama, a condor, and snakes have all been identified. One recent discovery is a structure that seems to cast a shadow rather like a puma's head when the sun rises on the winter solstice (21 June). You'll probably have already seen a photograph of this on the cover of *The Awakening of the Puma*, sold in every bookshop in Cuzco.

Salapunco

At Qenko it's best to ask someone for directions but you should follow the road uphill for about 50 metres; just before it joins the main road there is a path off to the left through the trees towards a village. Go down the path to a small gully, pass through a gate and turn left uphill along the side of the gully. Keep the village on your right and just past it you come to a crossroads. Take the diagonal path (east) across the fields to a large rocky outcrop ahead.

This is Salapunco, aka Cusilluchagoc, (always open, admission free) another carved limestone monolith riddled with passages and providing excellent views from the top. It isn't on the tour routes and so is often deserted.

Puca Pucara

If you stand on the top of Salapunco and look away from Cuzco, you can see directly below you a clear track. Follow the track to the left (west) towards a small depression where there is a junction with another path. There is a mound slightly to your right (north-west), and just before it a path heads uphill through a bog. Follow that path to the north. After climbing for about half an hour you pass a small village with a football field on your left, and beyond it you should be able to see the road running parallel to you. Shortly after this the path joins the road, and then Puca Pucara (7am-5.30pm, Visitor's Ticket) appears 50 metres away on the right.

Puca Pucara is probably a hunting lodge on one of the Inca's private estates near Cuzco. It was originally thought to be a military checkpoint or on a main Inca road. The name can be translated as 'red watchtower' or 'red fort'.

Tambo Machay

You can see the signpost to Tambo Machay from Puca Pucara. Return to the road, walk away from Cuzco and turn left (west) at the corner following the signpost to Tambo Machay (7am-5.30pm, Visitor's Ticket). It is about 200 metres away.

Tambo Machay (the name means 'inn cave') is known popularly as Los Baños del Inca, (the Inca's Baths), and was probably a centre of water worship. The whole complex is an architectural frame for a spring which falls from one terrace to another, slips underground, then emerges again in two cascades.

Returning to Cuzco

You can either retrace your steps, or catch a bus or taxi on the road by the turning to Tambo Machay.

THE SACRED VALLEY

The fertile valley of the Urubamba river, also called the Vilcanota, snakes its way through the old Inca province of Antisuyu, an area which the Incas valued greatly. There, beside this tributary of the Amazon, they built their retreats, palaces and sacred places: the fortress of Ollantaytambo (clinging to the steep sides of the river's gorge), Pisac with its Inca canal, three kilometres long, its imposing terraces and, of course, the once-lost Machu Picchu.

Urubamba means 'place of the bugs or spiders' but the area is called The Sacred Valley in all today's tourist literature. It's probably so called to attract tourists to the proliferation of ruins in the area, but some suggest the valley is sacred because it was Cuzco's granary, and others because it is connected with the sun and sky. One Quechua legend says that after the sun sets in the evening it passes through the underworld beneath the Urubamba where it drinks the chill water to refresh itself before emerging at dawn. Another legend says that the Urubamba is the earthly mirror of the celestial river, the Milky Way, and that water flows from one into the other.

There are many good hikes around the Sacred Valley. Hilary Bradt's *Backpacking and Trekking in Peru and Bolivia* describes some splendid little walks, as does Charles Brod's *Apus & Incas*, although this book is hard to obtain. Regular buses run from Cuzco to the towns in the Sacred Valley (see towns below and also p125), and there are many hotels out here where you can stay to escape Cuzco's bustle.

Pisac

Viceroy Toledo, who supervised the crushing of the last Incas, built Spanish Pisac on an Inca settlement in the shadow of the great terraces of the Inca ruins known as the Citadel. Many tombs have been found here, and there is a rare Intihuatana – a sacred carving or 'hitching post of the sun' (see p222-3), many of which had their tops broken off by the Spanish. The site is open 7am-5.30pm (Visitor's Ticket) and is definitely worth visiting. It's a fair climb up to the Citadel, and if you're not yet acclimatised you'll need to take your time.

There are markets here on Tuesday, Thursday and Sunday mornings at which you can pick up well-made souvenirs. A shop on the Plaza de Armas is worth mentioning because it sells fabrics produced by a weavers' collective, and all profits the shop makes go straight back to the weavers. It's run by an interesting woman called Doctora Gail Silverman.

Pisac is 32km from Cuzco. To get here catch a minibus from Calle Huascar or Inticahuarina in Cuzco.

Chinchero

There are Inca remains here (7am-5.30pm, Visitor's Ticket) and the church has paintings from the Cuzco School. The Sunday market (crafts as well as local produce) is worth coming for, particularly since it attracts fewer tourists than the Pisac markets. Buses from Cuzco leave early in the morning, usually from Calle Huascar.

Urubamba

Urubamba is a largish town, and the centre of the bus network; this is where you change if you're travelling between Cuzco and Ollantaytambo. It also has a local market but primarily it is a good base from which to explore other parts of the Sacred Valley.

Two to three hours' walk from Urubamba is the site of **Moray**, an Inca experimental farm, where a natural depression has been transformed into circular terraces of different sizes. This strange place was probably used to study the effect of altitude on different plants. You can walk from Moray (two hours) to the **Maras Salinas**, another bizarre site, where layers of beige and white salt-pans are still used to crystallise salt from water.

Where to stay and eat There are plenty of hotels in Urubamba, which range from the expensive and rather flash English-owned *Hotel Valle Sagrado de los Inkas* (☎ 201117/126-7, 🖹 201071) who even offer balloon rides (contact the New Yorker Jeff Hall at the hotel, cost US$300 per

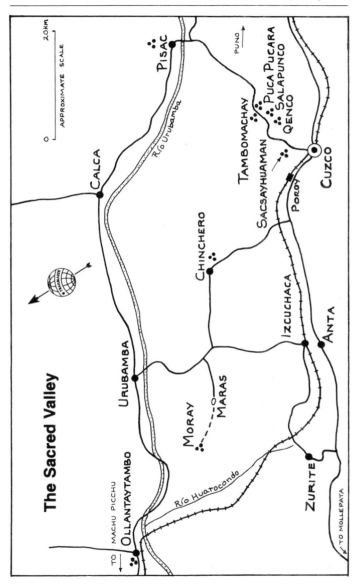

The Sacred Valley

hour) to the mid-priced *Los Girasoles* (☎ 201390) on the outskirts of town beyond the Torrechayoc Church. Los Girasoles has camping sites, dormitory beds as well as doubles and singles. There are some cheaper places too, like the *Hostal Urubamba* (no phone, Jirón Bolognesi).

Transport Urubamba is a 2¹/₂-hour minibus ride from Cuzco (from Calle Huascar or Inticahuarina). It's 1¹/₂ hours from Pisac and about 50 minutes from Ollantaytambo.

Ollantaytambo

At the end of its flat, verdant plain, the Urubamba river flows faster and enters a gorge which leads down from the Andes to the Amazon. It was in this beautiful, strategic spot, 60 kilometres from Cuzco, that the Inca Pachacutec built his fortress of Ollantaytambo. It's a lovely place, green and relaxed, enclosed in hills that hide some of the most impressive ruins in the valley. Stay here if the strains of Cuzco are getting you down, or if you want to explore the Sacred Valley or Machu Picchu from closer than Cuzco itself.

The fortress temple Myth has it that the name comes from an Inca captain, Ollanta, who fell in love with Pachacutec's daughter. Pachacutec forbade them to marry, at which Ollanta rebelled. Pachacutec himself was killed in the ensuing battle, and Ollanta almost defeated the army of the empire but was betrayed. The new Inca took pity on him because of his great prowess in war and allowed him to marry the princess.

It was to the forbidding fortress temple (7am-5.30pm, Visitor's Ticket), high above the valley floor, that Manco Inca retreated when he was being pursued by the Spanish (p99), and from here that he defeated a raiding party sent to seize him. The steep terraces seem to bar your route up to the fortress, and walls rise from the near-vertical cliff faces – you can see why the Spanish failed to capture this place. At the top lies the unfinished Sun Temple, consisting of massive mortarless slabs perfectly slotted together and stained with orange lichen. The double doorjambs you'll see here are rare in Inca buildings and indicate that this was a very important site.

❏ **Ollantaytambo Museum**
A burnished plaque on the museum in Ollantaytambo records its opening by none other than HRH Princess Anne. Many people wonder what she was doing out here. The answer is that Catcco, the organisation that runs the museum, was set up as a joint project by the Cusichaca Trust (see p89), the University of Cuzco, local community groups, and the British Embassy. It's an attempt to harness the tourist dollar to benefit the local people of Ollantaytambo directly, in a way that helps people come away with a greater understanding of campesino life and history. It's a very good museum, and is well worth a visit.

Old town Below on the valley floor lies the old town of Ollantaytambo – one of the best surviving examples of Inca urban planning. The Incas built their towns in blocks called *canchas,* and one cancha was home to several families. In most of Peru these canchas have long since been knocked down and the ancient Inca streets built over, but both remain here. Keep an eye out for more double doorjambs which show that this town itself was as important as the ruins that cling to the hills above.

The Rebel, Manco Inca
FELIPE HUAMÁN POMA DE AYALA (c1590)

Where to stay and eat There's the excellent if expensive North American-owned *El Albergue* (☎ 204014), Casilla 784 Cuzco (entrance on the platform of the station), and the cheaper but very good *Hostal Las Orquideas* (☎ 204032), on the right coming up from the station just outside town. *La Fortaleza* is a good restaurant on the Plaza de Armas.

Transport From Cuzco you can get here on the train (about two hours, see p125) by colectivo or minibus. The railway station is about a 10-15 minute walk from the town centre.

Colectivos and minibuses from Cuzco leave from Calle Huascar or in the side street of Inticahuarina. You'll have to change in Urubamba.

Aguas Calientes

This village is pretty much the end of the line, unless you're heading out towards the jungle at Quillabamba or searching for Vilcabamba. Really just a dormitory town for Machu Picchu, you'll either find it a useful place to stay while you explore the ruins or an ugly rash in the pristine forest of the Sanctuary. The trail up the mountain Putucusi starts here (ask at Gringo Bill's), and there are hot springs where you can rest your aching bones after you return. Also here, rather surprisingly for this remote place, a first-class restaurant and the best hotel in the whole valley.

Where to stay The top hotel is the *Machu Picchu Pueblo Hotel* (☎ 211032, ▤ 211124); reservations in Lima (☎ 422 6574, ▤ 422 4701, email: reservas@inkaterra.com.pe, website: www.inkaterra.com. pe), a beautiful place with bungalows set in the enclosing forest. A double with attached bathroom costs $173 (not including breakfast).

Other accommodation includes *Gringo Bill's* (☎ 211046, email: gringobill@yahoo.com), Pasaje Ccolia Raymi 104 – just off the Plaza – an imaginative place run by a disillusioned North American. A double is s/40. Nearby is the cheaper *yellow house* (no name), on the north-west corner of the square just before Gringo Bill's sign. Ask in the gift shop just by the sign. A double room with bath costs s/20. You can also look for accommodation in Avenida Pachacutec which is dotted with places to stay and on either side of the railway tracks.

Where to eat The best restaurant is the French-run *Indi Feliz,* Calle Lloque Yupanqui Lt 4 – if you walk up to the springs it's on the left just after the school on Avenida Pachacutec. Dishes here include freshly-baked quiche lorraine and Urubamba trout smothered in melted butter. Prices are quite reasonable and portions large.

Transport The village boasts two **train stations**, the modern one for the Autovagon and the old one for the local train. The place where the old train stops is more a halt than a station; just a rail track with pizza restaurants either side. Autovagon train tickets are sold at the modern station, but local train tickets must be bought from the booth in a beaten-up old building to the west of the police station.

The **bus for Machu Picchu** leaves from the bus 'station', just a patch of concrete where the train tracks pass over a small stream. You can buy tickets at a half-built concrete house near where the bus leaves.

See p227 for more information on transport from Aguas Calientes and Machu Picchu.

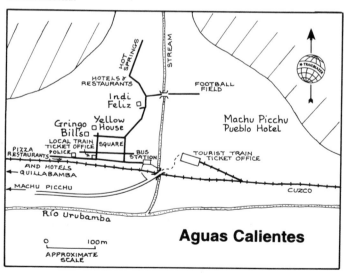

PART 6: MINIMUM IMPACT/SAFE TREKKING

Minimum impact trekking

There are problems on the Inca Trail. Some are unavoidable: people are attracted to the spot because of its solitude, and when they arrive they turn it from an unvisited oasis to a tourist attraction. Some of the problems however can be avoided, such as those of litter and erosion, of pollution and destruction of the ancient Inca sites.

A lot of the damage done by tourists flows from selfish thoughtlessness. They forget that they're not the only people who'll walk in these hills: others, too, will be tempted to light a little cooking fire and save money by camping in the ruins – a knock-on effect that endangers the environment. We who have the privilege of walking in this place must also accept the responsibility of helping to preserve it, at the very least by removing our rubbish.

ENVIRONMENTAL IMPACT

Continue to contaminate your bed, and you will one night suffocate in your own waste. Chief Seattle, taken from *Chief Seattle's Testimony* (Pax Christi and Friends of the Earth, 1976).

We are not entering a wilderness when we come to the Machu Picchu Historical Sanctuary. People, plants and animals have been living here for centuries in harmony. The influx of tourists threatens to ruin this delicate balance and we are part of the problem. By following a few rules, however, we can be part of the solution.

Pack it in, pack it out
If you've carried something into the Sanctuary, carry it out again. Some suggest burying litter but this isn't a solution as there are too many people walking these trails. Put your used packets and empty tins in a large plastic bag and dispose of them in Cuzco.

The rubbish bins along the trail are usually full to overflowing so it would be helpful if you took away some of the litter left by other people, too.

● **Is it OK if it's biodegradable?** Not really. Of course, things like an apple core will rot away in no time but orange peel takes six months to biodegrade, and clothes will take 15 years.

● **Lavatory paper** Lavatory paper is a vexed subject. Some people keep a lighter in a bag with their loo paper to burn the stuff. I find it difficult to get it to catch light so I pack it out along with everything else I've brought in. Put one plastic bag inside another (in case of ruptures), put the used paper inside and seal the top with a piece of wire. When you get to a lavatory (there are five on the trail) you can just flush the paper away. It might be biodegradable but if you leave it on the ground it will flutter around for a long time, a sordid reminder of your passing. Pack out sanitary towels, too.

Bury your excrement
Bring a little trowel to bury excrement. Make sure you do it *well* away from the trail.

Don't pollute water
Don't relieve yourself within 20m (70ft) of a stream or other water supply. People have ignored this rule, and as a result giardia (see p164) has infected the streams in the Sanctuary.

Don't pollute streams with soap. Some people bring a collapsible plastic bucket to collect water to wash in from a stream. Dirty water should be poured away at least 20m from the water source.

Avoid using detergent to clean pans; use a wire scrubber in swiftly flowing water. If you must use detergent, wash up in a collapsible bucket away from the stream. I think 'biodegradable camping detergents' are a con, because all detergents are biodegradable – the problems only start when they've biodegraded.

Erosion
Inca roads were designed for llama hooves and bare human feet, and there wasn't much traffic in those days as no one could travel without a permit. Today the old stones bear the weight of thousands of tramping boots and running porters, and the old paths have become deeply scored into the mountainside.

There have been efforts to deal with the problem, and the section up to Abra de Huarmihuanusca (Dead Woman Pass) has recently been paved. However, you can help things get better by sticking to the paths and camping only where you're supposed to.

Camp-fires
It's a park rule that you're not allowed to have a camp-fire, so don't. This is because the wood you're burning is not unlimited and also there's the danger of camp-fires getting out of control: there were large fires in 1988, 1994 and 1997 that were probably caused by careless tourists or their porters.

❏ **Machu Picchu cable car**
Some threats to the Sanctuary are caused by the desire to improve the locals' standard of living and attract more tourists. There are plans to drive a road up to Huayllabamba and expand the village of Aguas Calientes. By the time you read this work may have started on a $6 million cable car project. This is planned to run from the valley floor 1500 feet up to Machu Picchu; it will have a capacity of 400 tourists per hour. About 300,000 tourists visit the ruins each year – can the old stones really take this capacity?

Camping in the ruins

Inca ruins that have stood for hundreds of years are being damaged by selfish hikers who want the experience of sleeping in them, and think that it won't do any harm. But it does. Just peek over the other side of Sayacmarca and you'll see a pyramid of turds and a field of paper dropped by people who think that they're the only ones who've ever camped here.

Litter's not the only problem. Camp-fires can cause damage to the ancient walls, and careless campers knock off stones. And there's the more intangible way that people stake ownership with their sweaty bodies and nylon tents to the ruins that should belong to everyone.

Obey the park ruling and don't camp in the ruins, tempting as it might be. Wardens occasionally patrol the ruins to catch people camping illegally.

Don't pick flowers or disturb animals

You will be walking in a UNESCO natural World Heritage Site. It's a sanctuary where plant- and wild-life are supposed to exist without human interference, so don't pick the plants and leave any animals you see in peace.

The authorities may also be responsible for damage to the place, sometimes by accident, at other times on purpose. An example of accidental, well-meaning damage happened at the site of Intipata (see p180). Intipata was regularly cleared of encroaching plant life until it was discovered that it was a haven for a rare orchid. It's now once more abandoned to nature, and the ruins are being returned to the jungle.

ECONOMIC IMPACT

If tourists were more aware of the power of their money and the responsibility that goes with it, they could do a lot of good.

The power you have to do good

Some locals are as guilty of not looking after the Sanctuary as the tourists and authorities. The villains are often cheap tour operators, who drop litter and exploit their porters: porters are often paid very little for the back-breaking work of carrying your bags, and may not be provided with either food or shelter.

● **Pay a fair price for a fair service** If you take a cheap tour, the misery of the porters and the filth that's dropped on the ground is your responsibility – you're the one who's saving the price of a trip to the cinema by not giving these people a living wage. Don't encourage this situation. Go for the more up-market tours where the porters are more realistically paid and more effort is made to ensure that litter is destroyed or removed.

There's nothing worse than the shameful sight of a Westerner bargaining with a porter over what is to him the price of a newspaper and to the porter a square meal. Of course you may need to bargain and you shouldn't allow yourself to get ripped off, but find out from other hikers what the current fair price is, and pay accordingly.

The power you have to do bad

Well-meaning trekkers have created a begging culture amongst the children who live along the trail. In the busier villages, you'll be swamped with little hands and engulfed by children's voices piping: *'Dame dulce'*, *'Dame regalo'* (give me a sweetie/candy, a present). Because of their success with other tourists, little kids now associate gringos with an unlimited supply of money and sweets.

What you do about it is a matter for you. It's hard to resist the plaintive faces and grubby hands. I think that giving makes the situation worse: if they've done something helpful, reward them. Otherwise, sing them a song or make them laugh and they'll begin to see you more as a person, and less as an animated gum-ball machine.

CULTURAL IMPACT

Many campesinos get a pretty odd idea of life outside Peru as all they see of the world is well-dressed, apparently rich, tourists. Explain to them what the cost of living is like back home – how much does a loaf of bread cost, or a pint of milk – in soles, and how many hours you worked to earn the money to come to their country. Help them put your holiday into perspective and realise that we're not all Bill Gates.

Consider the feelings of local people

Some tourists leave their basic tact at home and forget that the locals they meet on holiday can be offended just as easily as they can themselves. It's often simple things, caused by thoughtlessness, that can really irritate.

● **Photographs** Ask permission before you take a photo and if your subject doesn't want you to take one, don't. Some children dress up and look deliberately cute, and then charge money when you ask to photograph them. Don't rip them off, but if you pay too much it becomes demeaning when they earn the same amount in ten seconds as their parents earn in ten hours.

SESTA CALLE
CORO·TASQVE

Lama herder spins as he walks
FELIPE HUAMÁN POMA DE AYALA (c1590)

● **Camping** If you're planning to camp somewhere near a village, ask permission: making contact can also help with safety.

● **Clothing** Although it matters less in Peru than in Islamic countries, wearing inappropriate clothing can still offend. In churches you should show proper respect by covering normally exposed skin. Don't bathe naked in mountain streams where you could be overlooked.

● **Don't flaunt your wealth** However poor you may be by Western standards, your wealth is way above the wildest dreams of most campesinos so don't flaunt it. Never leave valuable items such as cameras or watches lying about.

● **Be polite** Some campesinos can be offended if they offer you a place to stay the night and you refuse and set up your tent in their fields instead. Not surprisingly, they can also get offended if they offer you food and you turn it down and cook your own. Wouldn't you be? Be aware of this, and try not to step on any toes. Some campesinos are over-friendly in a way that's not helpful; they might point you in a direction you know is wrong, or proffer unwanted help. Keep your patience and just decline pleasantly.

● **Always keep your sense of humour** If things aren't working out as you want don't lose your temper. It's more likely that the person you're talking to does not understand what you want than that they're being deliberately obstructive. A smile costs nothing.

Return hospitality

You'll probably encounter hospitality that will make you swell up with guilt, as someone who can afford nothing gives you much and won't accept repayment. If you find yourself in this position, don't force money on people who don't want it as they have their pride just as you do. Share your food with them, and try and give them something of yourself in return: try and speak Quechua, listen to them (some shepherds are just lonely), and tell them about your home or how much you like their country. Campesinos are as proud and patriotic as anyone.

Safe trekking

SAFETY IN THE HILLS

If you're properly prepared for your trek, you should have no problems, just a wonderful time.

Weather

The weather in the Machu Picchu Historical Sanctuary is very changeable. Expect rain and carry warm clothing, even if the sun's out and it's a beautiful day, because while the valleys are bathed in beautiful sunshine the high passes may be enveloped in cloud. For more information about the climate see p19.

Getting lost

In good weather most of the trails described in this book are clear and easy to follow. I don't believe it's possible to get lost on the stretch from Huayllabamba to Machu Picchu, as it's a heavily beaten path and there'll be many other people walking at the same time as you. In bad weather, however, there are points on the more remote trails where the path will disappear, and there's one section of the Mollepata trek that's difficult in any weather.

Therefore a **compass** is absolutely essential if you're walking the longer trails. Some people bring a handheld GPS (Global Positioning System), but they really aren't worth it unless you head off into the wilderness.

Tell people where you're going

Before you leave on your trek, it's wise to inform someone at home and to tell your hotel manager or a fellow traveller where you're going and when you plan to be back; they should be aware of what to do if you don't get back, and how long to wait before raising the alarm.

Dogs

Dogs can be dangerous if they're carrying rabies and a nuisance when you're hiking. They'll often bark as you pass, but they seldom attack. If they look threatening, throw stones at them – this is what the locals do. The mere act of bending down to pick one up often scares them off.

A note of caution

Sadly there are some theft problems on the Inca Trail, and you'll hear some scare stories from other travellers but only believe one tenth of what you hear. Remember many thousands of hikers walk these trails each year without meeting any trouble at all.

The problems seem to be centred around the village of **Huayllabamba**; tents were slashed there when I was walking the trails for this book. You can easily reduce the risk of being a target by not camping near Huayllabamba, by travelling in groups, by stuffing your valuables deep down into your rucksack when you walk and by not leaving anything tempting outside your tent when you zip-up for the night. The SAEC in Lima is a good source of information as to the current situation.

Other villages on these trails are usually trouble free, but when you camp near one it's best to ask a local family for permission, partly out of politeness but also to come under their protection.

HEALTH IN THE HILLS

Walking in the Sanctuary is invigorating. It's generally a very healthy place, the blustering winds blow the cobwebs away and the sun warms your heart. When you come down from the high altitude, you'll feel like Superman. Nevertheless, you should be aware of illnesses associated with altitude above 3000m (10,000ft).

AMS – acute mountain sickness

AMS and the medical conditions, High Altitude Pulmonary Oedema (HAPO or HAPE) and High Altitude Cerebral Oedema (HACO or HACE), that can result from it are all entirely preventable if certain precautions are taken.

The important thing to remember is that **it is the speed of ascent not the altitude itself that causes AMS**. The body takes several days to adapt to an increase in altitude. The higher you go above sea-level, the lower the barometric pressure, resulting in less oxygen reaching your lungs with each breath you take. At 2500m/8202ft it's about 25% lower but up to this altitude the effects of the altitude are rarely felt; at 5000m/16,400ft the pressure is almost 50% lower.

AMS is uncomfortable but not dangerous unless it's a severe case. You'll feel a headache and nausea. In bad cases you may start vomiting. It's a bit like having a hangover, and it usually passes after one to three days. You can take painkillers (but not sleeping tablets) and acetazelomide (see below), but the best thing to do is rest, and if it gets worse, descend.

HAPO and HACO are very serious, and potentially life-threatening. You should know both how to recognise them and what to do if you suspect someone's got them, but if you take care you're very unlikely to come across either. **HAPO** occurs when the lungs get waterlogged. Symptoms include not being able to breathe properly and finding it more difficult to exert yourself than usual. It tends to progress from AMS, but it's not common in trekkers. The pulse increases, fluid is coughed up,

---

❑ SERIOUS AMS SYMPTOMS – IMMEDIATE DESCENT!

● **Persistent, severe headache**
● **Persistent vomiting**
● **Ataxia** – loss of co-ordination, inability to walk in a straight line, making the sufferer look drunk.
● **Losing consciousness** – inability to stay awake or understand instructions.
● **Liquid sounds in the lungs**
● **Very persistent, sometimes watery, cough**
● **Difficulty breathing**
● **Rapid breathing or feeling breathless at rest**
● **Coughing blood, pink phlegm or lots of clear fluid**
● **Severe lethargy**
● **Marked blueness of face and lips**
● **High resting heartbeat – over 130 beats per minute**
● **Mild symptoms rapidly getting worse**

---

there's fever, and your extremities go blue (compare fingernail beds with a healthy person). Sometimes there's also chest tightness, and the lungs sound crackly. Once the person descends recovery is usually quick and complete.

HACO is a build-up of fluid in the brain. Anyone who gets it will suffer from loss of balance, severe lassitude and will eventually fall into a coma. There may also be an altered mental state – hallucinations, weakness or numbness on one side of the body, and an inability to talk or make sense. Headache, nausea and vomiting are also symptoms. Death occurs quickly if the person remains at altitude, and even if you get them down, there can be long term neurological damage.

All are caused by the body's response to the lower oxygen pressure in the air, and all can be largely treated by descending promptly.

● **Headache** Headache is an important warning sign of trouble. If you have a headache follow Dr Peter Hackett's headache rule: rest, don't ascend, eat snacks, drink plenty of fluids, take mild pain medicine. If it's not going away or you suspect altitude sickness, don't ascend. If you suffer from severe shortness of breath at rest (you don't get your breath back after 15 minutes) or if you have any of the symptoms in the boxed text above **descend immediately** – even if it's the middle of the night.

● **Ataxia** Ataxia is altered balance and muscular coordination. You can test for it by drawing a 2m (6ft) line on the ground and walking heel-to-toe along it. If you can't walk in a straight line, then fear the worst and descend.

(Opposite): Waterfall near Huinay Huayna.

● **Acetazelomide** Acetazelomide (Diamox) is a drug that can prevent and treat AMS (not HAPO or HACO). It's a diuretic and so will make you urinate more, and it makes your fingertips tingle. It's widely available in Peru. The dose is 125mg twice a day, usually taken before you go to sleep. You can stop taking it after a couple of days at altitude. Some doctors recommend taking the same dose as a treatment for AMS, though by far the best thing is to descend. Don't take acetazelomide if you're allergic to sulpha drugs.

● **Coca leaf** Coca leaf (see p47) has been used for centuries to reduce the effects of AMS. You chew it in a quid in your mouth, with a little *llibita* (a catalyst). Some say it works; all it did for me was turn my shirt green when I spat out the juice and missed the ground.

Injury
An elementary knowledge of First Aid is useful. In an emergency the basics are ABC: first check the **airway's clear**, then ensure that they are **breathing**, and then check their **circulation**.

● **A Airway** Make sure the mouth is clear and the tongue is not obstructing the airway. Clean out vomit or anything else that's in the way.

● **B Breathing** Check they are breathing by putting your ear close to the victim's mouth. If there's no breath, give mouth-to-mouth resuscitation.

● **C Circulation** Check the heart's beating by feeling for a pulse on the wrist, groin or neck, or by feeling the chest. If there's no pulse, then start cardiac massage. Remember to stanch any wounds that are bleeding profusely (if it's arterial blood – red and spurting – press heavily on the bleeding point for 10 minutes, then apply a crepe bandage. Raise the wounded area above the level of the heart).

If the injury is serious and you need trained medical help you'll have to get the casualty out because there are no doctors on the remoter regions of this trail. Strap up suspected broken bones, try to keep the person as immobile and as warm as possible and ask the locals for help.

Animal bites
● **Rabid animals** If you get bitten by a dog, bat or other similar animal, there's a risk of contracting **rabies**, so wash out the wound with copious amounts of soap and water. Use a stiff brush if you have one, and get into the corners of the wound even if it hurts, then disinfect. Seek medical help as quickly as possible – there's a rabies centre in Lima (see p106).

● **Snakes** You are very unlikely to get bitten by a snake. If you do, don't try sucking the venom out or cutting into the wound. Keep still, wash the wound and surrounding skin with water to remove excess venom. It's reassuring to know that many snakes aren't venomous, and

---

(Opposite) Top: The campesinos won't be the only ones interested in your trekking. **Bottom:** Huinay Huayna (see p182).

many snake bites don't result in venom being injected. Remove any rings, watches or other constrictions because the bitten area may swell.

If you can, capture and kill the snake so it can be identified but make sure it's dead. I read somewhere the story of a paratrooper who was bitten by a snake. His colleagues did all the right things to the victim, caught the snake so that it could be identified by the doctor, beat it to death and stuffed it in a sack. The victim and sack were evacuated by air but in the plane, the 'dead' snake escaped from its sack and bit the pilot.

If a limb's been bitten, splint it, but don't apply a tourniquet unless you know what you're doing. Many limbs are lost through inexpertly applied tourniquets. One of the most important things to do is not to panic, **keep calm**, reassure yourself that even if you're bitten you're unlikely to die. Gene Savoy, the explorer of Vilcabamba, was bitten by a venomous snake forty years ago and he's still not dead.

Extreme heat and cold
● **Hypothermia** A person gets hypothermic when they are extremely cold, and this can kill them. If someone's hypothermic, they'll stumble, be confused, act oddly and be extremely cold to the touch. They may not notice they are ill, so if someone's acting like this warm them up. The best way to do this is to share bodily warmth, as James Bond said in *The Spy Who Loved Me*: strip the victim naked, get undressed yourself and jump into a sleeping bag together.
● **Sun-stroke and sunburn** The tropical sun in the high Andes burns quickly. **Sunburn** can be avoided by covering exposed skin (wear a long-sleeved cotton or linen shirt rather than a T-shirt) and putting sunblock on your face – especially your nose and ears. Always wear a hat.

When a person's temperature has been driven up dangerously high by the sun (usually above 40°C or 104°F), they've got **sun-stroke**. A sunstroke patient will be confused and possibly delirious. Breathing and pulse rate will be rapid (over 30 breaths a minute and a pulse of over 100 beats a minute). Reduce temperature by fanning, gradually cooling them by sponging frequently with a cool damp cloth. If the person loses consciousness you must get them to a doctor quickly.

Not dangerous but irritating
● **Blisters** If you feel skin rubbing, put a piece of moleskin on it or some of the new Second Skin (Compeed) you can buy in pharmacies. If you've got a blister you can burst it with a sterilised needle (hold it in a flame for a few seconds) then cover it with a sterile dressing. Alternatively cover the unbroken blister with a build-up of moleskin.
● **Cracked skin and lips** Carry moisturising cream and lip balm. Some people find the skin pulling back from their nails and cracking – it grows back when you descend to lower altitudes.

Cook it, peel it, wash it or forget it

Many of the bugs that travellers pick up come from dirty water or food that's been prepared by someone with dirty hands. The key to avoiding getting these diseases is hygiene, but that's not something you're going to have complete control over. If you are doubtful about something you're offered to eat – if it's had flies on it, if it's not piping hot, if it's raw – then leave it. The travellers' golden rule is if you can't cook it, peel it, wash it (in purified water) then forget it. Sadly that means that you should avoid ceviche (it's raw fish), which is a shame because it's a wonderful dish. I'm not encouraging you to go against sensible medical advice but it's worth saying that if you leave Peru without eating ceviche, you're missing out. If you do try it, perhaps wait until after you've been trekking.

Water purification

When you're hiking, you should purify your water unless you're getting it from a spring right at the top of a valley, as humans and livestock upstream from you are probably polluting it. There are a number of ways of doing this. You can use iodine tablets or drops, a water filter, or you can do it by boiling.
● **Iodine tablets** If you use tablets, use iodine not chlorine, as bugs like giardia aren't killed by chlorination. However, you shouldn't use iodine at all if you've got a thyroid problem, and it's not good for anyone to use it for long periods of time. It makes the water taste disgusting but you can add Vitamin C tablets or flavoured fruit powders to neutralise the taste. There are a number of brands on the market in the West (eg Potable Aqua and MicroPur). One tablet purifies a litre of water in about ten minutes.
● **Iodine drops** Using a 2% solution (Tinture of Iodine), the dose is 5 drops per litre of clean water which must then stand for 20-30 minutes. If the water is cloudy double the dose. You need a dropper to dispense the correct dose. Wrap the bottle and dropper in more than one plastic bag. An iodine leak in the centre of a pack can be a very messy business.
● **Water filter** This is a portable device that chemically or mechanically removes impurities from water, but they're expensive, and mechanical filters don't clean the water thoroughly enough to be much use.
● **Boiling** Current research shows that water need be brought only to the boil (even at altitude) to kill the bugs in it so drinks made from boiling water are generally safe.

Diseases from other people's filth

● **Diarrhoea** Despite the best precautions, just about everyone gets the 'Inca Two Step' in Peru. It's nothing to worry about, though.

   Don't plug yourself up immediately with Imodium: if your body wants to get rid of the contents of your bowels, let it. Drink lots of (uncontaminated) fluids: take a little weak soup or flat soft drinks, have some camomile tea with sugar and if you have re-hydrating powders, use them now. Only block yourself up if you have to travel or are becoming seriously dehydrated; avoid travelling if you can because it's best to rest for a couple of days. Be reassured that most of these attacks pass. However, if you're not better after 2-3 days, or if you get worse, you should try to see a doctor as you could have one of the following:

● **Dysentery** Dysentery is caused by drinking infected water or eating contaminated foods. It feels like diarrhoea with stomach cramps, and you may have blood in your faeces. Dysentery is treatable, but amoebic dysentery can cause difficulties if it's not caught.

● **Giardiasis** Giardiasis (giardia) is caused by eating or drinking giardia parasites that live in dirty water and food. The symptoms are foul smelling belches and wind and a distended belly. It often goes away on its own, but if it doesn't it's easily treatable by a doctor.

● **Cholera** Transmitted in a similar way, cholera is rare in travellers. It mostly afflicts those who live in poor conditions where there's little fresh water and is easily treatable.

Things not to worry about

I'm writing this last bit, not because you're in the least likely to come across any of these diseases, but to give you something to read on the bus.

● **Chagas disease** This is a rare, insect-borne disease transmitted by the bite of the assassin bug. The colourfully-named insect lives in the walls and roof of rustic huts, and comes out at night to feed on you. When it bites your skin, it tramples its faeces into the puncture hole and with the faeces go the germ that causes the disease. The bite hurts, so you'll know you've been bitten. If you're unlucky enough to be infected, the bite will swell and become inflamed. If this happens, get a blood test because the symptoms don't begin to appear properly for some years, by which time they're difficult to treat. Interesting fact about Chagas disease: Charles Darwin died from it, aged 73.

● **Leishmaniasis** This disease is transmitted by sandflies, and causes ulcers, most of which heal painlessly – but some don't. Interesting fact about leishmaniasis: this is the disease you can see afflicting some of the subjects of Moche pots who look like Boris Karloff. Obviously the people portrayed in the pots suffered from the unhealing kind of ulcer.

● **Oroya (verruga) fever** This is another rare disease, caused by the bite of the phlebotomus sandfly which lives only on Andean slopes between 800m and 2600m (2625ft and 8525ft). It's easily treatable with antibiotics, but if not caught will cause death by breaking down your red blood cells. The symptoms are bone and muscle pain, and anaemia. Interesting fact about Oroya fever: it's extremely rare, but everyone who gets a touch of fever thinks they've got it.

PART 7: TRAIL GUIDE AND MAPS

Using this guide

ROUTE DESCRIPTIONS

In the route descriptions which follow, directions are given as a compass point and an indication of whether you need to go right or left. An example might read: 'turn north (R)' which means north is to your right, or 'turn left (W)' which means left is a westerly direction.

Direction

On all the trails except three you can walk in the opposite direction to the one given here. The exceptions are that you're not allowed to start at Machu Picchu and walk to Huayllabamba, or to Chachabamba (Km104), and it wouldn't be sensible to do the Chilca Circuit in reverse because you'd have to pay the Inca Trail fee without actually walking it.

ROUTE MAPS

(See pp22-3 for Route Planning map)

Scale and walking times

These maps are drawn to an approximate scale of 1:50,000 (20mm to one kilometre). Remember that much of the walking is up and downhill, and the mere length of a trail is no indication of how long it's going to take you. Walking time is of greater interest to the hiker. In the margin of the maps, you'll see the time it takes to get from one '▲' to the next '▲'. Timings usually run in both directions and are approximate: some people are going to walk much faster, and some slower than I did. If you've got a mule to carry your kit, you'll take only about a half to three quarters of the time given.

Note that **the time given refers only to time spent actually walking,** so you will need to add more time to allow for rest stops. This will obviously vary from person to person but as a rough guide add 20-30% to allow for stops.

Up or down?

The trail is shown as a dotted line. Many of the trails are up or down. One arrow indicates a steep slope; two arrows indicate a very steep slope. Note that the arrow points towards the higher part of the trail. If, for

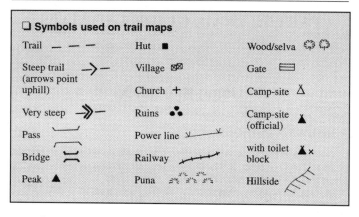

❏ **Symbols used on trail maps**

Trail — — —	Hut ■	Wood/selva 🌳 🌳
Steep trail →— (arrows point uphill)	Village	Gate
	Church +	Camp-site △
Very steep →»—	Ruins ••	Camp-site (official) ▲
Pass	Power line ⌄—⌄	
Bridge	Railway	with toilet block ▲×
Peak ▲	Puna	Hillside

example, you were walking from A (at 900m) to B (at 1100m) and the trail between the two were short and very steep, it would be shown thus: A - - - >> - - - B.

Altitudes
The altitudes in this book were taken from GPS and altimeter readings and have an average margin of error of +/– 150m.

Place names
Quechua words can be spelt in a number of different ways. In this section of the guide, places are spelt in the Hispanic way, because it's more familiar and because that's the spelling used on most maps.

Some places have more than one name: for example, Ancascocha is Silque on some maps, Patallacta is sometimes called Llactapata, and Paucarcancha often goes under the name of Inca Raccay ('raccay' means 'ruin' in Quechua, so 'Inca Raccay' indicates any Inca ruins). Where there's a potential cause for confusion I've given all the names.

Practicalities

FOOD AND WATER

Many of the smaller streams shown on the maps are seasonal and may be dry when you walk, so you should carry more water than you think you need. Note that there's **nowhere to buy food on these trails**: you need to carry everything you're going to eat.

TICKETS AND PRICES

The Classic Inca trail (Km88) and the trails from Km82, Mollepata, and Chilca cost US$17. The Km104 trail is US$12. (All half price with ISIC card).

On all trails except the Mollepata hike there's a checkpoint near the start of the trail where you buy your ticket; keep it safe as you'll be asked to produce it when you reach Machu Picchu. On the Mollepata run you buy your ticket at Machu Picchu.

GETTING TO THE TRAIL HEADS

The train from Cuzco to Machu Picchu leaves regularly each day from San Pedro station (see p142). It stops en route at Chilca, and Kms 82, 88 and 104.

Buses to Mollepata leave from Cuzco's Calle Arcopata at 4am. The later 5am bus to Abancay from the same place can drop you at the bottom of a track that leads up to Mollepata – both buses charge s/2. These details change often, so ask at your hotel for the latest information (don't trust what they tell you at the tourist information office because they often get it wrong).

The classic Inca Trail

Starting through the eucalyptus forest on the banks of the Urubamba river, the trail quickly turns into a steep series of climbs and descents. There are three passes to go over, the highest being 4200m (13,750ft) and it takes three to four days to reach Machu Picchu.

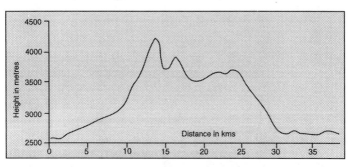

**How high you'll climb and how far you'll walk
Km88 to Machu Picchu**

❏ **Walking times on trail maps**
Note that on all the trail maps in this book the times shown alongside each
map refer only to **time spent actually walking**. When planning your walking
for the day you should add about 20-30% to allow for rest stops.

KM88 → HUAYLLABAMBA [MAP 1]

Km88 to Patallacta

The train stops very briefly at **Km88** – watch the kilometre markers by
the side of the railway or ask someone to tell you when it's near so you
can be prepared to gather your kit and make your way to the doors. Jump
off, pass along the tracks in the direction the train's been going (W) and
follow a little path down to the river, where you'll find a **bridge** and a
park warden's booth. Here you pay the trail fee. Km88 is sometimes
known by its Quechua name, Corihuayrachina.

Across the bridge, you can go either left (E) or right (W). To the right
there's a detour to the seldom-visited ruins of **Huayna Quente** and
Machu Quente (see below), a 20-minute walk away. The main trail goes

❏ **Huayna Quente and Machu Quente**
The people who lived by the Urubamba before the coming of the Incas never
ventured further downriver than the site of Huayna Quente and Machu
Quente, and no sign of their settlements has been found beyond these sites.
This all changed after the Inca Pachacutec conquered this region (see p80),
and the Incas drove roads along both the north and the south banks of the
Urubamba river, deep into the Amazon rain forest. Huayna Quente and
Machu Quente were two sites along the southern road, and like most of the
sites on the Inca Trail were some sort of combination of a tambo (an inn or
waystation), a gateway, a religious site and an agricultural station.

Huayna Quente was the more important and built in a different style
from the sites further upstream of Patallacta and Huillca Raccay (see p187).
Huayna Quente in some ways resembles Machu Picchu itself, built with fine
stonework and after intricate planning. Scholars think it was built around the
end of Pachacutec's reign, or at the beginning of the reign of his successor,
Tupac Yupanqui (Topa Inca), in the second half of the fifteenth century. This
high-status stonework suggests that it was primarily a small pilgrimage centre on a road to Machu Picchu. Its two stone baths were associated with the
ritual worship of water, and its two sacred rocks and a sacred cavern were
huacas (sacred spots). Like most of the Inca sites on the trail it was probably
self-sufficient agriculturally – it might even have exported some maize – and
it's surrounded by extensive terraces and canal systems. Thirty-four thousand
square metres of terracing has been uncovered.

Machu Quente is much less interesting, and seems to have been a more
utilitarian agricultural site; there is also a large building that could have been
a barracks.

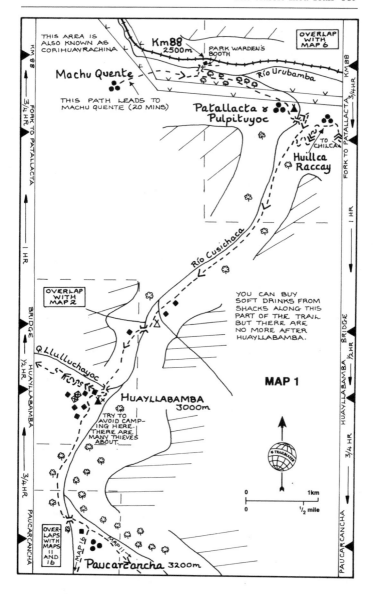

THIS AREA IS ALSO KNOWN AS CORIHUAYRACHINA

Km88 2500m

PARK WARDEN'S BOOTH

OVERLAP WITH MAP 6

Machu Quente

Río Urubamba

THIS PATH LEADS TO MACHU QUENTE (20 MINS)

Patallacta & Pulpituyoc

TO CHILCA

Huillca Raccay

Río Cusichaca

OVERLAP WITH MAP 2

YOU CAN BUY SOFT DRINKS FROM SHACKS ALONG THIS PART OF THE TRAIL BUT THERE ARE NO MORE AFTER HUAYLLABAMBA.

Q.Llulluchayoc

MAP 1

Huayllabamba 3000m

TRY TO AVOID CAMP-ING HERE. THERE ARE MANY THIEVES ABOUT.

0   1km
0   ½ mile

© TRAILBLAZER

OVER-LAPS WITH MAPS 11 AND 16

Paucarcancha 3200m

KM 88
¾ HR.
FORK TO PATALLACTA
1 HR.
BRIDGE
HUAYLLABAMBA ½ HR.
¾ HR.
PAUCARCANCHA

KM 88
¾ HR.
FORK TO PATALLACTA
1 HR.
BRIDGE
HUAYLLABAMBA ½ HR.
¾ HR.
PAUCARCANCHA

❑ **Patallacta and Pulpituyoc**

Patallacta is one the largest and most important sites in the whole area. It was first discovered by Hiram Bingham in 1911 and, while it was excavated when Bingham returned in 1915, most work on the area has been done in the past twenty years by Dr Ann Kendall and the Cusichaca Trust; you can see the results in the museum at Ollantaytambo.

Patallacta was primarily an agricultural station set amongst extensive terraced land that was used for growing maize, the staple of the Incas, and it supplied Machu Picchu and Ollantaytambo with part of their food. It's also near the high altitude lands up the Cusichaca river where potatoes and other root crops were grown, produce that probably made its way through Patallacta for shipment to other parts of the district. In its buildings lived the labour that tended the fields, both local and *mit'a* workers, and the soldiers who manned the hill fort of Huillca Raccay (see p187). It was probably built around 1450 as it's a classical Inca settlement, and it consists of one hundred and sixteen buildings and five baths, all laid out on a regular pattern. The main canal that fed the town's baths fell into disuse shortly after the Spanish conquest, which suggests that Patallacta was abandoned around 1540.

The other function of Patallacta was strategic. Inca roads run along both the north and the south banks of the Urubamba and up the Cusichaca, and Patallacta was built at this major road junction rather as Birmingham in England grew up at another major transport intersection. Built where it was, Patallacta could provide a reservoir of loyal Incas producing food for the region at this strategically important cross-roads.

Pulpituyoc is the religious or ceremonial complex of Patallacta, and consists of eleven buildings, two baths and a carved rock. Unlike Patallacta, Pulpituyoc was built on virgin ground, uninhabited before the arrival of the Incas. The exact nature of the religion or ceremonies carried out at Pulpituyoc remains a mystery.

---

off to the left (E), following the southern banks of the Urubamba through a eucalyptus forest. After three quarters of an hour you'll reach the valley of the **Cusichaca river** and the extensive ruins of **Patallacta** (see above) where you can *camp*. (On some maps Patallacta is shown as Llactapata). The small round tower on the ridge by the river is called **Pulpituyoc** which means 'containing a pulpit'. The Incas built only round walls when a building was particularly significant, so this was an important place.

Patallacta to Huayllabamba

Passing by the foot of Patallacta, the trail crosses over the Cusichaca and hairpins up the opposite slope. It's a bit steep here, a foretaste of the rest of the trail. It settles on the eastern bank, and you begin to follow the Cusichaca towards Huayllabamba. Ten to fifteen minutes after you enter the Cusichaca valley, you'll see a path joining from the left (W); this leads to Huillca Raccay and on towards Chilca (see p186).

After about an hour of gentle but steady climbing, you'll come to a **bridge** over the river. Just before the bridge there are huts from which you can buy soft drinks. Half an hour after the bridge you cross a bridge over a tributary of the Cusichaca, the Llulluchayoc, and arrive on the outskirts of **Huayllabamba**.

Huayllabamba is the largest village you'll pass through, and it's the last place where you can buy anything before the Trekkers' Hotel at Huinay Huayna. It's also a place you can hire porters. There is a *campsite* here, but people who've slept here have had things stolen (the SAEC – see p106 – report a person being physically attacked in 1997) so it's best to press on up the trail and camp somewhere else.

HUAYLLABAMBA → PACAMAYO CAMP   [MAP 2 p172]

Huayllabamba to Llulluchapampa camp-site
From the bridge over the Llulluchayoc the path heads uphill on the river's left-hand (S/W) bank; it doesn't go down through Huayllabamba itself. It hairpins and gets very steep, and after a pretty exhausting hour you reach a pleasant *camp-site* which has a river running close by. Just before this there's a **fork** with a rusty signpost pointing up to the left (W): take the right (N) fork.

Pass through the camp-site and over a **bridge** across a river called the Chaupihuayjo on some maps, Huayruro on others. Then head steeply uphill through a clearing, before ending up following the left-hand (S/W) bank of the Llulluchayoc as it veers to the west. You'll soon enter a beautiful **cloud forest** or *polylepis* woodland, rare in the Andes because it's self-contained. The path climbs steeply up an exhaustingly large number of steps, following the river up through the wood, at times going right down to the river, at times rising up the valley side away from it.

A little under two hours from the camp-site by the river there are another two *camp-sites*. The first is just inside the forest, but if you keep walking for another 20 minutes, just beyond the edge of the forest you'll reach another: **Llulluchapampa.** This is a much better place to camp, with running water and wonderful views down the valley. There's also a toilet block here, which is on the top tier of camp-sites, just by the thatched shelter with a cross on top.

Llulluchapampa to Dead Woman Pass/Abra de Huarmihuanusca
You can see the first pass – no one knows who the dead woman was – from Llulluchapampa. It looks deceptively close but in fact it's a gruelling one and a half hours' walk. The trail runs parallel to the river and climbs up into the hills above the river's spring, through windy puna, over the newly-laid paving that protects the mountain from erosion.

Dead Woman Pass to Pacamayo camp
Here begins the first of three tiring descents you'll face on the trail, considerable strain on your knees as you go down 800m (2624ft) over about

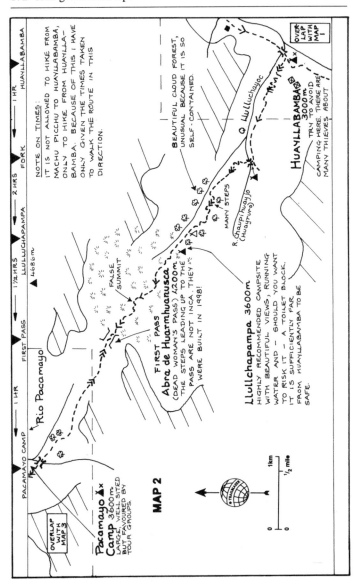

NOTE ON TIMES:

IT IS NOT ALLOWED TO HIKE FROM MACHU PICCHU TO HUAYLLABAMBA, ONLY TO HIKE FROM HUAYLLA- BAMBA. BECAUSE OF THIS I HAVE ONLY GIVEN THE TIMES TAKEN TO WALK THE ROUTE IN THIS DIRECTION.

BEAUTIFUL CLOUD FOREST, UNUSUAL BECAUSE IT IS SO SELF-CONTAINED.

Huayllabamba 3000m. TRY TO AVOID CAMPING HERE. THERE ARE MANY THIEVES ABOUT

First Pass
Abra de Huarmihuañusca
(DEAD WOMAN'S PASS) 4200m
THE STEPS LEADING UP TO THE PASS ARE NOT INCA, THEY WERE BUILT IN 1998!

MANY STEPS

R. Chaupihuayjo
(Huayruro)

Llullchapampa 3600m.
HIGHLY RECOMMENDED CAMPSITE WITH BEAUTIFUL VIEWS, RUNNING WATER AND — SHOULD YOU WANT TO RISK IT — A TOILET BLOCK. IT IS SUFFICIENTLY FAR FROM HUAYLLABAMBA TO BE SAFE.

Pacamayo Camp 3600m.
LARGE, WELL SITED BUT FAVOURED BY TOUR GROUPS.

OVERLAP WITH MAP 3

Rio Pacamayo

FALSE SUMMIT

Llulluchayoc

OVERLAP WITH MAP 1

4686m

PACAMAYO CAMP — 1 HR — FIRST PASS — 1 HR — LLULLUCHAPAMPA — 1½ HRS — 2 HRS — FORK — 1 HR — HUAYLLABAMBA

MAP 2

1km
½ mile
0

TRAILBLAZER

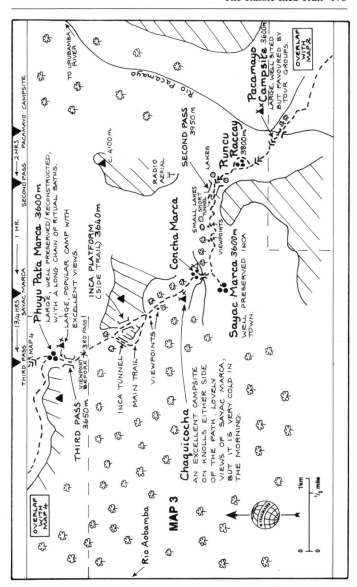

1¹/₄ miles. At the bottom there's a very large *camp-site*, nestling in some trees on the floor of the valley of the river Pacamayo. There's a toilet block here, and it's large so it's a favourite place for tours. It's a good idea to fill your water bottles at the stream here as the water from here to Sayac Marca can be unreliable and brackish.

PACAMAYO CAMP → THE THIRD PASS   [MAP 3 p173]

Pacamayo camp to the second pass
From the Pacamayo camp the path climbs very steeply up a series of **steps**; you'll be glad to pause every now and then at viewpoints over the valley below. After about an hour, you reach the Inca ruins of **Runcu Raccay**, a circular structure with a rectangular outbuilding. This was probably a tambo, where chasquis rested, but some think it was a guard post, or even because of the circular walls, a ritual building.

The second pass (sometimes called Abra de Runcu Raccay) isn't far now but there are a couple of **false summits** to get over first. Just before the real pass there are a couple of **lakes**, beside which you can *camp*. Down by the lakes there's a sign saying 'Deer Area', though if you see any deer these days, you'll be very lucky.

The second pass to Sayac Marca
From the second pass the trail heads generally eastwards. It passes through a short tunnel, the first of two on the route, and begins to switchback steeply as it descends to a small viewpoint, after which it descends more gently. To your right (N), you'll see some lakes and in front (W), clouds permitting, you'll see Sayac Marca. The trail descends quite steeply again, and just before it makes a hairpin bend, there's a staircase going up on the left (SW). About 50 metres (150ft) up this staircase lies **Sayac Marca** (see p176).

Sayac Marca to the third pass
In the shadow of Sayac Marca, tucked away in a little valley, is the small Inca dwelling of **Concha Marca**. There's a stream nearby, and it's a good place to fill up with water as there are no more streams until the third pass, but in the interests of health make sure you purify your water carefully because there's a small *camp-site* here, and the stream could be contaminated.

The section of trail from here to the third pass is very, very beautiful. The paving is for the most part original Inca, and the path crosses high stone embankments as it skirts deep precipices. You're enclosed in a cathedral of forest. If you find yourself walking this part of the trail in the mist, it's a sensible idea to camp and wait for the weather to clear: it's such a wonderful view, missing it would be a crime. There's a good *camp-site* about 20 minutes' walk from Sayac Marca, called

Chaquicocha, where there's a toilet block and space for about 15 tents on grassy knolls either side of the path.

Just after Chaquicocha the path heads steeply uphill and passes two **viewpoints**. Near the second viewpoint a side trail heads off the main path to the right (N). This path returns to the main route about a kilometre (half a mile) further on, but it bypasses the main Inca tunnel so few people take it and it's now very overgrown. It leads to a pleasant remote platform before descending again to the main trail.

❑ **Runcu Raccay**

The small, circular site of Runcu Raccay was discovered by Hiram Bingham when he was searching out the entrance roads to Machu Picchu. He considered it to be a fortress, dominating the highway.

It was explored in more detail in 1940 by Dr Paul Fejos, who thought it was a tambo, a rest-place for passing travellers. In design it's a transitional building, a bridge between the practical styles of the Cusichaca river and the more elaborate designs of Machu Picchu and the Cedrobamba sites (Cedrobamba is the name given to the areas around Machu Picchu).

It's interesting to note that the ruins of the Inca Trail were excavated during two periods when the northern nations of the world were embarking on the two most murderous wars in history. Bingham's second expedition was digging quietly in these hills in 1915 while the fields of Flanders were soaked in blood, and Fejos was busy excavating these ruins in 1940.

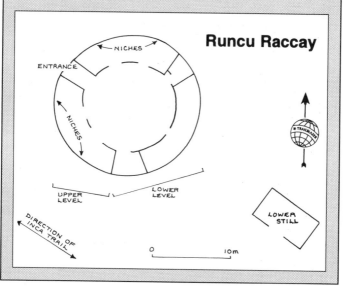

The main trail skirts a spur, turning from the north-west to the north-east. It descends, going through an impressive **Inca tunnel**, before climbing again to the third pass. A little before the third pass you'll reach a spot from which you can see down to two different river valleys, the Urubamba and the Aobamba. It's a spectacular view. Just after this is a large *camp-site*, right on the top of the pass. It's a beautiful spot.

❏ Sayac Marca and Concha Marca

Sayac Marca was discovered by Hiram Bingham when he followed an Inca road across the hills from Machu Picchu, but the name Sayac Marca was coined by the Fejos expedition in the 1940s. Bingham's half-Spanish, half-Quechua name for these ruins, Cedrobamba (Cedar Plain), actually refers to the elongated spur on which all the sites close to Machu Picchu are built. Fejos changed the name to Inaccessible Town, a name that describes the position of the ruins perfectly, protected as they are on three sides by a precipice that descends to the dense jungle of the valley of the river Aobamba below.

The dramatic setting of Sayac Marca was no accident as it's built at a fork in the old Inca road. Today's Inca Trail follows one fork to Machu Picchu, but the other fork descends to the bottom of the Aobamba valley. From here it's been traced up the other side of the valley, where it passes through some ruins called Llactapata, and then descends to the Santa Teresa river. Here it climbs again to more ruins, Ochopata, about 15km from Sayac Marca, and then it becomes lost in the jungle. This road is completely overgrown these days, and you shouldn't attempt to follow it without a map, compass and experience in jungle hiking.

There is some very impressive stonework here, indicating that this was an important place. Look for what Bingham called 'eye-bonders', holes drilled in corners of buildings and edges of walls, which were used for securing roofs of thatch (you can see reconstructions of Inca roofs in Machu Picchu). Notice also the characteristic way that the Incas incorporated and emphasised the natural features on which they built – a large outcrop is the unadorned centrepiece of Sayac Marca, and the whole structure is built on and emphasises a prow of rock.

Bingham thought that Sayac Marca was a fortified outpost of Machu Picchu, but Fejos wasn't so sure, saying that if the Incas wanted to build fortifications they could do a much more impressive job – he takes Sacsayhuaman as an example. Nevertheless it's unlikely that the site was a tambo (as were the nearby buildings of **Concha Marca** with their small terrace system): there isn't enough agricultural land for Sayac Marca to be a farming outpost, nor is the stonework impressive enough for it to be a religious centre. No one has come up with a conclusive answer as to what the ruins were.

While the function of Sayac Marca isn't clear, the date when it was constructed is more certain. The planning of the site is elaborate; the layout is flexible and responds to the terrain, which makes archaeologists think it was built after the classical period of Inca construction, and the ruins are dated to the last half of the fifteenth century.

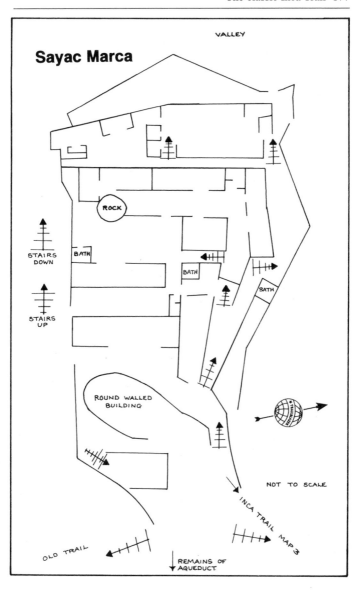

Sayac Marca

THE THIRD PASS → MACHU PICCHU   [MAP 4]

Phuyu Pata Marca

The other side of the pass there's the most impressive Inca site yet: **Phuyu Pata Marca**. Once more, this name comes from the Fejos expedition, and it means 'Cloud-Level Town'. The name's well chosen: you'll often see banks of clouds billow over this pass and you may be engulfed in a field of seamless white. It was once a remote, magical place, but it's surrounded by a large *camp-site* now which makes it lose much of its mystery.

Look for the six 'Inca baths' which you'll walk through on your way to the ruins. Despite the name, these are probably not baths, or even public hydrants, which is what Bingham thought they were. More likely they are a feature of ritual worship of water, and there are similar structures at Huinay Huayna, Tambo Machay (see p147) and Machu Picchu itself. The stonework you'll see in Phuyu Pata Marca is by far the most impressive you've come across so far, but it will get even better.

From Phuyu Pata Marca, there are **two options**: the usual route and the less travelled old route.

❏ **Phuyu Pata Marca**

Phuyu Pata Marca is another site that was discovered by Bingham but fully excavated by Fejos. When Bingham passed by, all he noted were the baths and the tops of some of the walls of the upper-most buildings; everything else was covered by the jungle. When Fejos set about digging he discovered a much larger and much more important site than Bingham had ever imagined existed, and in two months of work he managed only partially to clear the area. He discovered two plazas, four house groups and one intriguing house hidden in a terrace, discoverable only by a door in the terrace wall (it's to the east of the site near the lower road).

Phuyu Pata Marca, like Sayac Marca is built in a late Inca style, when the formalism of classical Inca planning had given way to a more fluid style. Archaeologists think that it was put up late in Pachacutec's reign or early in that of his his successor, Tupac Yupanqui (Topa Inca), late in the fifteenth century. The stonework on the upper terrace is particularly fine, with a wall where the stones are almost perfectly slotted together. Towards the bottom of the site, to the north-west, there is a group of caves that have been enlarged and extended by the Incas. When they were discovered the roofs were blackened and the floors were covered with a thick layer of ash, but all this was recent not related to the Incas. Only a few Inca remains were found, pottery of a plain type used for cooking.

Phuyu Pata Marca's function, like that of Sayac Marca, is unclear but the fountain of baths suggests that the site was associated with the ritual worship of water, and perhaps it was a place for ritual cleansing on the final leg to Machu Picchu. It could also, of course, have been a guard settlement, or a remote hunting lodge of the Inca's.

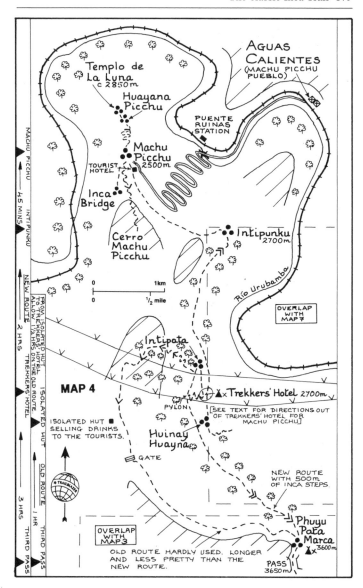

AGUAS
CALIENTES
(MACHU PICCHU
PUEBLO)

Templo de
La Luna
c 2850m

Huayana
Picchu

PUENTE
RUINAS
STATION

Machu
Picchu
2500m

TOURIST
HOTEL

Inca
Bridge

Intipunku
2700m

Cerro
Machu
Picchu

Río Urubamba

0   1km

0   ½ mile

OVERLAP
WITH
MAP 7

MACHU PICCHU ← 45 MINS INTIPUNKU

NEW ROUTE 2 HRS TREKKERS' HOTEL

FROM ISOLATED HUT
TO TREKKERS' HOTEL
ALLOW 1½ HRS ON THE OLD ROUTE

ISOLATED HUT

Intipata

MAP 4

✕ Trekkers' Hotel 2700m

PYLON

[SEE TEXT FOR DIRECTIONS OUT
OF TREKKERS' HOTEL FOR
MACHU PICCHU]

ISOLATED HUT ■
SELLING DRINKS
TO THE TOURISTS.

Huinay
Huayna

GATE

→ TRAILBLAZER

OLD ROUTE 3 HRS THIRD PASS

NEW ROUTE
WITH 500m
OF INCA STEPS.

OLD ROUTE 1 HR THIRD PASS

OVERLAP
WITH
MAP 3

OLD ROUTE HARDLY USED. LONGER
AND LESS PRETTY THAN THE
NEW ROUTE.

Phuyu
Pata
Marca
✕ 3600m

PASS
3650m

❏ **Walking times on trail maps**
Note that on all the trail maps in this book the times shown alongside each map refer only to **time spent actually walking**. When planning your walking for the day you should add about 20-30% to allow for rest stops.

The usual route

This takes you down the most impressive flight of Inca steps on the entire trail. The Incas turned a 500m (1500ft) hillside into a staircase. Be careful of your knees, which will feel the strain by the end of the day. It will take about three hours to reach the Trekkers' Hotel, and you'll pass through increasingly dense forest as the path twists and turns its way down. This is a lovely walk.

To get to 'the usual route', walk to the other side (W) of Phuyu Pata Marca from the baths. There you'll see **descending stairs**; this is where you start. There's usually a beaten path to this spot around the lower terraces of the ruins.

After about an hour, you'll be able to see the tin roof of the Trekkers' Hotel: a monstrous incongruity in the virgin forest. This is where the trail is heading. After about 2½ hours, you'll reach a **pylon** just off the trail. A path descends east (R) from this pylon, switch-backing steeply as it loses a lot of height, and heading towards the hotel itself. The main path that continues on under the wires leads to the Inca site, **Intipata**.

❏ **Intipata**
Intipata is once more being abandoned to the jungle. It was cleared, and discovered to be an extensive terrace system, but as the habitat of a rare species of orchid it is now being allowed to sink back into the forest. This would no doubt disappoint Dr Fejos, who in 1940 spent four months clearing over 40,000 square metres of the forest, discovering and mapping forty-eight of the site's terraces. Despite these four months Dr Fejos didn't feel he'd discovered everything and was sure that there were many more terraces. In his record of the expedition he describes Intipata, almost despairingly, as 'extending indefinitely to the south'. Like Phuyu Pata Marca, three of Intipata's terraces are hollow and hide what Fejos called 'terrace houses'.

The name Intipata was thought up by a member of his expedition, and means Sunny Slope. Not only because of the number of terraces, but also because of the absence of plazas, religious structures or fortifications, there's little doubt that Intipata was primarily an agricultural settlement, but it probably had a strategic function as well. From Intipata you can see across to the lookout platform on the top of Cerro Machu Picchu, and down to the Inca site of Choquesuysuy. Messages could be transmitted to mountain city of Machu Picchu from the floor of the Urubamba below through the lookout point on the top of Intipata.

The route less travelled
This used to be the route everyone took until the Inca staircase mentioned above was discovered about 20 years ago. This route adds another couple of kilometres (one mile or so) to the total length of the trail, but you do get a stunning view of Machu Picchu in the valley a kilometre below.

This path also leaves Phuyu Pata Marca from the west but instead of heading downhill it stays on the same level as the ruins. (Fill up with water before you leave; there are no streams along the way.) For the first hundred metres along the path you may be tiptoeing through the turds left by inconsiderate campers. Soon you'll be out into the open puna, skirting a small depression and gazing at stupendous views over the Urubamba a good mile below you. After an hour or so, you arrive at a rustic **gate** and, a little further on, a rustic **hut**. The man who lives here sees hardly any tourists and is very welcoming. He sometimes sells drinks and cigarettes. Watch out for his ferocious dog.

From the hut, the Trekkers' Hotel is about an hour further on. Note that the current edition of the SAEC's map is confusing here; I got dreadfully lost trying to follow it. You should head down the spur, under the first set of electricity wires, then the path turns right (E) before you come to the second set of wires. Skirt the forest, go under the second wires, then hairpin down. The jungle gets quite close here, but the path is obvious. You're likely to be the only people on it. Half an hour of descent later, you'll come out on a large, paved trail. Left (N) there's Intipata, right (S) there's the quick route to the Trekkers' Hotel: follow the paved trail, then turn left (E) by the **pylon** after you walk under the second set of electricity wires, and follow the steeply switch-backing path down.

Trekkers' Hotel
The *Trekkers' Hotel* (not to be confused with the expensive, plush Tourists' Hotel at Machu Picchu) isn't a pleasant place. It's all concrete-walled tin shacks, and the place has a bad reputation for theft. It's crowded, smelly and cramped, but it's the **last place where you're allowed to camp** before Machu Picchu – hence it's always full. In high season, tours send porters running along the track before dawn to book sites, so you must get here early in the day to get a decent spot to camp. There's a restaurant here (main course s/10), some beds (s/15 a night) or you can sleep on the floor for a couple of soles. There's also piped water, a lavatory block and a mediocre **museum** full of stuffed animals.

A 10-minute trail leaves from the southern end of the hotel to the ruins of **Huinay Huayna** (see p182), a glorious terraced complex with a flight of 10 baths and some very impressive stonework. It's currently being restored, but that should have been completed when you visit, and it's well worth seeing. If you do come here, don't leave anything valuable in your tent.

❏ Huinay Huayna (Wiñya Wayna)

The name means 'forever young' in Quechua, and the place is named after a pink orchid of that name that grows here.

The similarities between Huinay Huayna and the nearby Intipata are startling, as both are sites where the Incas terraced the whole side of a mountain. Obviously they both were used for growing food, but Huinay Huayna was more important – there are more buildings, the stonework is higher quality and there is a magnificent sequence of fifteen baths. All this suggests that the site was a religious centre, probably associated with the ritual worship of water, although some think it was a high-status hunting lodge where the Inca or his highest caste retainers might escape the trials of public life. The upper terrace, which incorporates some of the largest polygonal blocks in the whole area, contains some particularly fine masonry, and all over the site you'll find gabled houses, exterior pegs used for securing thatch and recessed niches. This, coupled with the flexible way the settlement was planned, suggests that it was built after the classical period of Inca architecture in the latter part of the fifteenth century.

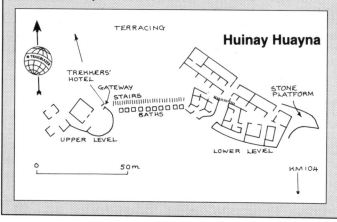

Trekkers' Hotel to Machu Picchu

To see the sun rise over Machu Picchu you'll need get up two hours before dawn to reach **Intipunku** (the gateway of the sun) in time. Machu Picchu is 45 minutes further on. **You are not allowed to camp at Intipunku**.

The only difficult thing about this part of the trail is finding the gate out of the Trekkers' Hotel; look for it before you go to bed to avoid a frantic search in the small hours of the morning. It's in the lower northern corner of the Trekkers' Hotel site: find the three doorless privies and the path that descends from them, and follow that down to an unimposing wooden

❏ **Beware of the Pishtaco**

On your walk in the hills, if you come across a pale gringo wearing a dark robe – beware! He could be a vampire, or as they're known locally, a Pishtaco.

These apparitions were first seen about the time of the conquest. They take the form of pale-skinned strangers, and carry with them a bag of dust, the powdered bones of their victims. They'll creep up on you when you're unaware, and blow this magic powder in your face, rendering you completely insensible. Then they'll drag you off to their lair, where they hang you upside down and let your fat drip into large bowls beneath your body. In the old days, it was said that this human fat that they collected was used to make church bells, now the story goes that it's used to power the space shuttle.

The anthropologist, Robert Randall, has pointed out the myth of Pishtacos has a basis in truth, allbeit allegorical truth. These pale-skinned strangers who kidnapped locals and used their fat are a symbol of the conquering Spanish, who worked the Incas to the bone and used their sweat to grease the wheels of the Spanish Empire.

gate, the gateway to Machu Picchu – a gate which looks as though it leads to the rubbish bins not to one of the greatest archaeological sites on the planet.

The trail from this point is mostly flat. It goes up and down a little, passes a couple of apparently impassable sheer rock faces, before climbing about 14 very steep steps to what you think is Intipunku. It's not. Intipunku is just around the corner, up steps with a more gentle gradient. This is an awe-inspiring approach, the architecture reinforcing your sense of anticipation. When you finally reach **Intipunku**, you look down across the wide bend of the Urubamba and can see, sheltering under the sugar loaf mountain of Huayana Picchu, your journey's end, **Machu Picchu** (see Part 8, p212).

Variations on the classic trail

These variations add an extra half-day to a day to the classic trail by starting further up the Urubamba. You won't see much more from starting at Chilca than you would if you started at Km82.

STARTING AT CHILCA   [MAP 5 p184]

You can reach Chilca by road or by train – most independent travellers go by train but the tour companies drive here. Chilca, also known as Km77,

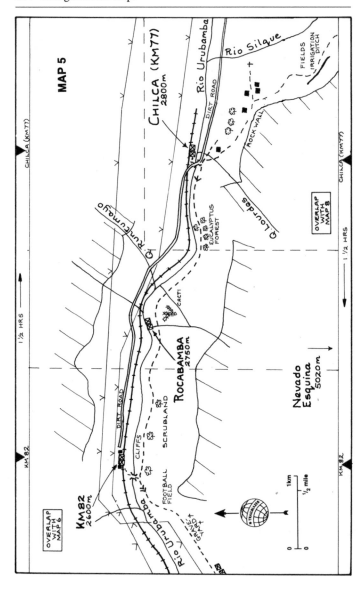

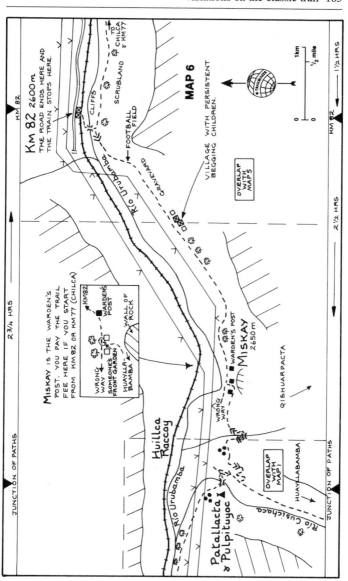

Km 82 2600 m.
THE ROAD ENDS HERE AND
THE TRAIN STOPS HERE.

KM 82

TO CHILCA & KM 77

SCRUBLAND

CLIFFS

FOOTBALL FIELD

Rio Urubamba

GRAVEYARD

MAP 6

VILLAGE WITH PERSISTENT BEGGING CHILDREN.

OVERLAP WITH MAP 5

A TRAILBLAZER

0 1km
0 ½ mile

KM 82

1½ HRS

2½ HRS

2¾ HRS

MISKAY IS THE WARDEN'S POST. YOU PAY THE TRAIL FEE HERE IF YOU START FROM KM 82 OR KM 77 (CHILCA)

KM 82

WARDEN'S POST

WRONG WAY

SOMEONE'S FRONT GARDEN

HUAYLLA-BAMBA

WALL OF ROCK

WARDEN'S POST

MISKAY 2650 m.

WRONG WAY

QISHUARPACTA

Huillca Raccay

Rio Urubamba

Patallacta & Pulpituyoc

OVERLAP WITH MAP 1

HUAYLLABAMBA

Rio Cusichaca

JUNCTION OF PATHS

JUNCTION OF PATHS

is a very small village, but there's more to it than there is to either Km88 or Km82. Make sure you're prepared to get out of the train in good time. The **bridge** across the Urubamba is slightly to the west of where the train stops – travel south through the houses towards the river bank, and you'll see it. Cross the bridge, and turn right (W). The path to Km82 continues west, following the southern bank of the river. It's a steep descent at first, then the trail heads through a eucalyptus forest, before turning northwest. Shortly before you come to the village of **Rocabamba**, where there's a stream, you'll walk through some interesting tree-like cacti. The trail and river then both turn west again, and pass through scrub before heading towards the Km82 bridge. See below for directions from Km82.

STARTING AT KM82   [MAP 6 p185]

Once more, the train only stops briefly at **Km82**, so ask your fellow passengers where to get off and prepare yourself to jump. Walk along the tracks (W), and down towards the river where you'll find a new bridge, which you should cross. (There is a dirt road out to Km82 down which the occasional brave truck makes its way but traffic is rare here.)

On the south side of the Urubamba, turn right (W) and follow the trail as it climbs steeply up from the river. Soon it levels out and passes through a football field following the river's south-westerly course. You walk through a graveyard and a small village full of children who will fearlessly pester you for presents and sweets. Just where the river turns due west again, you'll come to the village of **Miskay**. The park wardens' booth where you pay your trail fee is here.

Just after the booth, you'll come to a place where there's a path heading south off the main trail; apparently going through someone's front garden. Turn left (S) here, heading towards a wall of rock where the trail veers to the right (SW) again.

Follow the path as it goes westward. It soon leads down one side of a deep gully to a stream and then up the other side. Shortly after this you come to the ruins of the Inca hillfort **Huillca Raccay** (see opposite) high above the mouth of the Cusichaca and the extensive site of Patallacta. Huillca Raccay is a very ancient site, and it's been inhabited since 500BC. The Incas, when they conquered the area, took over this place and built a fort here because it commands the entrance to the Cusichaca valley.

From here it's simple to descend to the **main trail from Km88 to Huayllabamba**, which follows the eastern bank of the Cusichaca river though there are lots of paths down through the bush and it's easy to think you've got lost. You'll be fine as long you continue generally west and downhill towards the Cusichaca. You'll soon come to a large, heavily-beaten trail heading north-south. This is the path you want, turn left (south) and follow this trail to Huayllabamba. (**Route continues on p171**).

❏ **Huillca Raccay**

Huillca Raccay is one of the most fascinating sites in the whole area, and one of the earliest, and has been extensively excavated by Dr Ann Kendall. She's discovered that people lived here for many years before the arrival of the Incas, and that it was the first site that the Incas developed when they arrived. They built a fort here, called by some Chuncuchua, and Dr Kendall discovered a nearby site where the builders of the fort lived when they were working on its construction. Judging from modern experiments and archaeological discoveries, the fort itself was erected in just one season.

It's easy to see why the Incas built here. High up in this eyrie, Inca soldiers had an excellent view up and down the Urubamba river and controlled the mouth of the Cusichaca. And if the area had once been a centre of pre-Inca power, the building of an Inca fort was a visual statement of the arrival of the Inca Empire. Later, when Inca control was secure and Patallacta was built (see p170), Huillca Raccay could oversee, protect and control the agricultural settlements below it on the floor of the Urubamba valley.

It's quite a complicated site. Dr Kendall has discovered 37 buildings, including storage lofts, control buildings (gate-houses) and what are possibly barracks, as well as seventy pre-Inca buildings on the tableland behind.

The shorter trail

The attraction of this trail is that it's only a day's walk up a grassy hillside and a couple of hours further to Machu Picchu; it is designed for those who haven't got time to spare.

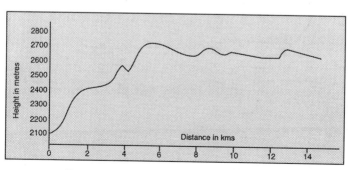

**How high you'll climb and how far you'll walk
Km104 to Machu Picchu**

KM104 → EL CAMINO SAGRADO DEL INCA [MAP 7]

The train pulls up at **Km104**, deep in the selva. Km104 is low, my altimeter read 2100m, and the heat can get oppressive down here on the valley floor. The trail up to Huinay Huayna and the Trekkers' Hotel is mainly across the exposed flank of a mountain with **no shade** and the sun burns and dries you out. The weather is very changeable so bring **rain-gear**. You must take **water**, or you will have a very miserable couple of hours. Fortunately there is a small stream of sweet water at the beginning of the trail where you can fill your water bottles. You are also under a little **time pressure**. The best camp-sites at the Trekkers' Hotel fill up quickly, so if you arrive at sundown you can expect to be left only the grotty spots.

Km104 to Huinay Huayna

As at Km88, the train stops only briefly at Km104, so be prepared to jump out at a moment's notice. The trail heads down to the river to your left (S), but depending where you got off the train you might have to walk a little along the tracks to find the **checkpoint**: a gate that guards the bridge over the river. Here you pay the trail fee.

After crossing the river, the trail heads off to the right (W) towards the ruins of **Chachabamba** (see opposite), then goes south and begins to climb the mountain, entering some pleasant woods, and crossing a stream.

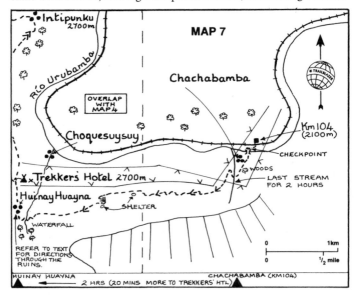

❑ Chachabamba

Chachabamba sits on the old Inca road along the southern bank of the Urubamba river, most of which is lost in the undergrowth. The ruins have been cleared; they were built in a sophisticated style, a style that's more reminiscent of Machu Picchu than of the earlier site of Patallacta. Archaeologists think it dates from the late fifteenth century.

There are both open and closed buildings (three-walled and four-walled), a boulder shrine, 14 baths – one of the largest sequence of baths on the Inca Trail – and a circular stone reservoir, all of which suggests that Chachabamba was an important religious site. This may have been combined with a gate-keeping function, with both Chachabamba and the site of Choquesuysuy lower down the Urubamba guarding this entrance to Machu Picchu.

Chachabamba was uncovered by Dr Paul Fejos in 1940. Before he stumbled across it no one knew it was there, although the railway had already been built along the northern bank of the river.

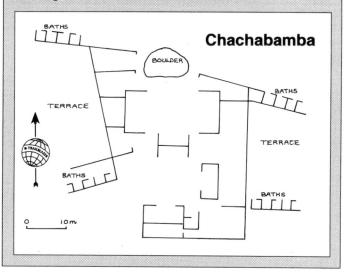

This is a good place to fill up with water. The path then heads westward and upward, leaving the woods for open grassland, soon passing under electricity pylons. The river itself is now far below you to your right (N). After 1½km (just under a mile) you are treated to a sight of the wart that is the Trekkers' Hotel, and a little further on you pass a shelter that's been built by the trail. A little further still and you get your first view of **Huinay Huayna** itself (see p182), an island of stone enshrouded by the deep green of the surrounding forest. Down to the valley floor there's

Choquesuysuy, a site that's currently being excavated. Choquesuysuy is larger and more important than was first thought, and new terraces are still being dug out of the forest. There was an **original Inca trail** from here up to Huinay Huayna, but this cannot be opened to the public because of the closeness of the hydroelectric project that fills up the whole of the valley floor.

The path continues as before west and up, past another shelter, then at last descends into a forest and shade. It rounds a small spur and then reaches a beautiful waterfall and forest. You pass close to Inca walls still lost in the green clutches of the jungle, before stumbling out into clear light at the foot of Huinay Huayna.

Huinay Huayna to the Trekkers' Hotel
To get to the Trekkers' Hotel, pass up the stairway to the urban area of the terraces, follow the stairs off to the right, and then ascend by the series of Inca baths, and turn right (NW). It's a 10-20 minute walk. See p181 for information about the Trekkers' Hotel.

Chilca up the Silque valley

This beautiful walk takes you up the Silque valley, over a 4800m (15,740ft) high pass and down the other side to Huayllabamba, taking in fertile low-lying areas and high puna. It takes six or seven days to get to Machu Picchu.

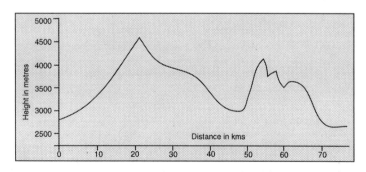

**How high you'll climb and how far you'll walk
Chilca to Machu Picchu**

CHILCA → HALF WAY UP [MAP 8]

You can reach Chilca by road or by train – most independent travellers go by train but the tour companies drive here. **Chilca** (also known as Km77) is a very small village, but there's more to it than Km88 and Km82. Make sure you're prepared to get out of the train in good time. Once you get off

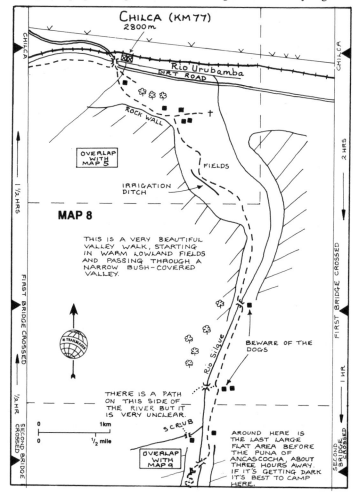

CHILCA (KM77)
2800m

CHILCA

CHILCA

Rio Urubamba

DIRT ROAD

ROCK WALL

†

OVERLAP WITH MAP 5

FIELDS

IRRIGATION DITCH

2 HRS

MAP 8

THIS IS A VERY BEAUTIFUL VALLEY WALK, STARTING IN WARM LOWLAND FIELDS AND PASSING THROUGH A NARROW BUSH-COVERED VALLEY.

½ HRS

FIRST BRIDGE CROSSED

FIRST BRIDGE CROSSED

TRAILBLAZER

Rio Silque

BEWARE OF THE DOGS

1 HR

THERE IS A PATH ON THIS SIDE OF THE RIVER BUT IT IS VERY UNCLEAR.

SCRUB

0   1km
0   ½ mile

½ HR

SECOND BRIDGE CROSSED

OVERLAP WITH MAP 9

AROUND HERE IS THE LAST LARGE FLAT AREA BEFORE THE PUNA OF ANCASCOCHA, ABOUT THREE HOURS AWAY. IF IT'S GETTING DARK IT'S BEST TO CAMP HERE.

SECOND BRIDGE CROSSED

the trail, look south-east and you'll see the valley of the river Silque. This is where you're heading.

The **bridge** across the Urubamba is slightly to the west of where the train stops. Travel south through the houses towards the river bank, and you'll see it. Cross the bridge, and turn left (E), and you'll shortly come to a fork by a hut; take the right-hand, more southerly, fork. A little later the path hugs a rock wall and heads east, then the wall falls away near some huts, and the path forks again. Take the right (more southerly) fork, and head up the valley away from the Urubamba. It's a pleasant walk along tractor ruts through the fields.

After about an hour, the valley begins to narrow and the path turns more to the south. After two hours, you come to a **bridge** over the river, guarded by a hut and ferocious dogs. You need to cross this bridge and get onto the left (E) side of the river. Carry on walking south past a couple more huts, ignore the next bridge you'll see across the river and, an hour after the bridge you crossed over, the path becomes steeper, passes another hut and reaches a third **bridge**. Cross this.

HALFWAY UP → PAST ANCASCOCHA   [MAP 9 p193]

There's no flat place to camp for the next couple of hours, so if it's getting late you should *camp* around here. The path, now on the right-hand side of the river (W), climbs steeply through scrub and hairpins back and forth, before descending to the river again and passing over to the other side (E). It crosses the river five more times before settling for the west (right-hand) bank. This final **bridge** is just above the confluence of the Silque and another river.

Once settled on the western bank, the path climbs steeply up the side of the valley – the floor's pretty flat and you can *camp* there. You'll pass an isolated hut set in mountain fields that almost everyone thinks is Ancascocha (a couple of hours further on) but this is actually **Sayllapata**. You'll know you've really arrived in **Ancascocha** because the village nestles in a flat area of puna at the confluence of three rivers. It's a very small place, so don't expect to be able to buy any provisions here, but it's a good place to *camp* (do make contact with the villagers first – see p157).

Ancascocha to the fork in the rivers

At Ancascocha the path, valley and river all turn to the right (W), and you should cross the river near to some huts – there's a footbridge just by them. The path then climbs gently away from the valley floor, and when

---

(Opposite): Ancient Inca roads still cut through the high grasslands and low jungle.

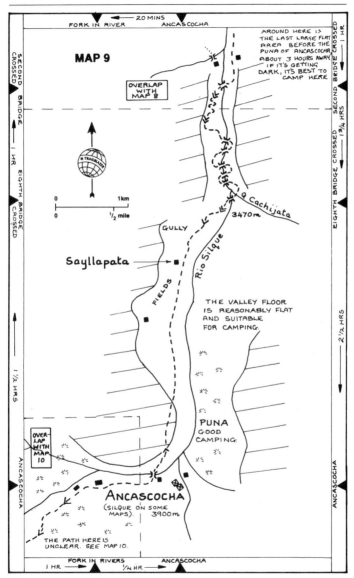

MAP 9

20 MINS
FORK IN RIVER   ANCASCOCHA

AROUND HERE IS THE LAST LARGE FLAT AREA BEFORE THE PUNA OF ANCASCOCHA ABOUT 3 HOURS AWAY. IF IT'S GETTING DARK, IT'S BEST TO CAMP HERE

OVERLAP WITH MAP 8

SECOND BRIDGE CROSSED

EIGHTH BRIDGE CROSSED

SECOND BRIDGE - 1 HR

EIGHTH BRIDGE CROSSED

TRAILBLAZER

0   1km
0   ½ mile

SECOND BRIDGE CROSSED - 1¾ HRS

EIGHTH BRIDGE CROSSED - 1¾ HRS

1 HR

La Cachijata
3470m

GULLY

Sayllapata

Rio Silque

FIELDS

THE VALLEY FLOOR IS REASONABLY FLAT AND SUITABLE FOR CAMPING.

2½ HRS

1½ HRS

PUNA
GOOD CAMPING.

OVERLAP WITH MAP 10

ANCASCOCHA

ANCASCOCHA
(SILQUE ON SOME MAPS).   3900m

ANCASCOCHA

THE PATH HERE IS UNCLEAR. SEE MAP 10.

FORK IN RIVERS   ANCASCOCHA
1 HR   ¼ HR

(Opposite): Below Salcantay on the Mollepata trek (see p206).

the river forks you follow the left hand (S/W) river. The other one leads to some beautiful **waterfalls** (which you can see off to the west across the grassy puna), where it's also possible to *camp*.

PAST ANCASCOCHA → VALLEY TURN   [MAP 10]
The fork in the rivers to the pass (Puerto Huyanay)
From the fork in the rivers you head south-west. The path here is unclear, it's just a collection of braiding cattle-tracks, but as long as you keep ascending gently and heading south-west you're doing fine. After a couple of hours you'll see in front of you a grassy spur which obscures your view – you need to keep on climbing up this at the same rate. On the other side of the spur you'll see some glorious red mountains and you cross a stream that runs from them. You can *camp* here.

The path to the pass doesn't go towards the red mountains, it continues across the side of the scree-slope ahead. Look down to the valley below and you'll see a lake, fed by a waterfall that flows over a cliff to the west. The path heads in the direction of the waterfall, but keeps above it. Soon you'll find yourself overlooking a corrie (cirque), with a small lake on its flat floor. A glacier is poised on the slopes of the mountain that's the other side (N) of the corrie to you. The floor of the corrie is a lovely *camp-site*.

To reach the pass (**Puerto Huyanay**) follow the path as it winds its way up to the head of the corrie – it gets steep and it switchbacks uphill. Just after the head of the corrie you walk across a large scree slope, following a little stream past some tiny lakes. Just a little more to the south-west (an hour and a quarter from the corrie) and you'll come to the pass, marked by an *apachita* (cairn – pile of stones) on a gently sloped puna hillock.

The pass to Inca Raccay
The pass and the area around it is all a bit flat and featureless, and it's easy to get lost up here, especially when the visibility is bad. Use your compass to get the right general direction. The valley you want heads north/north-west from the pass, away from the glacier-clad red mountains to your left. (You need to aim for the far side (W) of the river as you walk downwards and westwards).

There are several trails mostly heading in the right direction but to be on the safe side follow the one that looks most worn, tend to bear left (west) and always go down. You'll know you've got it correct because you'll begin to head south and cross a stream to find what looks like a **derelict hut**, then cross another stream and head off to the north-west. The derelict hut is, in fact, **Inca Raccay** – see p196.

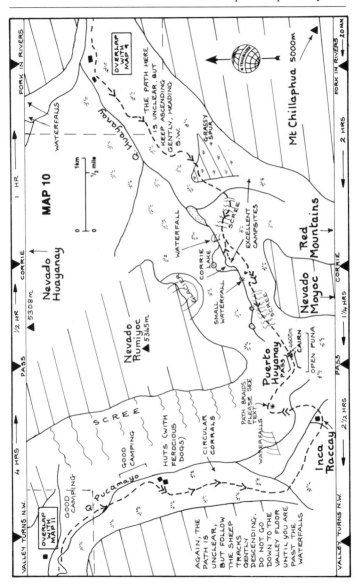

MAP 10

Nevado Huayanay 5308m.

Nevado Rumiyoc 5345m.

Mt Chillahua 5000m.

Red Mountains

Nevado Moyoc

Puerto Huayanay PASS 4600m. CAIRN

Inca Raccay

Q. Huayanay

Q. Pucamayo

OVERLAP WITH MAP 11

OVERLAP WITH MAP 9

THE PATH HERE IS UNCLEAR, BUT KEEP ASCENDING (GENTLY), HEADING S.W.

GRASSY SPUR

SCREE

EXCELLENT CAMPSITES

CORRIE LAKE

WATERFALL

GLACIER

SMALL WATERFALL

SCREE

OPEN PUNA

PATH BRAIDS, PLEASE SEE TEXT

WATERFALLS

SCREE

GOOD CAMPING

HUTS (WITH FEROCIOUS DOGS)

CIRCULAR CORRALS

GOOD CAMPING

WATERFALLS

AGAIN, THE PATH IS UNCLEAR, BUT FOLLOW THE SHEEP TRACKS GENTLY DESCENDING. DO NOT GO DOWN TO THE VALLEY FLOOR UNTIL YOU ARE PAST THE WATERFALLS.

VALLEY TURNS N.W. — 4 HRS — PASS — ½ HR — CORRIE — 1 HR — WATERFALLS — FORK IN RIVERS

VALLEY TURNS N.W. — 2½ HRS — PASS — ¼ HRS — CORRIE — 2 HRS — FORK IN RIVERS — 20 MN

0 1km
0 ½ mile

❏ **Inca Raccay**

Inca Raccay is the first Inca ruin on the old direct road from Cuzco to Machu Picchu, a road that rises from the plain of Anta up to the peaks of Salcantay, before descending along the Quesca river. The ruins don't look very impressive today, but they were originally a tambo – an inn, providing food and shelter to travellers. Remains of watchtowers have also been discovered close by, so it's likely that Inca Raccay was also an outpost which could warn the people of the lush agricultural lands down near the Urubamba river of any danger that came over the pass.

The ruins were constructed to a standardised plan which makes them difficult to date but suggests that they were built before the virtuoso stonework of Machu Picchu and Cedrobamba (the buildings close to Machu Picchu); the first half of the fifteenth century seems likely. Originally there were seven houses, including three large, two-door buildings that contained the storage lofts (marcas) where food and provisions were kept.

Inca Raccay to the turn in the valley

Continuing downhill and north-west from the hut you'll descend gently and, in time, ford another stream. Look back and you can see a high three-tiered waterfall at the head of the valley. Once you can see the waterfall, make your way down to the valley floor over the next couple of kilometres (a mile or so). The path here is once again not clear, and the intersecting cattle tracks are confusing. You should be down on the valley floor by the time you can see a hut by a stream – beware of the dogs who'll bark at you as you stumble downhill. Once on the valley floor, you'll see the path clearly on the left-hand (W) side of the stream.

Shortly after you reach the valley floor, it crosses over to the other side of the stream and then crosses back again, just before **the valley turns to the west**. Stand at this turning point and look down the valley and you can see laid out below a much more tropical landscape, dotted with houses and fields and smudged by the smoke of a dozen cooking fires. This is a good place to *camp*.

TURN IN THE VALLEY → PAUCARCANCHA [MAP 11]

The turn in the valley to Quesca

After the turn in the valley, the path switches from one bank to the other a couple of times before another stream joins from the south. Soon after, a fast-flowing river joins from the east. Your direction is straight ahead but if you can't ford the river walk a short way to the east and you'll find a rickety bridge.

Soon after this you'll pass a hut, and then two more huts beside a proper bridge, cross here to the left-hand (W) bank. From here **Quesca** is a 20-minute walk away. Quesca is the largest village in the area, but it's

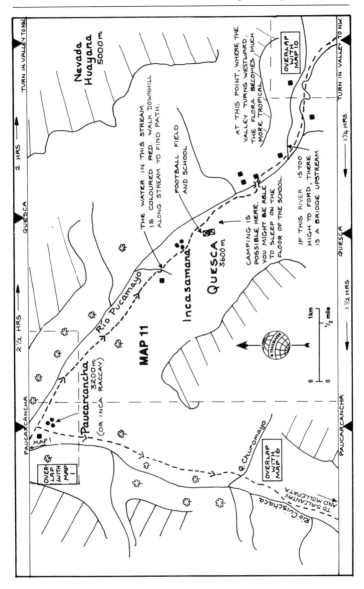

Nevada Huayana 5000 m.

TURN IN VALLEY TO N.W.

OVERLAP WITH MAP 10

AT THIS POINT, WHERE THE VALLEY TURNS WESTWARD, THE FLORA BECOMES MUCH MORE TROPICAL.

2 HRS

QUESCA

THE WATER IN THIS STREAM IS COLOURED RED. WALK DOWNHILL ALONG STREAM TO FIND PATH.

FOOTBALL FIELD AND SCHOOL

CAMPING IS POSSIBLE HERE. YOU MIGHT BE ABLE TO SLEEP ON THE FLOOR OF THE SCHOOL.

2½ HRS

Rio Pucamayo

MAP 11

Incasamana

Quesca 3600 m.

IF THIS RIVER IS TOO HIGH TO FORD, THERE IS A BRIDGE UPSTREAM.

TURN IN VALLEY TO N.W.

1¼ HRS

QUESCA

1½ HRS

1 km
½ mile
0
0

© TRAILBLAZER

Paucarcancha 3200 m. (OR INCA RACCAY)

PAUCARCANCHA

MAP 1

OVER LAP WITH MAP 1

Q. Churomayo

OVERLAP WITH MAP 16

Rio Cusichaca

TO SALKANTAY AND MOLLEPATA

PAUCARCANCHA

> ❏ **Incasamana**
> A half-day's walk from Inca Raccay along the Anta-Machu Picchu road is
> Incasamana, another tambo for weary travellers. Unlike Inca Raccay just by
> the pass, Incasamana is surrounded by land that was cultivated – over three
> hundred square metres have been discovered, and storage lofts have been dis-
> covered, too.
>
> Incasamana and Inca Raccay (see p196) were built along a similar stan-
> dardised plan, probably around the same time in the early stages of the Incas'
> domination of the area (early fifteenth century). Nearby there's a hot spring,
> and it's easy to imagine a weary Inca traveller soaking his bones in the water
> after crossing the high passes, knowing that he's only a couple of day's jour-
> ney from Machu Picchu.

not big. You'll only know you're in the middle of it when you walk past
a football field, where you can usually *camp* if you get permission.

Quesca to Paucarcancha

Quesca to Paucarcancha is mostly a straightforward path keeping to the
west bank of the widening river, but there's one difficult bit. Shortly after
you pass the ruins of a tambo called **Incasamana** (just off the trail to the
right – N/E), there's a small gully carved out by a stream (coming from a
hot spring) that runs through red rock and is coloured red itself. Walk
down the stream a little and you'll see the main path heading straight as
an arrow through the now dense scrubland towards Paucarcancha. This is
the path you want. Looking up on the skyline directly in front (N/W) of
you, you can see **Dead Woman Pass/Abra de Huarmihuanusca** (see
p171), which is the first pass on the trail from Huayllabamba to Machu
Picchu.

One and a half hours out of Quesca is the site of **Paucarcancha** (see
opposite). Paucarcancha is built at the junction of three valleys: the valley you've just walked down, the upper Cusichaca leading to Salcantay
and Mollepata and the lower Cusichaca leading to Huayllabamba and the
Urubamba river. Its position makes it a sensibly-placed fort but it was
probably a tambo as well.

OPTIONS FROM PAUCARCANCHA

From Paucarcancha, there are **three options**: the first is to turn left
(south) and walk towards Mollepata (see Map 16, p209); the second is to
turn right (north) and walk towards Huayllabamba, then turn up the
Llulluchayoc towards Machu Picchu (see Map 2, p172); the third option
is to walk to Huayllabamba, then down the Cusichaca river to the
Urubamba, where you could either pick up the train from Km88, 82 or
walk all the way back to Chilca and complete a circuit (see Map 1, p169).

❑ Paucarcancha

Standing on the walls of this reconstructed Inca fort and looking down at the Cusichaca and Quesca rivers, you can see one of the reasons why the Incas chose to build it. Paucarcancha dominates both valleys, valleys along which Inca roads ran. These roads led over the Salcantay watershed to the Apurímac river, a source of danger to Inca stability since the days of the Cancha invasion. Paucarcancha was, therefore, a guarded entry point to Machu Picchu and the Urubamba from the Apurímac to the south.

The archaeologist, Dr Ann Kendall, discovered that a large non-Inca population lived in the areas around Paucarcancha and Huayllabamba. These people were the indigenous inhabitants of the area, and the Incas pretty much let them be but the imposing walls of Paucarcancha must have been a permanent reminder of who was really in control.

Paucarcancha is the first large Inca site that's been discovered on the old Anta to Machu Picchu road and is probably a gateway to the region. It was built quite late in comparison with the tambos of Inca Raccay and Incasamana, after the early constructions in the area around Patallacta, around the mid to late fifteenth century. Within the complex are sixteen buildings, one of which looks a little like a barracks and could have held soldiers or perhaps mit'a workers. The people who lived in Paucarcancha had enough fields to grow all their food, and over ten thousand square metres of terracing have been discovered in the hills nearby. It's likely it also functioned as a tambo.

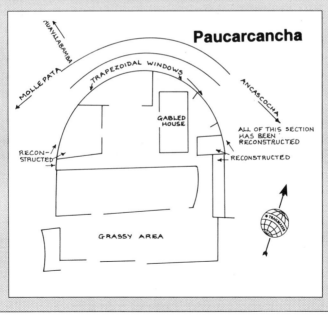

The Mollepata trek

This hike takes six or seven days, and is quite gruelling; the pass is at 5000m (16,400ft) on the shoulder of the mountain Salcantay. However it's a wonderful walk and takes you right from the watershed of the Apurímac to the Urubamba.

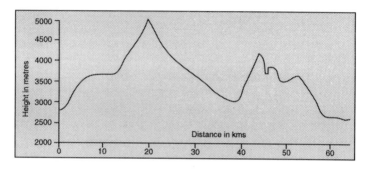

**How high you'll climb and how far you'll walk
Mollepata to Machu Picchu**

MOLLEPATA → ABOVE MARCOCASSA   [MAP 12]

Mollepata is a village at the end of a dirt track off the main Cuzco to Abancay road. The early bus from Cuzco (4am from Calle Arcopata) will take you right into the village, but the later one (5am) will drop you only at the bottom of the dirt track, down by the Apurímac river in the heat among the biting insects. It's a good few kilometres from the main road to Mollepata, and you *could* walk it but I wouldn't recommend that unless you like desert hiking. You can usually hitch up from the main road to Mollepata, but you should pay the driver s/2 or so.

There are arrieros for hire in Mollepata – the Perez family are often recommended and as a result they're a little more expensive than others: s/20-s/25 a day rather than the going rate of s/15-s/20. Be clear whether or not the sum decided includes your providing food.

Mollepata to the glade after the bridge

The trail leaves from Mollepata's Plaza de Armas. Take the road that leaves from the Plaza's north-west corner, and walk up the cobbles until

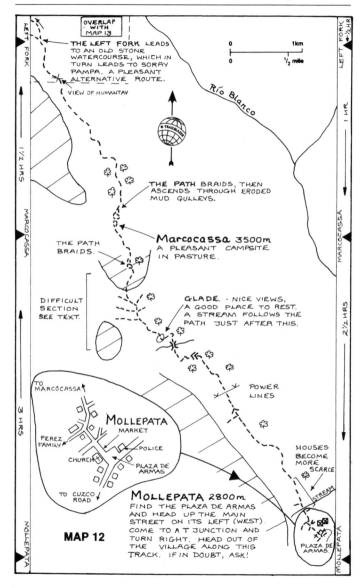

OVERLAP WITH MAP 13

THE LEFT FORK LEADS TO AN OLD STONE WATERCOURSE, WHICH IN TURN LEADS TO SORAY PAMPA. A PLEASANT ALTERNATIVE ROUTE.

VIEW OF HUMANTAY

LEFT FORK

LEFT FORK → ½ HR

1 HR

Río Blanco

0   1km
0   ½ mile

THE PATH BRAIDS, THEN ASCENDS THROUGH ERODED MUD GULLEYS.

½ HRS

MARCOCASSA

THE PATH BRAIDS.

Marcocassa 3500m
A PLEASANT CAMPSITE IN PASTURE.

MARCOCASSA

2½ HRS

DIFFICULT SECTION SEE TEXT.

GLADE. - NICE VIEWS, A GOOD PLACE TO REST. A STREAM FOLLOWS THE PATH JUST AFTER THIS.

3 HRS

TO MARCOCASSA

MOLLEPATA
MARKET

PEREZ FAMILY

CHURCH

POLICE

PLAZA DE ARMAS

TO CUZCO ROAD

MAP 12

POWER LINES

HOUSES BECOME MORE SCARCE

STREAM

PLAZA DE ARMAS

MOLLEPATA 2800m
FIND THE PLAZA DE ARMAS AND HEAD UP THE MAIN STREET ON ITS LEFT (WEST). COME TO A T JUNCTION AND TURN RIGHT. HEAD OUT OF THE VILLAGE ALONG THIS TRACK. IF IN DOUBT, ASK!

MOLLEPATA

MOLLEPATA

you arrive at a T junction. Turn right (N/E) and then the path veers around to the north-west. As you leave the village the houses become more and more infrequent. You're walking along the left (W) side of a valley that's heading just about due north-west. In a short time you'll pass under some power lines, and then a little further on the path will head uphill (W), hair-pinning steeply. You then cross a bridge and turn almost back on yourself as you climb up the valley side before coming to a pleasant glade. This is a place to catch your breath and prepare for the difficult bit to come.

The difficult bit

It's easy to get lost after the glade, though the campesinos around here are used to trekkers getting lost and often point out the way.

The main valley to Soray, where you're heading, runs from the north-west to the south-east in what's a straight line if you're a condor. In fact the line of the valley is broken by a large gully which appears as a fork in the valleys when you walk uphill. One valley heads off more to the west, one to the north. You want to take the valley that goes more to the north. There's an isolated hillock between the northern and western valleys that you should avoid.

Richard Derham who tested my maps gives this detailed advice:
1) Reach a house with three-way pylons and a tin and thatch roof.
2) About 100m further on, pass an irrigation channel on your left.
3) The main path leads (after 50m) over a bridge and up an isolated hillock.
4) Follow the channel for 600m.
5) The path then crosses the channel, so the water's now flowing on your right (E).
6) Follow this path for 50m past a house.
7) A cattle track goes to the left, a dirt road (through a wooden gate) to the right. Go straight up a track that leads uphill to two pylons close together. The trail becomes obvious again.
8) The channel is on your right, cross it after 50m, so it runs on your left. Head straight up the most used path, and don't veer off to the left into the valley on the other side of the crest of the hill.

You should then find yourself at **Marcocassa**, a green, open area which is a good place to *camp*. Marcocassa is three hours from Mollepata. Fill up your water bottles here, as the streams from here to Soray are season-al and unreliable.

From Marcocassa, head north and uphill through some deeply-eroded mud gullies and into a wood. The path then winds in a north-westerly direction and settles on the left-hand (W) side of the valley of the Blanco river. (If you find yourself on the right-hand (E) side of a river valley, you've gone the wrong way. Head back down to Marcocassa and try again.) You turn a corner and suddenly, four and a half hard hours out of Mollepata, you get your first view of a snow peak: **Mt Humantay**.

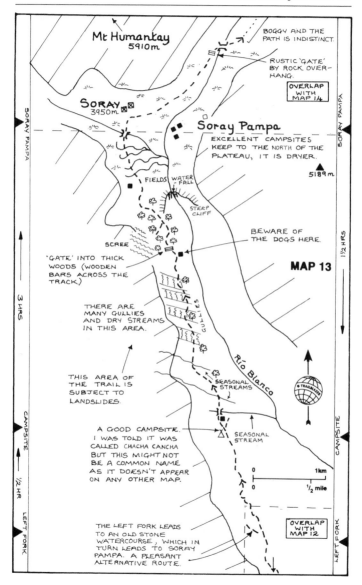

Mt Humantay
5910m

BOGGY AND THE
PATH IS INDISTINCT.

RUSTIC 'GATE'
BY ROCK OVER-
HANG.

OVERLAP
WITH
MAP 14

SORAY
3950m

Soray Pampa

EXCELLENT CAMPSITES
KEEP TO THE NORTH OF THE
PLATEAU, IT IS DRYER.

5189m

FIELDS WATER
FALL

STEEP
CLIFF

BEWARE OF
THE DOGS HERE.

SCREE

'GATE' INTO THICK
WOODS (WOODEN
BARS ACROSS THE
TRACK)

MAP 13

THERE ARE
MANY GULLIES
AND DRY STREAMS
IN THIS AREA.

GULLIES

THIS AREA OF
THE TRAIL IS
SUBJECT TO
LANDSLIDES.

Río Blanco

SEASONAL
STREAMS

A GOOD CAMPSITE.
I WAS TOLD IT WAS
CALLED CHACHA CANCHA
BUT THIS MIGHT NOT
BE A COMMON NAME
AS IT DOESN'T APPEAR
ON ANY OTHER MAP.

SEASONAL
STREAM

0   1km
0   1/2 mile

THE LEFT FORK LEADS
TO AN OLD STONE
WATERCOURSE, WHICH IN
TURN LEADS TO SORAY
PAMPA. A PLEASANT
ALTERNATIVE ROUTE.

OVERLAP
WITH
MAP 12

SORAY PAMPA

SORAY PAMPA

3 HRS

CAMPSITE

1/2 HR

LEFT FORK

1/2 HRS

CAMPSITE

LEFT FORK

ABOVE MARCOCASSA → SORAY   [MAP 13 p203]

The path from here to Soray is easy – you're walking in the same direction, along a valley towards an objective you can see at the foot of Mount Humantay. It takes a good 3½ hours to get there. There are two paths: the main one is the lower one, and there's an upper path that follows the route of an ancient Inca watercourse. The upper one isn't suitable for mules.

Half an hour after you get your first view of Humantay, you'll come to an open green field: the *camp-site* of Chacha Cancha (this is my approximation of what I was told it's called). I thought this a good place to camp but it appears the stream is seasonal and not reliable.

A couple of hours further, and you reach a gate across the path, next to a hut that's home to some very loud dogs. You'll then enter some woods – Soray is about another half hour's walk. You'll pass a large scree slope on your left (W), and after that if you look to your right (E), you'll notice a waterfall as the Blanco river flows over a steep cliff. Soon after, you walk out of the woods and onto some high puna fields – you've reached **Soray pampa**.

The pampa is often latticed with small drainage canals and streams that you'll have to cross (though these disappear in dry years). Keep to the left (W) side of the fields, close to the rock wall if you want to remain dry-booted. At the far (N) end of the pampa there's **Soray** itself, over the other side (N) of a stream – often there's a bridge but you might have to use stepping stones. This is a good place to *camp*.

SORAY → THE PASS   [MAP 14 p205]

You can hire arrieros in Soray. I hired Antonio Huari Huillca, who charged s/15 a day and was reliable, friendly and had sound animals; he'll probably double his rates when he finds out he's in this book.

Soray to Salcantay pampa

The trail heads up the valley to the north-east, to the right. The path takes the northern (left) side of the little valley and passes through a rustic gate by a rock overhang, then crosses to the right (S/E) bank. Mount Salcantay, the sacred mountain of the Incas, is ahead of you. The valley floor becomes boggy after the gate and the track indistinct. As long as you continue following the stream north-east you're doing fine. At the end of the boggy bit, the path crosses the stream to the left-hand side, then back to the right again.

You're now underneath a massive wall of scree at the end of this valley – it's the terminal moraine (end debris) of a glacier. The flat ground before the moraine is called Salcantay pampa, and is a great place to *camp*. The path follows the moraine round to the right (E) all the way up to the pass.

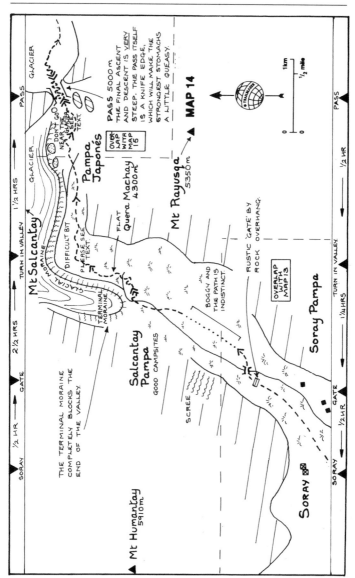

MAP 14

PASS 5000m
THE FINAL ASCENT AND DESCENT IS VERY STEEP. THE PASS ITSELF IS A KNIFE EDGE, WHICH WILL MAKE THE STRONGEST STOMACHS A LITTLE QUEASY.

OVERLAP WITH MAP 15

Pampa Japonés

Quera Machay 4300m

FLAT

Mt Rayusqa 5350m

RUSTIC GATE BY ROCK OVERHANG

OVERLAP WITH MAP 13

Soray Pampa

GLACIER

PASS

GLACIER

1½ HRS

TURN IN VALLEY

DON'T GO NEAR THE GLACIER SEE TEXT.

Mt Salcantay

DIFFICULT BIT

PLEASE SEE TEXT.

GLACIAL MORAINE

2½ HRS

TERMINAL MORAINE

THE TERMINAL MORAINE COMPLETELY BLOCKS THE END OF THE VALLEY.

GATE

½ HR

Salcantay Pampa
GOOD CAMPSITES

SCREE

BOGGY AND THE PATH IS INDISTINCT.

TURN IN VALLEY

1¼ HRS

½ HR

GATE

PASS

SORAY

½ HR

Mt Humantay 5910m

SORAY

½ HRS

Soray ⌧

1km
½ mile
0
0

SALKANTAY

Salcantay pampa to the pass

To get to the pass, follow the path which switchbacks steeply up the right-hand (E) hillside that faces the moraine. You'll soon reach a small, flat spot called Quera Machay, which is another great place to *camp*. The path heads north from Quera Machay, then round to the right (E), steeply uphill. Don't go down to the lateral moraine of the glacier, keep the river between you and it. As you climb, the gully gets narrower and narrower, until the path seems to disappear when you reach the top. There's another stream here which you need to keep on your right – it's not the same as the one that runs down by the glacier. You'll know you've got it correct when you can look back over the wall of the lateral moraine and see two lakes.

From here, you should be able to see the pass at the top of a very, very steep path, surrounded by little ridges. Don't be tempted to cut out the pass and go over the watershed by the glacier – there are dangerous holes under the glacier and you could easily slip down into them. The **pass** is the most knife-edged of passes I've ever seen – it's just a metre or so wide. You can look down into the great valley up which you've come, and over into the wide valley where you're now headed.

THE PASS → PAMPA CAHUANA   [MAP 15]

From the pass, head steeply downhill. Go over and have a look at the glacier on your left (N) which is the origin of the river Cusichaca. It's worth stopping and thinking that this is one of the origins of the Amazon, and the melt-water from this mountain flows to the Atlantic Ocean.

The trail from here to Paucarcancha is easy – you just follow the valley down – first east-north-east to Pampa Cahuana, then north-east.

Taking it step by step, the path first heads south-east, then bends round to the north-east and descends quite steeply. Just before a ridge, there's a beautiful *camp-site*, flat, green and protected from the wind but it's often occupied by tour companies. Down the other side of the ridge, the path crosses a plain of glacial out-wash before settling on the northern (L) bank of the river. This area is flat and good for camping too, it's called the **Quebrada Sisay pampa.**

Keep on this side of the river, and skirt around two gullies with seasonal streams running in them. The land gets very steep. In a short while you'll see on the other side of the river a couple of huts and a large stream coming down from the south – there is a path on this side of the river too, but the main path's on the north. Just after the huts and stream the valley turns north-east and looking down you can see an Inca canal, glistening in the sun (there's a better view from the southern path). This area's called **Pampa Cahuana.**

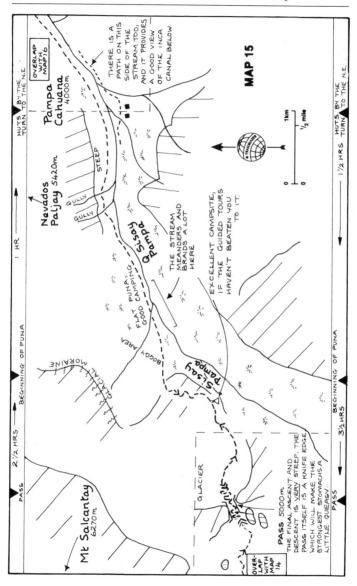

MAP 15

OVERLAP WITH MAP 16

HUTS BY THE TURN TO THE N.E.

THERE IS A PATH ON THIS SIDE OF THE STREAM TOO, AND IT PROVIDES A GOOD VIEW OF THE INCA CANAL BELOW.

Pampa Cahuana 4000m

Navados Paljay 5420m

STEEP

GULLY

GULLY

Q Sisay Q Pampa

THE STREAM MEANDERS AND BRAIDS A LOT HERE

EXCELLENT CAMPSITE, IF THE GUIDED TOURS HAVEN'T BEATEN YOU TO IT.

1km

½ mile

0

0

HUTS BY THE TURN TO THE N.E.

1 HR

BEGINNING OF PUNA

PUNANG GOOD FLAT CAMPING AREA

BOGGY AREA

GLACIAL MORAINE

Mt Salcantay 6270m

GLACIER

PASS 5000m. THE FINAL ASCENT AND DESCENT IS VERY STEEP. THE PASS ITSELF IS A KNIFE EDGE WHICH WILL MAKE THE STRONGEST STOMACHS A LITTLE QUEASY.

2½ HRS

PASS

Sisay Pampa

BEGINNING OF PUNA

3½ HRS

PASS

OVERLAP WITH MAP 14

PAMPA CAHUANA → PAUCARCANCHA   [MAP 16]

The path passes by two huts, and then crosses a **bridge** to the right-hand (E) bank of the river. You are crossing over the Inca canal. Then, after a narrow gorge, the river, valley and path all turn northwards. The valley descends gently, and the flora changes from high puna to scrub, bathed in warmth and flourishing with butterflies and insects. One and a half hours after the bridge you arrive at the ruins of **Paucarcancha** (see p199).

OPTIONS FROM PAUCARCANCHA

From Paucarcancha, you have **three options**: walk to Huayllabamba and complete the Inca trail (see Map 1, p169); walk down the Cusichaca where you could either take a train out or walk to Chilca (again, see Map 1); turn up the valley you find on your right (E) and walk up to Puerto Huyanay (see Map 11, p197).

Other trails

CHILCA CIRCUIT (5-6 DAYS)

(To follow this route description look at the Route Planning map on pp22-23). A Chilca circuit would take you up the Silque valley, down the Cusichaca valley and back around to Chilca along the Urubamba river. It would take about five or six days. Remember that it's not a good idea to do this circuit anti-clockwise because you'd have to pay the Inca Trail fee twice.

THE FULL MOLLEPATA (2 WEEKS)

(See Route Planning map on p22-23). An extended Mollepata hike would take you from Mollepata, over the Salcantay pass, down the Cusichaca to the Urubamba, along to Chilca, then up the Silque valley. At the top of the Silque valley you'd turn right and head up to the pass of Puerto Huyanay. You'd then follow the Quesca valley and down to Paucarcancha and then Huayllabamba where you'd pick up the classic Inca Trail to Machu Picchu. This hike would take you about two weeks.

VILCABAMBA (7-10 DAYS)

There is also a trek to another famous Inca city – but it's a very different walk, through steamy jungle away from the Machu Picchu Sanctuary. The route to the ruins of **Vilcabamba**, the lost Inca capital that was

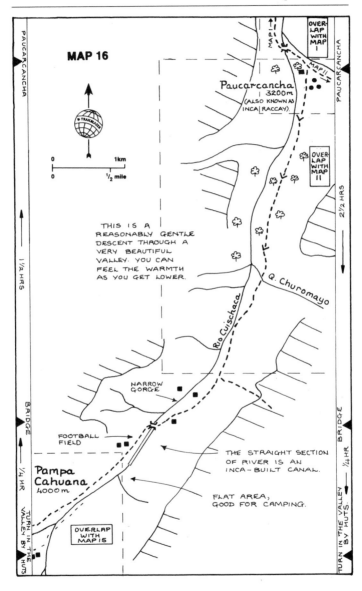

MAP 16

0   1km

0   ½ mile

PAUCARCANCHA

PAUCARCANCHA

Paucarcancha
3200m
(ALSO KNOWN AS
INCA RACCAY)

OVER-
LAP
WITH
MAP
I

MAP I

MAP II

OVER-
LAP
WITH
MAP
II

2½ HRS

THIS IS A
REASONABLY GENTLE
DESCENT THROUGH A
VERY BEAUTIFUL
VALLEY. YOU CAN
FEEL THE WARMTH
AS YOU GET LOWER.

Q. Churomayo

Rio Cusichaca

1½ HRS

NARROW
GORGE

FOOTBALL
FIELD

THE STRAIGHT SECTION
OF RIVER IS AN
INCA-BUILT CANAL.

BRIDGE

BRIDGE

¼ HR

Pampa
Cahuana
4000m

FLAT AREA,
GOOD FOR CAMPING.

¼ HR

TURN IN THE
VALLEY BY HUTS

TURN IN THE VALLEY
BY HUTS.

OVERLAP
WITH
MAP 15

founded by Manco Inca after he had fled Cuzco (see p99), is a 65km hike mainly through a humid low-altitude region. Unless you're particularly interested in jungle wildlife and Inca history it's a much less enjoyable walk than the Inca Trail and consequently it's infinitely less popular. It probably appeals more to serious birdwatchers than anyone else.

To reach the trailhead take the train from Cuzco to **Chaullay Puente** (seven hours). Then it's a 5-7 hour truck ride to the trailhead at **Huancacalle**. You'll need a guide as the ruins, which are above **Espíritu Pampa**, are spread out in the jungle and not easy to locate.

If you're thinking of taking this walk, buy *Sixpac Inca* by Vincent R Lee (self-published 1985, available in Cuzco), which contains the only detailed maps available.

PART 8: MACHU PICCHU

The Lost City?

I felt infinitely small in the centre of that navel of rocks, the navel of a deserted world, proud, towering high, to which I somehow belonged. I felt that my own hands had laboured there at some remote point in time, digging furrows, polishing rocks. **Pablo Neruda**, *Memoirs.*

For many people, the words Machu Picchu conjure up an image of a lost Inca city, swathed in the green creepers of an encroaching jungle, hidden behind the years, waiting to be discovered by intrepid explorers armed with machetes and attended by armies of porters. It was like this, there's no doubt – all you have to do is look at the photographs of the Hiram Bingham expedition to be reminded of Indiana Jones from the film *Raiders of the Lost Ark* – but today, sadly, some of the mystique has gone. You can now make a day trip to the site by train or helicopter, and if you want to spend the night near the ruins there is a reasonable hotel close to the old stones.

A thousand people a day visit this 'lost' city in high season, and with these people come inevitable problems: overcrowding, garbage and hotels built like concrete bunkers. But Machu Picchu hasn't been ruined – it would take the most insensitive of philistines not to be impressed by the sight of the sun rising over the rim of the mountains that enclose this awe-inspiring place. This *is* still a Lost City and still a place of magic especially when you come upon it after three days hiking in the wilderness.

Practicalities

Machu Picchu is 2400m (7800ft) above sea level, and it nestles on a ridge between Machu Picchu mountain and the sugar loaf of Huayna Picchu. When the sun's out, it burns, so bring sun barrier cream and a hat. It can also get cold up here when the sun's not out, and it sometimes rains unpredictably, so bring a jumper and a waterproof.

ARRIVAL

You've either come off the trail or come up by bus from the valley below. If permission is granted for the building of the cable car (see p155) this will be another way of getting here.

If you're going back to Cuzco in the afternoon, check the train timetable as it changes often. They normally have the times at the reception desk in the hotel. See p227 for the timetable at the time of writing.

ORIENTATION

If you've just come off the Inca trail, you'll be led by officials down a winding path to the entrance booth. Here you must leave your kit at a left luggage hut (s/2 a day) because you won't be allowed in the ruins with it. The large ugly bungalow you can see is the restaurant and hotel. If you've come by train, the bus from the station will deposit you in the car park in front of the hotel. The entrance to the ruins is just up some stairs to the right of a map of Machu Picchu.

Passing through the entrance booth and around a shoulder of rock, you'll reach an open area. Straight ahead are a couple of thatched cottages through which most visitors enter the site. Before this there is a path uphill, indicated by little white arrows painted on stones. If you follow these (back up the little hill you just climbed down if you've come along the trail) you'll get to a place just below a thatched hut on the top of a promontory. This is the Watchman's hut, the best place to start your tour – see 'A guide to the ruins' (see p220).

OPENING TIMES AND TICKETS

The ruins are open 7am-5pm daily, and entrance costs US$10 and US$5 for a second day. If you've walked the trail the price of one day's entrance is included in your trail fee, which you should have paid already (unless you hiked from Mollepata, in which case you pay here).

WHERE TO STAY

You can't camp in the ruins – so don't try. I'm told there's a *shed* where you can occasionally put up your tent, 20 yards down the road to Aguas Calientes on the right (S), with a water pipe outside and a strip-light inside. If this is closed there's a free *camp-site* at the foot of the hill: cross over the Urubamba, and it's to the right (E) of the bridge. It's filthy, and don't leave kit unattended here or you'll lose it.

You can stay in the *Machu Picchu Ruinas Hotel* (☎ 211054, ▤ 211039, Carreterra Bingham, Monumento Histórico Machu Picchu, Urubamba), which at US$190 (double, att) is overpriced, but it is the only hotel in the world so close to these legendary ruins so they can charge what they want. You can also make bookings for Hotel Machu Picchu Ruinas through Peru Hotel (☎ 84-240742), Officina Principal, opposite Calle Palacio, No 136 and at the Plazoleta de las Nazarenas No 144, Cuzco, or reserve in Lima: (☎ 01-211 0826/440 8043, 🖺 440 6197).

There is a much wider selection of places to stay in Aguas Calientes (see p151).

WHERE TO EAT

You can have an excellent buffet breakfast and an overpriced canteen lunch at the *Hotel Machu Picchu Ruinas*. The 'all you can eat' breakfast is expensive but worth it at s/56. Lunch, too, is expensive at s/45 and isn't worth it; pick up a hot dog or burger instead from the barbecues on the terrace by the gift shop above the lavatories. There's also a cheapish restaurant a ten-minute walk down the road in a building on your left.

History

People have been arguing about what Machu Picchu was and why it was built almost from the moment Hiram Bingham rediscovered it. It all seems a bit clearer now, since a lot of light was thrown into this dark corner of history by an old copy of a sixteenth-century document found by the scholars Luis Miguel Glave, María Remy and John Rowe in the library of a Cuzco monastery.

MACHU PICCHU REVEALED TO THE WORLD

A young graduate from Yale University named Hiram Bingham had been bewitched by the stories of lost Inca cities ever since visiting a pre-Hispanic ruin called Choqquerquirau. (Bingham was originally an expert on Bolívar, not an archaeologist, and he was rather at a loss for what to do when he made it to his first ruin. In the best tradition of the amateur he did his best, helped by a book published by the Royal Geographical Society with the quaint title *Hints to Travellers*.) Bingham raised enough money to lead a seven-man expedition to Peru under the auspices of Yale University and the National Geographic Society. In 1911 he and his team started to explore the uncharted hills around the ancient Inca capital, Cuzco.

Uncharted is not the right word: these hills weren't completely unknown territory. The mountain Machu Picchu appears on a map in the 1910 edition of a book on the Incas written by the English historian,

Clements Markham, and Bingham himself used a map of the area prepared by Antonio Raimondi. There had even been some reports of ruins around the lower Urubamba. Bingham describes both the failure of a Frenchman, Charles Wiener, to find them in 1875, and what he rather unfairly referred to as the 'treasure hunting' of a Peruvian called Lizárraga.

So in July 1911, Bingham and his team headed out of Cuzco down the Urubamba, and almost immediately they discovered a major Inca site which they named Patallacta (it's the site on the corner where the Cusichaca river meets the Urubamba, see p170). After walking a little up the Cusichaca, the team also discovered Huayllabamba and Paucarcancha. Bingham and his companions then travelled on.

On July 23, just a week into the expedition, they camped off the trail at Mandorpampa. A local man, one Melchor Artega, was suspicious of these foreigners, and came over to see what was going on. When they explained that they were looking for ruins, Artega told them that there were some fine ones up in the hills above their camp.

The next day it rained. No one else in the expedition wanted to climb up the steep side of the Urubamba canyon, so Bingham went on his own, accompanied by the expedition's guard, Sergeant Carrasco, and Artega. After an unpleasant crossing of the Urubamba on a flimsy log bridge and a perilous climb through snake-infested forest, he reached a grass-covered hut. There he was welcomed by two men, Richarte and Alvarez, who had been living up on the hillside for four years to escape the army and taxes. They gave Bingham water and fed him, and he describes not really wanting to have a look at the ruins because he was tired, the water was cool and the heat of the day was great. But he did have a look. And the rest, as they say, is history.

WHAT BINGHAM FOUND IN THE JUNGLE

Bingham named the ruins Machu Picchu because that was the name of the mountain on which they were found. Machu means old or big, and Picchu is the name of the area. The sugar loaf mountain that overlooks the ruins is called Huayna Picchu (small Picchu).

Bingham believed that he'd stumbled upon the rebel Incas' stronghold, Vilcabamba (see p208), the site of the last independent Incan state and their place of final refuge in the days when the Spanish were hunting them down. For a number of reasons it's now thought that these ruins aren't Vilcabamba, not least because the routes the Spanish took to get to Vilcabamba don't match the routes you'd need to take to get to Machu Picchu, and the descriptions of the site of Vilcabamba don't fit with the geography around Machu Picchu.

But what Bingham did find is no less impressive: he'd discovered not only a lost city of the Incas but a whole lost province that the Incas had miraculously concealed from the Spanish conquistadors. (How they managed to do this is a good question). Within the mountains now enclosed by the Machu Picchu Historical Sanctuary are numerous Inca roads and ruins, towns, cities, forts and outposts – everything from humble mud-and-rock structures to castles of magnificent dressed stone – which have only survived the centuries because no one knew they were there.

Keeper of the royal bridge
FELIPE HUAMÁN POMA DE AYALA (c1590)

Most people now think that Vilcabamba is much further into the jungle at a place known as Espíritu Pampa. Bingham would not really mind if he knew this as he also rediscovered Espíritu Pampa.

MACHU PICCHU AS PACHACUTEC'S ROYAL FRONTIER

According to the old papers found by Rowe and his colleagues, the lower Urubamba valley was conquered by the Inca Pachacutec in his expansionist wars of the fifteenth century. It's likely, then, that Pachacutec built the hilltop city of Machu Picchu to celebrate his greatness; he decorated the banks of the Urubamba with Ollantaytambo for the same reason. Machu Picchu was the royal estate at the end of the line, also perhaps a religious centre, the capital of a frontier province, and an impregnable watchtower that guarded the route from Antisuyu to the civilised uplands of Cuzco.

The Urubamba route to Antisuyu became less important in later years. All traffic for the *cejas de la selva* (the eyebrows of the jungle) headed down the Lucumayo, and Machu Picchu became a backwater rather than a frontier. By the time of the conquest, it's probable that Machu Picchu was already just an abandoned shell, and when the archaeologists arrived there wasn't much they could dig up.

It's not clear why the city was quite so thoroughly deserted. Perhaps the water ran out – there were hardly enough springs to provide water for Bingham's expedition, so water must have been very scarce when the city was fully inhabited. Perhaps the Incas evacuated the place to create an uninhabited buffer zone between their rebel capital of Vilcabamba and the Spaniard's base in Cuzco.

At any rate, Rowe's document says that by the time of the conquest, part of the area was used for growing coca. It was given to Hernando Pizarro when the Spanish carved up the old empire, and it passed from him to the encomienda of a man called Arias Maldonado.

OTHER THEORIES

Tour guides give explanations as to Machu Picchu's past, varying from the plausible to those which have now been disproved by research, and on to the absurd. It's not just a case of guides making it up to impress the tourists: not everyone agrees on the interpretation of Rowe's document, and archaeologists may yet come up with tenable theories.

Incorrect

The idea that Machu Picchu was a convent of acllas (Inca nuns) was based on evidence that eighty per cent of the bones that Bingham dug up were those of women. This has been disproved by recent re-examination of the bones which showed that the sexes were equally represented.

Alternatively, you might read that Machu Picchu is laid out to resemble both a condor and a cayman (South American crocodile) and that Huayna Picchu is carved into the shape of a large puma. You can believe that if you want to, but I think that if the Incas wanted to make Machu Picchu look like a condor or a puma they'd have done a much better job.

Unlikely

An interesting theory of Bingham's suggests that Machu Picchu was between eight hundred and a thousand years old by the time of the Spanish invasion.

According to legend, the Incas had their origin in a sacred cave called Tambo-toqo (see p80), and the mythical first Inca, Manco Capac, built a three-windowed temple on this site to celebrate its significance. Bingham suggested – quite sensibly – that the Temple of the Three Windows in Machu Picchu (see p222) commemorated Manco Capac's temple. However, he went on to suggest that the structure in Machu Picchu was, in fact, the actual one built by Manco Capac, and that Machu Picchu is therefore the primeval home of the Incas. There is little evidence to support this theory and much against it: few pre-Inca objects have been found, the style of the Temple of the Three Windows is fifteenth-century Inca (not fifth century), and anyway Machu Picchu is completely the wrong side of Cuzco to be Tambo-toqo.

Plausible

Some say that Machu Picchu was an **agricultural outpost** of the Incas. It was used, they say, to maximise the rare and valuable growing zone between the jungle and the high valleys of Cuzco, a suggestion backed by the large tracts of land in the district that have been irrigated and terraced for agriculture. Other people expand on this, suggesting that the area around Machu Picchu was a place where sacred plants were grown by priests.

There are theories that Machu Picchu is a big **observatory**. It's recently been discovered that at dawn on the winter solstice (21 June) the sun shines right through the middle of the window in the Torreon (see opposite p225), casting a shadow. This isn't the only building that was built with an eye on the heavens. The Temple of the Moon, on the far side of the sugar loaf mountain that dominates Machu Picchu, was built to face the Pleiades (also worshipped by the Incas), and some say the Intihuatana (see p222) is a place where the sun could be ceremonially tied and prevented from falling lower in the sky in winter.

Johan Reinhard, a respected anthropologist, suggests an interesting idea in his short book *The Sacred Centre*. Reinhard suggests that Machu Picchu was the focal point of a constellation of sacred geographical features: the city is built on a spur of one of the Inca's most important mountains called Salcantay; it perches above the sacred river the Urubamba and it is on a sighting line from other important mountains Pumasillo and Veronica. Machu Picchu is, like Cuzco, the focus of religion. The city should not be looked at as a citadel but as a religious symbol, a sacred centre. This theory links in with what we know about the Inca religion – the sacredness of certain spots (huacas) and the sacred lines (ceques) which joined them to other spots. It's true, too, that there is a large amount of ornate Inca architecture in these hills. If Reinhard is right, this means that the Inca Trail is more than just a road – it's a sacred route of pilgrimage.

Of course, these theories aren't necessarily contradictory. It's possible that Machu Picchu was a citadel built to the glory of Pachacutec, on a place found to be sacred in Inca religion, designed in a way so that the heavens could be observed, accessible only after a ritual journey.

A guide to the ruins

This was the habitation, this is the site:
here the fat grains of maize grew high
to fall again like red hail.

The fleece of the vicuña was carded here
to clothe men's loves in gold, their tombs and mothers,
the king, the prayers, the warriors.

Up here men's feet found rest at night
near eagles' talons in the high
meat-stuffed eyries.
Pablo Neruda, from *The Heights of Machu Picchu*.

This walking tour covers the main buildings at the site and summarises what's known about (or guessed about) each one. The rest is up to your imagination.

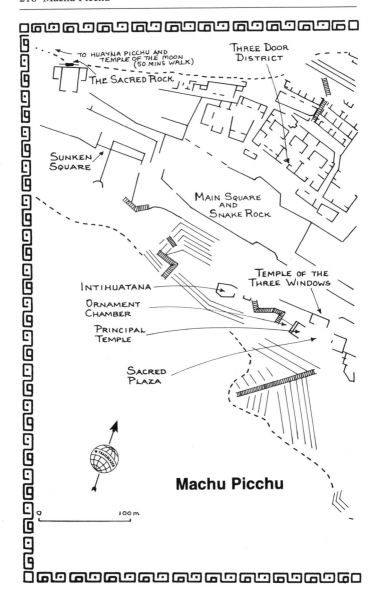

Machu Picchu

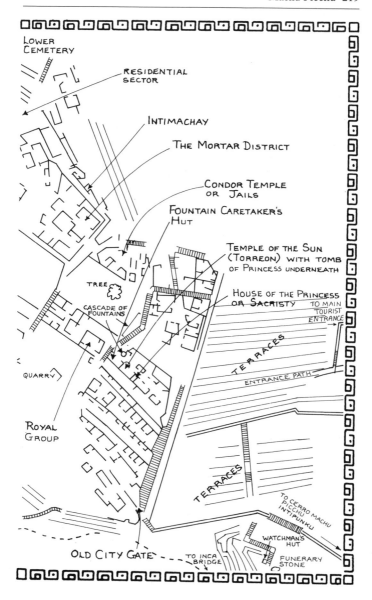

LOWER CEMETERY

RESIDENTIAL SECTOR

INTIMACHAY

THE MORTAR DISTRICT

CONDOR TEMPLE OR JAILS

FOUNTAIN CARETAKER'S HUT

TEMPLE OF THE SUN (TORREON) WITH TOMB OF PRINCESS UNDERNEATH

HOUSE OF THE PRINCESS OR SACRISTY

TO MAIN TOURIST ENTRANCE

TREE

CASCADE OF FOUNTAINS

TERRACES

ENTRANCE PATH

QUARRY

ROYAL GROUP

TERRACES

TO CERRO MACHU PICCHU PICCHU INTIPUNKU

WATCHMAN'S HUT

OLD CITY GATE

TO INCA BRIDGE

FUNERARY STONE

The best place to start is up at the Watchman's hut – for directions from the entrance booth, see 'Orientation' above.

AROUND THE WATCHMAN'S HUT AND FUNERARY STONE

This lone hut gives such a perfect view over Machu Picchu that it has been called **the Watchman's Hut**. It guards any entrance to the site from the road to Intipunku (p183), the trail up Machu Picchu mountain, or the road to the Inca Bridge (see p221). It's unlikely that this was a hut for a mere gatekeeper as the stonework's too good.

The oddly shaped rock nearby is known as the **Funerary Stone**, but it's probably a sacrificial altar. The Incas often sacrificed llamas, and sometimes even humans. In the festival of Inti Raymi (see p55), there's a llama sacrificed (allegedly – it still looked pretty alive to me), and the remains of the occasional human sacrifice have been found in such places as the volcano of El Misti near Arequipa. Note the strange carvings in the stone of a ring and something a bit like a staircase: no one knows what they're for, but there's one of these rings carved in a rock in Vilcabamba and the Incas often carved their huacas with stair-like designs, Qenko (see p146), for example.

The rock was named the Funerary Stone because Bingham found and excavated many tombs near here, which leads some to think that this stone was the place where the privileged dead were laid out for embalming – a Funerary Stone. Because of these finds, the area around here is often called the upper cemetery.

Machu Picchu's districts

Looking out over the city you can see the division of the land into terraces (an agricultural zone) and buildings (an urban zone). The terraces in the agricultural area were primarily for growing foodstuffs, and there are many more at nearby Choquesuysuy and Huinay Huayna (p182). Dr Ann Kendall thinks that there were about 677 hectares (1670 acres) of land under cultivation in the Sanctuary, and that there was a four-fold over-capacity. In other words, the Machu Picchu area was a breadbasket.

There are other suggestions as to what the terracing was for. Some have suggested that they were a defence measure against potential attackers, and others have suggested they were for decoration: the Chronicles say that the terraces at Ollantaytambo were used for growing flowers.

From the terracing you can clearly see another division of the city; the division into Hanan and Hurin districts to the left and right of the main plaza. The Incas often divided their towns into these two sections, which were probably inhabited by different clan groups. There's an interesting theory that every feature in one district (Sun Temple, etc) has a mirror image in the other district.

This is the ideal place from which to take a picture of Machu Picchu.

The Inca Bridge and Machu Picchu mountain

If you're looking down at the town, the path for the Inca Bridge goes off from your left, snaking around the top of the amphitheatre of terraces. The path leads along a sheer rock face to an abyss. In Inca times, there was a wooden drawbridge across this void that could be drawn up in times of trouble. The path's closed at the time of writing, because of the 1997 fire. The path for Machu Picchu mountain (cerro Machu Picchu) is on the right if you head back up towards Intipunku. It takes about an hour to get to the top and it's a tiring climb.

THE MOAT AND GATE

You can see from the Watchman's Hut a moat and long stairway that divides the agricultural terraces from the buildings. Walk along the path in front of the Hut to the top of the **moat**.

According to Bingham, there are 150 steps in the main staircase in the moat and about 3000 in the whole city. Because this is the main route along which an army could approach Machu Picchu, it's thought by many that the moat was a defence feature. Precipices and rock walls guarded the city's other flanks. However, those who prefer to regard Machu Picchu as a sacred rather than a military city see it as an architectural way of excluding the outside profane world from the inside sacred city.

The **Old City Gate** is at the top of the moat, and is an impressive trapezoidal arch with a vast lintel. When Bingham discovered this doorway it was in the process of collapse, so what you see has been repaired. If you stand in the gateway, there is a large wall to your left that overlooks you, which was probably built to protect the door from attackers. If you were standing here with a battering ram, there'd be nowhere to hide from any rocks and arrows thrown at you. Go through the door and look up at the big ring in the lintel and at the bars sunk in the doorposts to the left and right. These probably provided a method of securing the door.

Bingham found the remains of 41 containers of liquid refreshment in this place and thought that the chicha sellers of the old city were stationed here, selling drink to tired travellers.

THE QUARRY

Walk on through the gateway and along the street and you'll see in front of you a place where there are large boulders lying around. Go down some steps to get there.

Bingham found tombs around here and thought this was a cemetery, but it's now thought that this place was the **Quarry** for the stones used to build the city. You can see some rocks that are in the process of being split: tiny stones have been fed into small cracks. These stones kept the cracks open, which were then worked open until eventually the rock was split. This 'Inca work-in-progress' is eagerly pointed out to tourists by guides, but it was in fact an experiment conducted by a modern researcher, Dr Manuel Chavez Ballon.

THE SACRED PLAZA GROUP

Walk on through the quarry and straight ahead rising above the rest of the city, you'll see a mound on top of which is the Intihuatana. You're about to walk into the Sacred Plaza at its base.

The sacred plaza was named by Bingham because Machu Picchu's finest buildings are set around it. On one side the **Principal Temple**, on another the **Temple of the Three Windows**, and looming above it the **Intihuatana** itself.

Bingham's archaeologists dug up the floor of the sacred plaza as a good place to look for artefacts but found nothing. They did, however, find an enormous amount of smashed pottery on the ground outside, beneath the Temple of The Three Windows, which leads many to think that pots were ritually broken here and thrown out of the window as part of some ceremony.

The three-windowed temple is a very important place – Bingham used it as the centrepiece in his theory that Machu Picchu was about a thousand years older than anyone else thought (see p216). The three windows refer to the creation myths of the Incas. An enormous amount of effort has gone into the building of this place: look downwards out of one of the windows and you'll see that the terrace on which this place was built has been clad in massive, beautifully carved rocks. If you can't quite see from this angle, look back at it when you're walking along the other side of the city.

The principal temple was so called because it is so impressively built. The ranks of regular bricks have slipped a bit in the years as a result of subsidence. In front of them there's a large altar.

Walk to the left of the principal temple and along a path. You'll see on your right the doorway of the **Ornament Chamber**. Put your head in and have a look at the corners of this room – they're not built from stone blocks but carved from rock – one of these stones has 32 angles in three dimensions. This isn't building, it's sculpture.

THE INTIHUATANA

Continue walking past the ornament chamber and you'll start to climb the stairs up to the **Intihuatana** (see photo opposite p224). The importance of this place is emphasised by its architecture: you have to climb to reach it, and you can't go straight there, you have to turn corners. You get almost the same sense of awed anticipation as you do climbing to Intipunku to get a first sight of Machu Picchu.

Inti means sun and *hata* means to tie, and 'intihuatana' has been translated as 'hitching post of the sun'. The word doesn't appear in the ancient vocabularies of Quechua; it seems it was first noted by the nineteenth century North American traveller, George Squier. Squier came across an Intihuatana in Pisac and thought that it might be a place where the sun was ritually stopped, perhaps when it reached its lowest point in the winter skies, and encouraged to rise higher once more.

Spanish priests, when they came across these sacred rocks of the Incas, used to lop the tops off them or ritually exorcise them and it's rare for one to survive intact.

Unlike the Torreon (see below), no one has yet found a precise astrological function for the Intihuatana – the various edges and angles are carved into the mother rock with considerable exactitude but no one knows why. Some archaeologists don't think of it as a ritual hitching post; it's been renamed simply as a gnomon (a carved block), although a gnomon is also the name for the arm on a sundial.

AROUND THE SACRED ROCK

Pass through the space around the Intihuatana, and go down the other side. As you're walking, look down at the minute terraces on your left, apparently too small to be purely for agriculture, yet on such a steep slope that it's doubtful whether they were either necessary or effective for defence purposes.

In front of you to the left is the **Sunken Square**. This area has been carefully terraced to make a little enclosed square apart from the main plaza, and in one corner there are the remains of what looks like a tomb under a large rock. It's overgrown, and by looking at it you can get an idea of what Machu Picchu must have looked like when Bingham first stumbled up here – that is, unless they've cut the plants back again.

The **Sacred Rock** is to your right, tucked away under the shadow of Huayna Picchu, across the main square. There's a path that leads to it. This rock's called 'sacred' because it has been exposed in such a way that its shape is emphasised, fronted by a plaza and enclosed on two sides with well-built Inca houses. Why it's been exposed like this isn't clear, and you'll hear some bizarre theories: that the rock is a statue of Pachamama, the earth goddess, that it's a puma or that it's a guinea pig. The most likely theory is that the shape of this rock mimics the mountains around it. The plaza makes you want to look at the rock from one side, and you'll notice that it's a good representation of the mountain Putucusi that looms behind. Some, however, have pointed out that the rock's an even better copy of Pumasillo (Puma's Claw), a mountain many miles away on the opposite horizon behind you.

HUAYNA PICCHU

The path for Huayna Picchu leaves from the little caretaker's hut to the left of the Sacred Rock. It's about an hour's climb to the top, and in places the path takes you up near vertical faces with ropes and iron steps driven into the rock. Tiny terraces cover the top of Huayna Picchu, and the view of the sunrise from up here is even better than that from Intipunku.

A side path on Huayna Picchu leads to the **Temple of the Moon** which is around the other side of the mountain, about 50 minutes' detour down a very steep path (with the occasional ladder). The Temple of the Moon has very high-quality Inca stonework and was orientated to face the Pleiades, who were worshipped by the Incas. Fire damaged the whole mountain in 1997, and it was out of bounds until late 1998. The trail opens early, at 7am, and it's best to get up here before the crowds arrive at around 10am.

> ❏ *From the narrow saddleback on which the ruined city stands, the precipices plunge headlong into the raging brown river, fifteen hundred feet below. Looking up makes you even giddier than looking down, for all around the valley are black snow-streaked mountains, looming over you through the driving clouds, and right ahead, at the end of the ridge, towers an appalling berg of rock, like the fragment of a fallen moon. This is called Huayna Picchu. The Incas, who must have been able to climb like flies, built a watchtower on top of it, to guard the approach to the citadel.*
> **Christopher Isherwood** *The Condor and the Cows*, 1949.

THE THREE DOOR DISTRICT AND LOWER CEMETERY

Turn right from the Sacred Rock and walk behind a large boulder. You'll come to a flat rock that hangs a little over the precipice leading down to the Urubamba below. There's an unforgettable view from the edge of it.

Continue walking and follow some little white arrows painted on rocks, and the path will take you to the **Three Door District** (so named because it's got three main doors). This is a clan group area of Machu Picchu, and the houses are arranged in a small labyrinth. Note the pillars sticking out of the building's gables, and also the little carved projecting holes that run along the edge. To these the Incas tied the thatch that made up their roofs – you can see reconstructions of this in the Watchman's Hut, the huts around the sacred rock and the storehouses on the way out. Looking downhill you can see a terraced area connected to the three-door district by tiny paths and stairways. This is the **lower cemetery**, another

(Opposite): The Intihuatana (see p222) – 'hitching post of the sun'. (Photo © Bryn Thomas).

area where Bingham found many tombs, but it's very steep – you should only visit it if you have a head for heights and are sure-footed.

THE MORTAR DISTRICT

Back up in the main housing district, the next clan group to the south (straight on) is the **Mortar District**. It's thus named because Bingham found some interesting solid stone circles carved into rocks set into the floor of one of these houses, which he thought were mortars used for crushing maize in the house of an important chief. They don't bear much relation to the mortars commonly used by local people today so this theory isn't believed any more, but what they are actually for, no one knows. This district's sometimes called the Industrial Sector.

THE CONDOR TEMPLE OR JAILS

Leave the Mortar District, and go down a flight of stairs bordering the main plaza. Look back across at the marvellous stonework of the Temple of the Three Windows, if you haven't already. At the bottom of the stairs, turn left, and then right. This is the district that Bingham thought contained the **Jails** of the city. He noticed the small alcoves with tying places bored into the niche frames at about the height for manacling a prisoner to the rock. People no longer think these were jails – it seems that death was a punishment for many crimes against Inca laws, and there would be no need of jails. It's thought by some that these niches used to contain something sacred and holy: mummies perhaps, guarded by a taboo stick tied onto the rings.

On the floor further around the corner is a rock that looks a little like a condor with a white ruff, which gives this area its other name: **the Condor Temple**. There's also an altar in a natural fissure in the rock here, a bit like the one in Qenko (see p146). The condor was a sacred bird, sometimes a messenger or an embodiment of the huacas, especially of the apus (mountain spirits). Different birds could represent different things, the smallest bird representing a small mountain and the largest – condors – the sacred mountains of Salcantay, Veronica and Pumasillo. However, not every bird was a messenger – some were just birds, and it took an expert to be able to tell the difference.

THE FOUNTAINS AND THE ROYAL GROUP

Come out of the Condor Temple group, and make your way up the large flight of stairs to a **cascade of fountains**. These little square structures

(Opposite) Top: The Torreon (see p226). The curved wall indicates that this was probably a Sun Temple. **Bottom:** Beneath the Torreon is the Tomb of the Princess.

with water flowing through them are probably something to do with the ritual worship of water: there are similar structures in Phuyu Pata Marca, Sayac Marca and Tambo Machay. Bingham again thought them something different, believing that they were the main water supply for the city. The spring that used to feed these now feeds the hotel, and rather prosaically they can be switched on and off like a tap.

At the head of the cascade is the most carefully worked fountain. Uphill from this is the **Fountain Caretaker's Hut**, which, like the Watchman's Hut, is too ornate to be that of a mere caretaker. It is likely to be a place associated with water worship like the fountains it oversees. There are niches and stone pegs inside for hanging things, and there's a theory that it's where a priest supervised the rituals of water worship. It's good to sit in the place and absorb the atmosphere.

On the right (looking from below) of the caretaker's hut is **The Royal Group**. This is an area of particularly fine buildings, which Bingham took to be the place where the highest status person lived. The stone is nicely carved, but what draws most attention is the massive lintel over the main door. It weighs about three tons and was probably placed where it is by being dragged up an earth mound, which was then swept away. There's also an enclosed area in this group, possibly a garden, which the historian, Garcilasco de la Vega, describes as being common in the dwellings of people of high status, and often filled with golden statues.

THE TORREON OR SUN TEMPLE GROUP

The circular tower to the left of the Fountain Caretaker's Hut (if you're looking uphill) is the **Torreon** (see opposite p225).

The Torreon was probably a Sun Temple, as it has a curved wall and the Incas seemed to have used curved walls only in temples; but it does not have six chambers as you normally find in a sun temple. Reminding you of the Serpent Window in the Coricancha in Cuzco is a window with holes drilled in the frame. These holes were probably for fixing shadow-casters or aids to astronomy, but some have suggested they concealed snakes – hence the name. It's recently been noted that at dawn on the winter solstice (21 June) the sun shines through the window in the circular wall highlighting the rock in the middle of the temple. You can't enter the temple as it's been roped off.

Beneath the Torreon is a wonderful place, where the rocks have been carved in three-dimensional asymmetry so that they look as if they're made of putty. This is called the **Tomb of the Princess,** or the Royal Tomb, but that's misleading because no bodies were found here. All the same it's likely that this was an important place for the Incas, judging from the work involved in enlarging and shaping this fissure. Just around the corner from the Tomb there is a flight of eight stairs carved from the

living rock, leading to a beautiful double-framed door. There are two of
these doors in Ollantaytambo, and they are very impressive, indicating an
important dwelling. Note the bars recessed deeply into both door frames,
similar to the ones in the Old City Gate.

To the right of the stairs is an entrance into a particularly fine walled
building called **The Sacristy** or **House of the Princess**. The walls of Inca
buildings are particularly remarkable and here both the internal and external walls are amazing pieces of workmanship, especially when you consider that the Incas didn't have iron, only small brass crowbars. Bingham
described it as 'the most beautiful wall in all America'.

THE WAY OUT

If you stand at the top of the cascade of fountains facing out into the void,
you can see two or three thatched huts away to your right, at the same
level as you are. A path leads there. This is the way out to the Tourists'
Hotel, the car park and the buses back to the valley floor.

Moving on

HELICOPTER TO CUZCO

For the adventurous and rich, there's a brightly-clad woman selling **helicopter** tickets who normally sits under an umbrella on the wall leading to
the entrance booth. A twenty-five minute ride in a chopper back to Cuzco
will cost you US$80. The flight generally leaves at 3.30pm, but there may
be more flights if there are enough people. If the woman isn't there, try
in Aguas Calientes at Avenida Imperio de los Incas 123 (☎ 211036 –
there's a public phone outside the hotel).

MACHU PICCHU TO AGUAS CALIENTES

Transport for Cuzco leaves from Aguas Calientes in the valley below
Machu Picchu. The **walk** down there takes three quarters of an hour (follow the signpost on the edge of the car park), or you can take the **bus**. A
man with an open briefcase sells bus tickets just by the restaurant; a one
way costs s/9 and a return costs s/18.

BY TRAIN TO CUZCO

From Aguas Calientes the most common way back to Cuzco is by **train**.
The timetable depends on the class of train and upon the vagaries of the

Peruvian railway system. At the time of writing, all trains were leaving from Aguas Calientes. The Autovagon left at 3pm and reached Cuzco at 6.30pm, the Pullman and Express left at 4pm and reached Cuzco at 8.25pm, and the local train left at 7.30pm and reached Cuzco at about 10pm.

DOWN INTO THE JUNGLE

If you are feeling more adventurous, you can jump on the train in Aguas Calientes and head away from Cuzco into the jungle, although the line was impassable at the time of writing. The tracks lead to Quillabamba, the massive district of La Convención and the start of the Amazon rain forest. Legend has it that there are other completely undiscovered cities out here, lost far in the selva and guarded by fierce tribes, cities like the mythical Paititi. You could discover one of them.

APPENDIX A: QUECHUA AND SPANISH

QUECHUA

There are very few readily-available Quechua-English dictionaries or phrasebooks except for Ronald Wright's *Quechua Phrasebook* (Lonely Planet Publications). If you've access to a large library, however, have a look at the *Tri-lingual Dictionary: Quechua of Cusco/English/Spanish* by Esteban Hornberger S and Nancy H Hornberger (three volumes, Quechua Community Ministry 1977). This is a good book, but it sometimes goes over the top with religious vocabulary and doesn't translate words like 'chicha'!

There are many different ways of spelling Quechua. In most of this book I've used the Hispanic spelling because the maps use it, but in this section I've tried to use the version which is easiest for English speakers to pronounce (which also happens to be the accepted standard alphabet). Pronunciation of Quechua words is difficult, as the language includes glottal stops, aspirations and plosives not found in most European languages. Stress, as in Spanish, almost always falls on the second last syllable. Letters to watch out for are Q, Q', Qu, Qh, K, K' (glottalisations).

SPANISH

Peruvian Spanish differs from Castilian (Spanish Spanish) in pronunciation and vocabulary but is basically the same language.

The letters for an English speaker to watch out for are the LL (pronounced as an English Y), C (pronounced as an 'S' when followed by E and I, otherwise 'K') H (silent), HU (pronounced a bit like W), Ñ (the '~' puts an 'I' noise after the N), Q (pronounced K). Unlike Castilian, the S is pronounced as an S not a TH, and the V is usually a V not a B. The rule of thumb about stress is that it goes on the penultimate syllable, unless there's an accent, in which case it goes where the accent indicates.

ENGLISH	QUECHUA	SPANISH
Hello and goodbye		
Greeting!	*Napaykullayki!*	*¡Buenos días!*
How are you?	*Allillanchu?*	*¿Cómo está usted?*
See you later	*Ratukama*	*Hasta luego*
Goodbye (final)	*Kacharpari*	*Aiós*
sir	*tayta*	*señor*
madam	*mama*	*señora*
Excuse me (polite)	*Munayniykimanta*	*Con permiso*
oi!	*yaw!*	*¡oiga!*
Politeness		
Please	*Ama hiinachu kay, allichu*	*Por favor*
Thanks	*Añáy*	*Gracias*
Can I stay here? (spend the night)	*Puñupayukuykimanchu*	*¿Puerdo pasar la noche aqui?*

ENGLISH	QUECHUA	SPANISH
Yes and no		
yes	*arí, riki* (certainly!)	*sí*
no	*mana, ama* (don't!)	*no*
impossible	*mana atina*	*imposible*
that's good	*allinmi*	*está bien*
that's bad	*manan allinchu*	*no está bien*
Directions		
Where is...?	*maypin ...?*	*¿donde está...?*
...the river	*...mayu*	*...el río*
...the village	*..llaqta, marka*	*...el pueblo*
...the path	*...ñan*	*...el camino, el sendero*
...the pass	*...q'asa*	*...la abra*
...the bus /truck	*...omnibus /karro*	*...el bus/el camión*
...the railway	*...ferrocarril*	*...el ferrocarril*
...the toilet	*...bañu*	*...los baños*
...the hotel	*...qorpa wasi*	*...el hotel*
...the house	*...wasi*	*...la casa*
...water	*...unu*	*...agua*
...food	*...mikuna*	*...la comida*
...here	*...kaypi*	*...aqui*
...there	*...chaypi*	*...allí, allá*
...over there	*...haqay*	*...por ahí*
...up	*...wichay*	*...arriba*
...down	*...uray*	*...abajo*
...left	*...lloq'e*	*...izquierda*
...right	*...paña*	*...derecho*
...near	*...sispa*	*...cerca*
...far (far off)	*...karu*	*...lejos*
...straight ahead	*...dirichu*	*...derecho*
...everywhere, nowhere, anywhere	*...maypipas*	*...en todos partes, en ninguna dondequiera*
When is it?		
When?	*hayk'aq?*	*¿cuándo?*
now (soon)	*kunan*	*pronto*
right now	*kunallan, kunanpacha!*	*ahora mismo*
later	*qhepata*	*más tarde*
never	*manan hayk'aqpas*	*nunca*
Weather		
heat of the sun	*ruphay*	*calor del sol*
rain	*para*	*lluvia*
wind	*wayra*	*viento*
freezing wind	*qasa*	*viento helado*
snow	*rit'i*	*nieve*

ENGLISH	QUECHUA	SPANISH
How much?		
How much is...?	*hayk'atan kubrawanki...?*	*¿cuanto cuesta...?*
...that one	*...haqay, chay*	*...eso/a*
...it to hire a guide	*...pusawasqaykimanta*	*...arrendar un guía?*
...it to hire a horse	*...caballoykikunamanta*	*...arrendar un caballo?*
...it to hire a llama	*...llamaykikunamanta*	*...arrendar una llama?*
...each week	*...sapa semanan*	*...por semana*
...each day	*...sapa p'unchay*	*...por día*
Will you sell me...?	*icha ... ta bendiwankiman?*	*¿me vende ...?*
...money	*...qolqe*	*...dinero*
Food and drink		
meat (dried meat)	*aycha, (ch'arki)*	*carne (charqui)*
fish	*challwa*	*pescado*
chicken	*wallpa*	*pollo*
egg	*runtu*	*huevo*
bread	*t'anta*	*pan*
soup	*chupi*	*sopa*
maize (corn)	*choqllo, sara*	*maíz, choclo*
potato	*papa*	*papa*
fruit	*ruru, añawi*	*fruta*
roast	*kanka*	*asado*
boil	*t'impuy*	*hervir*
fry	*theqtichiy*	*freír*
raw	*hanku*	*crudo*
cooked	*chayasqa*	*cocido*
coca	*kuka*	*coca*
beer	*sirwisa*	*cerveza*
fizzy drink		*bebida gaseosa*
hot (temperature)	*q'oñi*	*caliente*
spicy	*haya*	*picante*
cold	*chiri, khutu*	*frío*
cold food	*kharmu*	*comida fría*
Quantity		
more	*aswan*	*más*
less	*aswan pisi*	*menos*
a little	*chika, pisi*	*un poco, poquito*
big, large	*hatun*	*grande*
small, little	*huch'uy*	*pequeño/a*
normal sized	*tinku*	*tamaño normal*
Numerals		
1	*huk*	*uno*
2	*iskay*	*dos*
3	*kinsa*	*tres*
4	*tawa*	*cuartro*
5	*pisqa*	*cinco*
6	*soqta*	*seis*
7	*qanchis*	*siete*

ENGLISH	QUECHUA	SPANISH
Numerals (cont)		
8	*pusaq*	*ocho*
9	*isqon*	*nueve*
10	*chunka*	*diez*
20	*iskay chunka*	*viente*
30	*kinsa chunka*	*trienta*
100	*pachak*	*ciento*
200	*iskay pachak*	*dos cientos*
1000	*waranqa*	*mil*
2000	*iskay waranqa*	*dos mil*
Help!		
Help me!	*yanapaway!*	*¡socorro!*
Take me to a hospital	*uspitalman pusaway*	*ilévame al hospital*
Ouch!	*achakáw!*	*¡ay!*
It hurts	*nanan*	*me duole*
I'm cold	*chiriwashan*	*tengo frío*
I'm hungry	*yarqawashan*	*tengo hambre*
I'm thirsty	*ch'akiwashan*	*tengo sed*
I'm tired	*sayk'usqa kan*	*estoy cansado*
Tie up your dog	*atahay alqoykita*	*ate su perro*

APPENDIX B: GLOSSARY

AMS	acute mountain sickness
abra	mountain pass
acetazelomide	drug taken for AMS
aclla	Inca nun
Almagro	(Diego) a leader of the Spanish conquerors of Peru, executed in 1538
alpaca	type of llama bred for its wool
amauta	keeper of Inca oral history
Antis	Inca word for the tribes of the rain-forest
Antisuyu	the forested eastern district of the Inca Empire
apu	mountain spirit
Apurímac river	the river to the south of the Urubamba
arriero	muleteer, donkey man
Atacama	desert running down the coast of northern Peru and Chile
Atahualpa	the last independent Inca ruler
audiencia	a seat of government of Spanish South America
Aymara	a people who live around Lake Titicaca
ayllu	Inca kinship group
Bingham (Hiram)	the man who rediscovered Machu Picchu in 1911
cacique	Spanish word for a local leader in the time of the Incas
cambista	money-changer
cancha	block of houses in an Inca town
caudillos	the military leaders at the time of Peruvian independence
calle	street
campesino	Peruvian peasant
cerro	mountain
ceviche	traditional Peruvian dish of marinated raw fish
chasqui	relay-running message carrier
chicha	drink of fermented maize
Chinchaysuyu	the northern quarter of the Inca Empire
chuño	type of traditional freeze-dried potato
Collasuyu	the far southern quarter of the Inca Empire
colectivo	South American form of transport, half-taxi, half-bus
conquistadors	the Spanish conquerors of Peru
Convención (La)	the district further into the jungle beyond Machu Picchu
Coricancha	Inca Sun Temple
Coya	the Inca's sister, and his official wife
Cuntisuyu	the south-western quarter of the Inca Empire
Curaca	Inca name for local noble
Cusichaca river	the river that runs from the mountain Salcantay to the Urubamba
Cusqueños	the people who live in Cuzco
Encomendero	man who owns an encomienda
encomienda	plot of land governed by a Spaniard
Espíritu Pampa	the modern name for Vilcabamba

guanaco	type of wild llama
Hanan	Inca clan division, also a part of an Inca town, the opposite of Hurin
HACO/HAPO	very serious forms of mountain sickness
huaca	sacred spot
Huascar	Atahualpa's brother and rival for the Inca throne, murdered in 1532
huayna	small or young
von Humboldt	(Baron Alexander) – European explorer of South America, died in 1859
Hurin	an Inca clan division, also a part of an Inca town, the opposite of Hanan
Inca	(properly) the ruler of the Incas
Inti	the sun, the Sun God
Intihuatana	the 'hitching post of the sun', an Inca ceremonial stone
Inti Raymi	a re-creation of the Inca festival of the winter solstice
jirón	street
llama	a South American relative of the camel
Limeños	people from Lima
machay	cave
machu	old, big
Manco Capac	the Inca crowned by the conquistador Francisco Pizarro, subsequently rebelled against the Spanish and was murdered in 1533
mestizo	a half-caste
mit'a	Inca tax, often paid in labour
mitimaes	Inca settlers
orejones	'big-ears', the Spanish name for Inca nobles
Pachacutec	the founder of the Inca Empire and folk hero
Pachamama	an earth goddess
pampa	plain
panaca	the tradition of preserving the estate of a dead person
parillada	plate of grilled meat
pirka	basic method of Inca construction
Pizarro (Francisco)	captain of the Spanish conquerors of the Incas, murdered in 1541
pucara	Inca fort
puna	high grassland
Punchao	a sacred idol of the sun from Cuzco's Sun Temple
Qenko	sacred spot near Cuzco
qollqa	Inca storehouse
Quechua	group of Andean campesinos; a name for the Inca language
quinoa	an Andean grain
quipus	strings and knots used by the Incas for record-keeping
raccay	ruins
Runasimi	the Quechua word for their language
Sacsayhuaman	the massive ruins near Cuzco
suyu	a division of the Inca Empire
Tahuantinsuyu	the original name for the Inca Empire

tambo	an inn, way-station or rest-house
Tiahuanaco	a pre-Inca Peruvian culture
tumi	an Andean knife
Tupac Amaru	the last Inca, executed in 1572
Urubamba	the river that runs below Machu Picchu
usno	raised ceremonial square in Inca city
vicuña	rare relative of llama with beautiful wool
Vilcabamba	site of the capital of the remains of the Inca Empire, 1537 to 1572
Vilcanota river	another name for the Urubamba river
Viracocha	the creator of the Incas, also the name of one of the early Incas

APPENDIX C: PERUVIAN EMBASSIES

Argentina
Av Del Libertador No 1720
1425 Capital Federal
Buenos Aires
(☎ 54-1 802 6427, 🗎 54-1 802 5887)

Australia
43 Culgoa Circuit
O'Malley, Act 2606
Canberra
(☎ 61-6 290 0922, 🗎 61-6 290 0924)

Austria
Gottfried-Keller-Gasse 2/8-35
1030 Vienna
(☎ 43-1 713 4377, 🗎 43-1 712 7704)

Belgium
Avenue de Tervuren 179
1150 Bruxelles
(☎ 32-2 733 3185, 🗎 32-2 733 4819)

Bolivia
Calle Fernando Guachalla Cdra.3
Sopocachi
La Paz
(☎ 591-2 353550, 🗎 591-2 367640

Brazil
SES Av das Nacoes, Lote 43
70428-900, Brasilia D.F.
(☎ 55-61 243 9933, 🗎 55-61 244 9344)

Canada
130 Albert Street
Suite 1901
Ottawa, Ontario, K1P 5GA
(☎ 1-613 238 1777, 🗎 1-613 232 3062)

Chile
Av Andres Bello 1751
Providencia, Santiago
(☎ 56-2 235 1640, 🗎 56-2 235 8139)

Colombia
Carrera 10 No 93-48
Bogota
(☎ 57-1 218 9212, 🗎 57-1 623 5102

Denmark
Rosenvaengets Alle 20, 2nd TV
2100 Copenhagen
(☎ 45-35 265848, ▤ 45-35 268406)

Ecuador
Av Republica de El Salvador 495 e Irlanda
Quito
(☎ 593-2 468410, ▤ 593-2 252560)

France
50, Avenue Kleber
75116 Paris
(☎ 33-1 53 70 42 00, ▤ 33-1 47 55 98 30)

Germany
Godesberger Allee 125
53175 Bonn
(☎ 49-22 373045, ▤ 49-22 456 1690)

Israel
37 Rehov Ha-Marganit
Shinkun Vatikim
52584 Ramat Gan
(☎ 972-3 613 5591, ▤ 972-3 751 2286)

Japan
4-4-27 Higashi
Shibuya-ku
Tokyo 150
(☎ 81-3 3406 4240, ▤ 81-3 3409 7589)

Netherlands
Nassauplein 4
2585 EA
La Hague
(☎ 31-70 365 3500, ▤ 31-70 365 1929)

New Zealand
Level 8 Cigna House
40 Mercer St
Wellington, PO 2566
(☎ 64-4 499 8087, ▤ 64-4 499 8057)

South Africa
Infotech Building Suite 202
1090 Arcadia St
0083 Hatfield
Pretoria
(☎ 27-12 342 2390, ▤ 27-12 342 4944)

Spain
C/Principe de Vergara No 36
5 to Derecha
28001 Madrid
(☎ 34-91 431 4242, 🖻 34-91 577 6861)

Switzerland
Thunstrasse 36
3005 Berma
(☎ 41-31 351 8555, 🖻 41-31 351 8570)

UK
52 Sloane St
London SW1X 9SP
(☎ 44-71 235 1917, 🖻 44-71 235 4463)

USA (Washington consulate)
1700 Massachusetts Ave NW
Washington DC 20036
(☎ 1-202-833-9860, 🖻 1-202-659-8124)

USA (Miami consulate)
444 Brickell Ave
Suite M-135
Miami, Florida 331313
(☎ 1-305-374-1305, 🖻 1-305-381-6027)

USA (New York consulate)
215 Lexington Ave 21st Floor
New York, NY 10016
(☎ 1-212-481-7410, 🖻 1-212-481-8606

APPENDIX D: BIBLIOGRAPHY

Some contemporary sources

Comentarios reales que tratan del origen de los Incas, Garcilasco de la Vega 1609
  trans Livermore, Texas 1966, trans CR Markham 1869
Crónica del Peru, Pedro Cieza de León 1553, trans CR Markham *The Travels of
Pedro Cieza de León,* Haklut Society, first series 1864
Historia del descumbriento y conquista del Peru, Agustín de Zarate, 1555, trans
  JM Cohen, Harmonsworth, 1968
Historia del Nuevo Mundo, Bernabé Cobo, 1653, trans Ronald Hamilton, *History
  of the Inca Empire* and *Inca Religion and Customs,* Univ of Texas, Austin 1979
  and 1990
Instrucción del Inga Don Diego de Castro Tito Cussi Yupangui, Titu Cusi 1570,
  in *En el encuentro de dos mundos: los Incas de Vilcabamba,* María del Carmen
  Martín Rubio, ed, Madrid 1988
Letter to a King (El Primera Coronice y Buen Gobierno), Felipe Huamán Poma de
  Ayala 1613, facsimile edition, *Travaux et mémoires de l'instiut de'ethnologie,*
  Paris 1936, vol 23
Relación del descumbriento y conquista de los reinos del Péru, Pedro Pizarro,
  1571, trans PA Means, *Relation of the Discovery and Conquest of the Kingdom
  of Peru,* Cortes Society, New York, 1921
Verdadera relacion de la conquista del Peru, Francisco de Xerex (Pizarro's
  scribe), July 1534, trans CR Markham, *Reports on the Discovery of Peru,*
  Haklut Society, first series 47, 1872

Modern historians of the Incas

Conquest of Peru, William Prescott, New York, 1847
Conquest of the Incas, John Hemming, Macmillan 1970, Penguin 1983,
  Papermac 1993
Everyday life of the Incas, Ann Kendall, BT Batsford, 1973
The Incas of Peru, Clements Markham, Smith Elder & Co, 1910

Inca studies

Inca Architecture and Construction at Ollantaytambo, Jean-Pierre Protzen, Oxford
  University Press, 1993
Inca Road Systems, John Hyslop, Academic Press New York, 1984
Inca Architecture, Louise Margolies & Graziano Gasparini, University of Indiana,
  Bloomington, 1984
Inca Settlement Planning, John Hyslop, University of Texas Press Austin, 1990
Monuments of the Incas Edward Ranney and John Hemming, New York Graphic
  Society, New York, 1982

Machu Picchu and the Inca sites around it

An introduction to the Archaeology of Cusco, John H Rowe, Papers of the Peabody
  Museum of American Archaeology, Harvard University vol 22, No 2, 1944
Archaeological Explorations in the Cordillera Vilcabamba, Paul Fejos,
  Publications in Anthropology No 3, The Werner Gren Foundation, 1944

Archaeological Investigations of Late Intermediate Period and Late Horizon Period at Cusichaca, Peru, Ann Kendall, in *Current Archaeological Projects in the Central Andes*, edited by Ann Kendall, BAR Int Series 210, 1984
Exploring Cuzco, Peter Frost, Nuevas Imágenes, 2000
Inca Planning North of Cuzco between Anta and Machu Picchu and along the Urubamba Valley, Dr Ann Kendall, BAR Int Series, 421, Oxford, 1988
Lost city of the Incas, Hiram Bingham, Duell, Sloan and Pearce, 1948
Machu Picchu, John Hemming. Readers' Digest, 1981
Machupicchu, Devenir Histórico y Cultural, Efrain Chevarria Huarcaya, UNSAAC, 1992
Machu Picchu Historical Sanctuary, Jim Bartle and Peter Frost, Nuevas Imágenes, 1995
The Sacred Centre Johan Reinhard, Nuevas Imágenes, 1995

Books on ancient Peru
Art of the Andes, Rebecca Stone-Miller, Thames and Hudson, 1995
Chavín and the Origins of Andean Civilisation Richard Burger, Thames and Hudson 1992
Peruvian Prehistory Keatinge (ed), CUP, 1988
The Ancient Civilisations of Peru J Alden Mason, Penguin 1957
The Ancient Kingdoms of Peru, Nigel Davies, Penguin, 1997
The Cities of the Ancient Andes, Adriana von Hagen and Craig Morris, Thames and Hudson 1998
The Incas and their Ancestors Michael Moseley, Thames and Hudson, 1992
The Pre-Hispanic Cultures of Peru Justo Caceres Macedo, Lima 1998

Modern Peru
A Fish in the Water, Mario Vargas Llosa, Faber and Faber, 1994
Fujimori's Peru, John Crabtree and Jim Thomas (ed), Institute of Latin American Studies 1998
Shining Path, Simon Strong, Harper Collins, 1992
The Peru Reader, University of Wisconsin Press Duke University Press, 1995

Latin America
A History of Latin America, George Pendle, Penguin 1963
Ancient South America Karen Bruhns, CUP, 1994
The Penguin History of Latin America Edwin Williamson, Penguin, 1992

Quechua
Quechua Phrasebook, Lonely Planet Publications 1989
Tri-Lingual Dictionary: Quechua/English/Spanish Esteban Hornberger S, Nancy H Hornberger, Quechua Community Ministry, 1977

Travel narratives
Antisuyu, Gene Savoy, Simon and Schuster, 1970
Cut Stones and Crossroads, Ronald Wright, Penguin 1984
Cuzco: A Journey to the Ancient Capital of Peru, Clements Markham, 1856
Inca Cola, Matthew Paris, George Weidenfeld & Nicholson, 1990
Inca Land Hirham Bingham, London Constable & Co, 1922

Memoirs General William Miller, London, 1828
Peregrinations of a Pariah Flora Tristan, Folio 1986 (trans)
Peru. Travel and Exploration in the Land of the Incas, E George Squier, NY1877
The Condor and the Cows Christopher Isherwood, Random House, 1948
Voyage a Travers L'Amerique du Sud, Paul Marcoy (Laurent Sant-Criq) Paris 1869

Other books
Death in the Andes, Mario Vargas Llosa, trans Faber and Faber 1996
Royal Hunt of the Sun, Peter Shaffer
The Bridge of San Luis Rey Thornton Wilder
The Heights of Machu Picchu, Pablo Neruda, trans Jonathan Cape 1966

Health and medicine
Altitude Illness: Prevention & Treatment by Stephen Bezruchka MD, Cordee 1994
Bugs, Bites and Bowels Dr Jane Wilson Howarth, Cadogan 1995
Medical Handbook for Mountaineers Peter Steele, Constable 1988
Medicine for Mountaineering Ed James Wilkerson MD, The Mountaineers 1985

Flora and fauna
Annotated Checklist of Peruvian Birds, Theodore Parker III and others, Buteo
    Books, 1982
Birds of the High Andes by Jon Fjeldsa and Niels Krabbe, Apollo Books, 1990
Orquídeas del Perú, Moisés Cavero and others, Centro de Datos para la
Conservación del Perú, Lima 1991

UPDATE: JANUARY 2001

Thanks to the South American Explorers' Club and to Roger Williams (USA) and Jon Doran (UK) for information used in the preparation of this update. I've organised this section to mirror the main book, and so that you can find your way around it both by using the headings and the page numbers. To contact me with any further updates, recommendations or comments write c/o Trailblazer or email me on ⌨ richardd@trailblazer-guides.com.

An end to independent trekking

There's no doubt that the popularity of the trail is becoming a problem and when I sat down to write the last update for this book in May 2000 the Peruvian authorities were about to restrict free access to the trail. It turned out not to be quite as imminent as implied. Everyone in Peru had other things on their mind in 2000 what with an election and the subsequent resignation of the president (see p244), the Inca Trail and Machu Picchu were no longer in the spotlight. But the final announcements have been made and from February 2001 everything's going to change. Well, maybe. It is, nevertheless, the end of an era and the price for access to the trail will increase; one can but hope that the whole Sanctuary will be the better for it.

The other hot potatoes last year were the plans to build a **large hotel** near Machu Picchu and **cable car** up to the ruins. The hotel plans, thankfully, have been scaled down, and the cable car will probably not be visible from the site itself, so it all sounds a bit more acceptable. I still have some reservations about the plans.

PART 1: PLANNING YOUR TRIP

With a group or on your own?
Page 11

From February 2001 the access rules for the Inca Trail will change and hiking will (generally) only be permitted in tours. There will be 23 companies offering these tours, and I'd love to be able to tell you who they are but the list has still not been confirmed. Your best bet is to check with your local Peruvian Embassy (see pp236-8) or, better still, ask the South American Explorers' Club (www.samexplo.org), an excellent organisation which anyone travelling to South America should seriously consider joining (see p106).

I said 'generally' there because there's an exception. The original plans, which were to prevent all access to independent hikers, have been amended and those who don't want to hike with a large group of strangers will still be allowed on the trail. But the new regulations say that they must hire a licensed independent guide. Again, I'd love to be able to tell you who these people are but so far no one really knows. Groups of these independent hikers must not comprise more than 10 people.

Restricting access is a pity but I hope it's for the best; there's no doubt that something had to be done, as unlimited access to the trail had caused filth to build up and damage to be caused to the old sites. But you can't help having some reservations as the Peruvian government do tend to see the Inca Trail and Machu Picchu as a cash cow, taking what they can and providing only limited support to locals and the local environment. (In September 2000, the whole site was blockaded by local farm workers, students and teachers protesting about lack of help from central government).

Tours and trekking agencies – Australia
Page 14
Inca Tours (☎ 02-4351 2133 or ☎ 1800 024 955, 🗎 02-4351 2526) 3 Margaret St, Wyong NSW 2259, offer a full itinerary from Sydney for around A$6000.

Getting to Peru
Page 16
Flights connecting Peru and Chile are now subject to a tax of US$50, payable at the airport. The (rather good) airline LanPeru were planning international flights but at the time of writing were not even operating internal flights.

Budgeting
Page 18
The price of a guided tour to the Inca Trail (now the only way of visiting the Sanctuary) isn't yet known but it's expected to be around US$150 for four days.

Route options
Page 20
The record time for running, (yes, running), the trail is held by Edgar Rodriguez, the President of the Cuzco Athletic League, who is said to have completed the distance of just under 40 kilometres in 3 hours 50 minutes.

Page 21
The blockage of the original Inca route from Choquesuysuy has been cleared and the walk has been christened 'The Purification Trail', picking up on the presumed function of Choquesuysuy as a place of ritual cleansing for those approaching Huinay Huayna.

Maps
Page 29
The IGN maps are now available at some specialised map shops outside Peru. Stanfords have them and take mail orders (☎ 020-7836 1321, 🗎 020-7836 0189, 🖳 www.stanfords.co.uk, 12-14 Long Acre, London WC2).

Web sites
Page 30
● A good Latin-American travel site is **www.amerispan.com/lata**.
● The best site on Machu Picchu and the Inca Trail, with links all over the web, is **www.ex.ac.uk/~RDavies/inca**.
● A good virtual guidebook can be found at **www.bestweb.net/~goyzueta/qos qo/index.html**.
● The site of Gene Savoy, one of the discoverers of Vilcabamba (see p99), is at **www.greatbasin.net/~genesavoy**, and Vincent R Lee, another Vilcabamba traveller, can be found on-line at **www.blissnet.com/~sixpacmanco/books.htm**.
● Also worth a look is **www.pacaritambo.com**, an informative (if a little odd) site specialising in ancient South American cultures,
● **www.machupicchuperu.com**, is the official site of Aguas Calientes (see p151).

PART 2: PERU

Facts about the country
Page 46
Politics Fujimori did stand for a third term and was re-elected in early 2000 but he was beset by allegations of fraud and impropriety. Just as he was settling in and thinking everything was in the bag his past caught up with him. His shadowy right-hand man, Vladimiro Montesinos, who had been his eyes and ears as the head of the state intelligence agency ('Servicio de Inteligencia Naciona', or SIN), fell from grace.

A video tape of Montesinos bribing a Member of Congress was leaked to the press. Montesinos fled to Panama, which resisted pressure from the United States to grant him asylum. He returned to Peru and went to ground. The suspicion was that his old friends in high places were hiding him. It was discovered that he'd salted away around $48 million in various foreign banks. Fujimori held on for a couple of months, declaring his intention of tracking Montesinos down, and then left Peru on a run-of-the-mill foreign tour. When he stopped off in Japan, home of his parents, he stayed. He told Peru he was resigning his presidency. In one final glorious irony, he declared that he was in fact – contrary to all the assertions he had given throughout the decade he was in power – a Japanese national. As it's illegal for anyone other than a Peruvian national to be president of Peru, this meant Fujimori had for ten years been an illegal president.

On 22 November 2000, Valentin Paniagua, a compromise candidate who'd been President of Congress for only a week, was sworn in as President of the Republic. New elections are expected in April 2001. The days of Fujimori are over.

The economy One of Peru's most eminent economists, Hernando de Soto, has recently suggested that there is a structural problem at the heart of Peru's (and the rest of the developing world's) economic troubles. In *The Mystery of Capital: Why capitalism triumphs in the West and fails everywhere else* (London, Bantam Press 2000), he suggests that capitalism succeeds in the West because people can liquidate the value of the land they occupy, by mortgages, for example. They can do this because they can prove they own the land. In other countries where it's difficult to prove title to land, the wealth bound up in your property is frozen and inaccessible. He estimates that in the developing world as a whole, US$29,000 billion of wealth is tied up. This figure has come in for criticism as being too high, and the book itself has come in for criticism for not suggesting a practical way of registering land claims.

Practical information for the visitor
Page 51
Money In January 2001 the exchange rate was s/3.4 to US$1.

Getting around
Page 52
Travelling between cities LanPeru (☎ 446-6995, 🖹 215-1818, Paz Soldan 225, San Isidro, Lima) was set up in 1999 and connected Lima and Cuzco twice a day (approximately US$49 one way). They had earned themselves a reputation as the best carrier on the route but suspended all flights in November 2000 and their

future is now in doubt. That leaves **Aero Continente** (☎ 242-4242 or 433-1667, 🖹 241-8098, Av Pardo 651, Miraflores, Lima) as the only airline servicing Peru's major airports.

The train from Lima to Huancayo is being privatised and is not currently operating.

Page 64
Flora and fauna In the early part of 2000 a remarkable discovery was made in the forests around Vilcabamba by the North American zoologist, Dr Louise Emmons. As she was walking through the undergrowth she scared a tree weasel, which dropped its lunch in her lap. Lunch turned out to be a completely new genus of mammal, never before known to science. It's a rat the size of a cat that lives in trees, and has been called *Cuscomys ashaninka*, after Cuzco and the Ashanika, the local people. It's heartening to know that there are still secrets waiting to be discovered in the forests of Peru.

PART 4: LIMA

Where to stay
Page 110
Lima Centro: Budget hotels The *Hostal de las Artes*, (☎ 433 0031, 🖥 http://clientes.telematic.com.pe/artes), 1460 Jiron Chota, has been recommended. Prices start at US$6.

Page 111
Miraflores: Budget hotels *The Hiker's Youth Hostel*, (☎ 271 7970, 🖥 a-mauriz@usa.net), Dona Catalina 358, Los Rosales 2da Etapa-Surco, has also been recommended.

Page 112
Expensive hotels The *Swissotel* (☎ 421 4400, 🖹 421 4422, 🖥 reservations@swisslim.com.pe), Via Central 150, Centro Empresarial Real, San Isidro, PO Box 270079, which has recently opened, is now one of the best places to stay in Lima. They charge from US$195 a night.

What to see
Page 117
The **Museo de la Nacion** no longer contains the exhibition of the Señor de Sipan. At the time of writing it was on a world tour, currently in Germany.

Moving on
Page 119
Highland routes The train from Lima to Huancayo is being privatised and is not currently operating.

PART 5: CUZCO

Page 124
Wandering around Cuzco, you'll notice a rainbow flag hanging from houses, shops and bars. It looks very much like the gay and lesbian banner and so at first sight you might think that Cuzco had a thriving gay and lesbian community. But the

flag's actually the emblem of the Quechua and is a different design, though only slightly, bearing as it does an extra blue line.

Services
Page 128
The **South American Explorer's Club** have opened a clubhouse in Cuzco. It's at 930 Avenida El Sol (☎ 223 102), and can be contacted on ▢ saec@way na.rcp.net.pe. For more details of what the SAEC have to offer, see p106.

The Cuzco regional tourism office now has an email address: ▢ turismo@ tourcusco.com.

Tours
Page 129
There are to be only 23 companies authorised to take tourists on the Inca Trail, but who they'll be isn't yet known. The best source of information (until the next edition of this book) will be your local Peruvian Embassy (see pp236-8), or the South American Explorers' Club (▢ www.samexplo.org). The price of a trip is expected to rise to around US$150. Tours can normally be booked a day in advance.

Where to stay
Page 131
The district of San Blas suffered a crime wave in 2000 with incidents of robbery and rape so be very careful there. The drivers of taxis hailed from the street are often accomplices of the attackers. Get your hotel to book your taxi.

Page 132
Mid-range hotels *Niños Hotel* (☎ 231 424, ▢ www.targetfound.nl/ninos/), Calle Meloq 442, has been recommended. Prices start at US$30.

The *Casa Real*, a new Novotel, is being built in Cuzco. It'll be a four-star place, and reports of what it's like are welcomed.

Moving on
Page 143
Rail Express and Pullman classes have been discontinued, and backpackers are being discouraged from taking the local train as it annoys the locals. An alternative 'backpacker' train is being laid on, at a relatively costly US$30 return. The website, **www.machupicchuperu.com**, lists train times but is not always up to date. (The 'newsflash' displayed at the time of writing was six months old). PeruRail, the private train operator, plans to invest US$2million in the line in 2001, which might mean the end of landslides in the area.

The Sacred Valley
Page 147
Ancient rock carvings connected with the Incas were found in March 2000 to the south of Cuzco, in the valleys of Huatanay and Vilcanota. They are thought to be associated with a temple dedicated to knowledge. Their exact location hasn't been released.

PART 6: MINIMUM IMPACT TREKKING

The weight of numbers on the trail makes it all the more important that each person takes seriously their responsibility to look after the place. There has been talk of creating a plan to preserve the trail but by May 2000 it had run into difficulties.

PART 7: TRAIL GUIDE AND MAPS

Page 167
Tickets and prices The fee for the main trails has gone up to US$50, and from Km104 and Salkantay to Km88 it's up to US$25. No more than 500 people will be able to start the trail in one day. (This sounds like a positive step to preserve the trail, but according to conservationists the trail has never had more than 494 people starting on any one day. They argue that this is only window-dressing). The price of a guided tour is likely to be around US$150 for a four-day trip.

Tickets can now be bought only at the INC (Instituto National de Cultura) on Calle Bernando.

PART 8: MACHU PICCHU

Page 213
Just as Rowe's old documents shed light on the origin and purpose of Machu Picchu, so have other recently discovered documents shed light on the man who revealed Machu Picchu, Hiram Bingham. Papers found in the family home by his son, William, show that Bingham, distinguished enough by his exploration and his being a US Senator, acted as an Oscar Schindler while a diplomat in Vichy in France. He helped 2500 Jews escape the Nazis.

Page 222
The Intihuatana In September 2000, the Intihuatana was damaged by a crane. The US publicity firm, J Walter Thompson, were filming an advertisement for Cusquena beer, when a crane they were using chipped a chunk out of the old stone. There's a rich symbolism in the fact that this ancient monument, which survived the Spanish invasion and centuries lost in the jungle, has now been damaged by the forces of modern capitalism.

Page 228
The train track to Quillabamba has still not been repaired; its future is in doubt.

INDEX